ADMINISTRATIVE ARGUMENT

Administrative Argument

CHRISTOPHER HOOD AND MICHAEL JACKSON

Dartmouth

Aldershot · Brookfield USA · Hong Kong · Singapore · Sydney

Published by
Dartmouth Publishing Company Limited
Gower House
Croft Road
Aldershot
Hants GU11 3HR
England

Dartmouth Publishing Company
Old Post Road
Brookfield
Vermont 05036
USA

British Library Cataloguing in Publication Data
Hood, Christopher *1947–*
    Administrative argument.
    1. Public administration. Theories
    I. Title   II. Jackson, Michael
    350.0001

ISBN 1 85521 023 1

Printed in Great Britain by
Billing & Sons Ltd, Worcester

Contents

List of Figures and Tables

FIGURES

TABLES

Preface

Administration, like religion and politics, is a field marked by multiple and competing doctrines about the road to salvation. What counts as heresy and what as orthodoxy is variable and problematic. The supersession of one ruling doctrine by another occurs through a rhetorical process, not by the marshalling of incontrovertible evidence from exhaustive examination of data. And the stock of basic doctrines itself is far more limited than one might think from the endless parade of neologisms and apparently new managerial fads. Every generation thinks that it has invented the fashionable administrative doctrines of the day. But this is an illusion.

We have written this book for tertiary students, practitioners and general readers in public administration and the many 'adjectival administrations'. We wrote it because of dissatisfaction with the standard texts on administrative ideas. Most of those books treat 'theory' and 'doctrine' as synonymous. This one explicitly focuses *only* on the latter. Further, most existing texts on administrative ideas are organized chronologically, typically beginning with late nineteenth or early twentieth century ideas. This one is built around a set of 99 doctrines, most of which far antedate the supposed 'fathers' of modern administrative science, such as Woodrow Wilson, Frederick Winslow Taylor and Max Weber.

We have three main purposes in writing this book.

The first is to start to identify systematically some of the major doctrines which appear and recur in administrative argument. The link between administrative argument and 'proverbs' has long been understood. But there is no book of proverbs, laying out and juxtaposing the commonest doctrines.

Our second and related purpose is to help readers to recognize standard lines of doctrine and justification in administrative argument, and hence to be aware of the range of available doctrines and justifications. There is a counterstroke to parry every thrust, and the aim of this book is to help readers find it. Administrative doctrines should not be taken as *arcanae imperii*, sacred mysteries to be known only to an elite of mandarins and management consultocrats.

A third purpose is to help readers to look critically at administrative arguments which sound persuasive - to learn to look for the private advantage behind the allegation of public good, to look for the evidence which has been conveniently omitted from the argument because it does not suit the conclusions, to find the rival proverbs and maxims which will challenge those which have been put into play, to identify and counter the ways in which disbelief is suspended.

In addition to these three purposes, the book contains an iconoclastic argument. It tries to show that there is an alternative way to conceive administrative 'science', apart from the mainstream approach on the link between administrative design and administrative performance, and to indicate how such an approach can be developed. It argues that such an approach to administrative analysis has a valid place alongside more orthodox approaches.

This book has been several years in the making, and we have many debts to acknowledge. We are particularly grateful to Andrew Dunsire, who read most of the chapters in draft, and helped us to improve on our early faltering efforts. We are also grateful to Hal Colebatch, Jack Hayward, Brendan O'Leary, Christopher Pollitt, Rod Rhodes and Len Tivey for advice, comment or encouragement. Parts of the book were read to a seminar at the Victoria University of Wellington in 1989 and at a panel session of the UK Political Studies Association in 1990. When we first showed Hal Colebatch a draft of what became Part One of this book, he urged us to organize a conference around it in order to produce an edited volume around the theme. Our response was that it would be much less effort to write the rest of the book ourselves. In fact, it turned out to be much more effort. Perhaps it is just as well that this is more a book of proverbs than a book of prophecies.

PART I
ADMINISTRATIVE ARGUMENT AND ADMINISTRATIVE DOCTRINE

It had become clear to the garrison that not only did the doctors sometimes apply different remedies to the same illness, in certain cases the remedies were diametrically opposed to each other. So what was a sick man to do? (Farrell 1985, 249)

1 Getting Organized

The doctrines that I was now encountering were intuitive and self-generated: those who held them thought that what they were saying was plain common sense, which needed no prompting or authority. (Henderson 1986, 10)

'Let's get organized!' Haven't we all heard that cry? Haven't we all said it ourselves? Everyone wants to get organized. The only question is: *how*, exactly, should we get organized? And that is the generic question of administration.

There are plenty of instant-management books which offer direct and simple answers to the question. This book is not one of them. Rather, we concentrate on the *way* that the administrative what-to-do question comes to be answered. What are the available doctrines and what arguments convince people to get organized in one way rather than another? What makes for a convincing administrative argument? These are the questions at issue in this book.

'How should we get organized?' The question may seem simple enough. But there are a surprising number of plausible answers readily to hand. Let's stop three passers-by in the street and put the question to them.

First Person (who has a military bearing): 'Get organized in the way the *army* does. Look at what can be achieved by a great military leader like Bonaparte. Run a tight ship. Make command and obedience the watchwords. Put the emphasis on leadership from the top, group pride, glorious deeds for the cause. That's the only way to motivate people to sacrifice their own interests for the group, to ensure that orders are carried out snappily and that lines of responsibility hold "under fire". Remember that the test of good organization is the ability to adapt and to function reliably even in worst-case conditions.'

Now there is food for thought. Armies often have an image of discipline and efficiency, do they not? But wait a minute: what about all those tales of spectacular military incompetence,[1] mindless ritual, monumental waste? Perhaps we need another opinion.

Second Person (whose appearance tells of an expense-account lifestyle): 'Get organized the way that *business* does. Look at what Lee Iacocca did for Chrysler. Focus on the bottom line. Work through material rewards, concentrating on the dreams that money can buy, not on tradition or mystique. So pay good wages to get and keep good people. Fire the non-performers. Keep paperwork and record-keeping to a minimum. That's the only recipe for motivating everyone to give of their best, to keep costs down and to search for innovations. Remember that the test of good organization is the ability to marshall the resources needed to perform a particular task competently, without waste, contradiction or muddle.'

That response makes sense, too. After all, business is said to face the discipline of the market and a lot is made of that today. But could there be another side to it? What about the recurring stories of mammoth corporate blunders, swindles, all-too-predictable collapses following bouts of irrational euphoria or speculative fever?[2] Perhaps we should stop someone else as well.

Third Person (who has an other-worldly air): 'Get organized the way that a *religious order* does. Look at Mother Theresa's work in Calcutta. Make the motivation come from within, not from outside. Get a commitment for life from everyone to asceticism and altruism, not to selfish gratification. Put each individual under constant review from the group as a whole so that you get strict and sceptical questioning of any new idea before it is accepted. Work out the objectives as you go along, by a continuous process of interaction and debate. That's the only way to check the evils of opportunism and put a brake on the rash adoption of half-baked ideas. Remember that the test of good organization is fairness, mutuality, the avoidance of corruption or error.'

Here is an altogether different perspective. Base organization on an inner sense of vocation. Make it a life's work. It seems attractive...but aren't there pathological forms of this type of organization too?[3]

Even so basic a question generates at least three fundamentally different approaches to organization. Of course, other respondents might well give answers different from these, or substantial variations. But these three answers alone, even without further explanation, tell us four things about administrative argument.

Table 1.1   Three administrative what-to-do stereotypes

	Military Stereotype	Business Stereotype	Religious Stereotype
Stereotype Slogan	Run it like the army	Run it like business	Run it like a monastic order
Stereotype Work Force	Limited career	Hired & fired as needed	Service for life
Stereotype Motivation	Fear of punishment Hope for battle honours	Fear of dismissal Hope for monetary gain	Fear of damnation Hope for spiritual or psychic satisfaction
External Control Stereotype	The 'audit of war'	Ruthless and impersonal market forces	Social acceptance or faith
Objective Setting Stereotype	Defined in orders of the day from the top	Defined in pursuit of profit	Worked out in lengthy processes of discussion & reflection
Belief Stereotypes	Obedience to discipline & leadership means commands are carried out snappily and lines of responsibility hold 'under fire'	Monetary incentives & hire & fire management means incentives to minimize waste & to search for innovations	Lifetime internal commitment limits opportunism, peer group control checks rash adoption of half-baked ideas

First, each of the 'philosophers' whom we consulted is putting forward one or more administrative *doctrines* – ideas which claim to answer the question 'What's the best way to...?'. Later, we shall distinguish between *doctrines*, *philosophies* and *justifications*, and we shall discuss the special features of administrative doctrines as a variant of political argument. For now, it suffices to note that a doctrinaire answer to the what-to-do questions of organization is typically based on simple maxims and snap judgements.

Second, each set of doctrines offers a *different* answer to the question as to how to get organized. To be sure, there are often overlaps. Some business firms may well be like military units. Some military units may be more like monasteries or universities. But the main thrust of each set of doctrines is different. We can sum them up in tabular form, as shown in Table 1.1.

Third, none of the doctrines advanced by the consultant philosophers is new. Of course, these particular philosophers might well have put their own special personal gloss on the doctrines which they advanced. But, whatever they might think, they are not the first people to come up with those ideas. Each set of doctrines has a long history. Few administrative doctrines are ever invented completely *de novo*. Like doctrines in economics, administrative doctrines are often re-invented, in complete or tactical ignorance of their past lives. Keynes' (1936, 383) famous remark about the recycling of economic ideas applies just as much to administrative doctrines:

> ...madmen in authority, who hear voices in the air, are distilling their frenzy from some academic scribbler of a few years back.[4]

For instance, martial doctrines about how to get organized were recommended for government by the eighteenth-century German cameralists, whose ideas we will be looking at later (Small 1909; Parry 1963). Such doctrines lay behind the idea of 'civil service' as a variant of military service by reformers such as Frederick the Great, Napoleon Bonaparte and Catherine the Great. In Third World countries today, the idea is commonly advanced that military organization can get a country back on its feet. And military expertise in administration has often been highly valued both in government and business.

'Business' doctrines, too are not an invention peculiar to the late twentieth century. They have been influential for at least a century, since the beginnings of the 'city manager' movement in the USA (Downs and Larkey 1986). In fact, some of their precepts pre-date the advent of modern corporate management.

Likewise, collegial doctrines of the kind advocated by our third consultant are ideas of great antiquity. Plato advanced them as a recipe for good government over 2000 years ago. They figure in Confucian doctrines of administration, which emphasize asceticism rather than greed as the mark of the good administrator. Variants of them are enthusiastically proposed today by those who believe that self-management or communal structures are the best answer to the failings of other approaches to public management (Martin 1983; Schumacher 1973). For instance, some feminist institutions have aspired to such an approach in order to remedy what are seen as the failings of a 'masculine' style of organization (Ferguson 1984).

Fourth, none of the respondents could *prove* the truth of the doctrines they assert in a way which would begin to satisfy a natural scientist or a professor of logic. There is neither sufficient evidence to satisfy the scientist nor adequate logic to convince the logician. Rival examples which might cast doubt on the validity of the doctrine are conveniently ignored – for instance, Lord Raglan rather than Napoleon as the archetype of military leadership, Lee Iacocca's role in creating the ill-fated Pinto at Ford rather than his days at Chrysler (Lacey 1986, 575–86), the Vatican hierarchy's involvement in the Banco Ambrosiano affair rather than Mother Theresa's work with the destitute.

We draw particular attention to this fourth point because it is typical of administrative argument, and it is not confined to the laity whom we consulted above. Most ideas about how to get organized – even those coming from 'experts' – are based on what Lindblom and Cohen (1979) call 'ordinary knowledge'. Ordinary knowledge means ideas based on common sense maxims linked with casually observed examples which happen to suit the argument.

Hence administrative argument consists of advocacy of doctrines by reference to 'common sense' maxims and selected examples that ostensibly vindicate the maxims. Over time 'common sense' changes and new maxims come to the fore, accompanied by a new selection of favoured examples. This process of defining 'common sense' and selecting sustaining examples produces a rotation of doctrines, each different from the other, none of them new and none of them proven superior. The result is that administrative argument has a rhetorical character. There is no basis for a *definitive* argument which would prove one doctrine to be superior to all others.

In the course of exploring the character of administrative argument, we deliberately use the word 'administration' very broadly. Our background is in government or public administration, and that is the main focus of the book. But we look beyond government administration to the generic phenomenon of administration as well. At its most general level, administration is government, whether it is the government of a nation, a crime syndicate, or a self-help collective. Likewise, we draw our specimens and examples from a wide range of political systems and historical periods. Looking at administration in a broad sense, rather than only at its specialized variants, increases the chances of our net capturing the variety of doctrines to be observed in administrative argument. And looking at a range of historical examples can help us to put current administrative doctrines into perspective.

This book can be read at different levels and in different ways. What integrates the whole of the book is a general argument about approaches to administrative science. Readers whose main interest lies in the state of that subject will want to focus on that; and the next chapter discusses the state of the art at greater length. But readers who are not primarily concerned with that issue may want to skip that chapter and use different parts of the book as stand-alone units.

Part II can be treated as a mini-encyclopaedia of administrative doctrines, foreshadowing the larger encyclopaedia that needs to be written. That Part is like an encyclopaedia, in that it is designed for selective reading, using an index of doctrines which appears at the outset. But some readers may want to read it 'linearly' from start to finish.

Part III picks up the analytic argument and builds on the index of doctrines in Part II, though Chapter 6 may be of interest to the general reader as an account of three classic cases of administrative argument.

Part IV concludes with a review of the general argument, returning to the three consultant philosophers who gave us their views about how to get organized at the outset. But Chapter 8 can be read as a stand-alone unit. It compares the latest how-to-get-organized doctrines in public administration – which we term 'New Public Management' – with the earliest version of public managerial philosophy offered by the eighteenth-century cameralists, in an attempt to demonstrate some unchanging features of administrative argument.

NOTES

1   As explored, for instance, by Dixon (1976).
2   See, for instance, Earl (1984) or Sykes (1988).
3   See, for instance, Cornwell (1989).
4   Equally (though Keynes did not, of course, say this), the 'academic scribblers' themselves may well be distilling their own ideas from earlier 'madmen in authority'.

2 Doctrines and Persuasion in Administrative Argument

As not one of our logical writers...have thought proper to give a name to this particular species of argument, – I here take the liberty to do it myself, for two reasons. First, ... to prevent all confusion in disputes.... And, secondly, that it may be said ... that he had invented a name ... for one of the most unanswerable arguments of the whole science. And if the end of disputation is more to silence than to convince, – they may add, if they please, to one of the best arguments too.

I do therefore, by these presents, strictly order and command, That it be known and distinguished by the name and title of the *Argumentum Fistulatorium*, and no other; – and that it rank hereafter with the *Argumentum Baculinum*, and the *Argumentum ad Crumenam*, and for ever hereafter be treated of in the same chapter. (Sterne, 1983, 56-7)

I ADMINISTRATIVE DOCTRINE AND ADMINISTRATIVE SCIENCE

What does the 'science' of administration or management have to do with what-to-do doctrines of the kind that we encountered in the last chapter? There are two stock answers to that question.

One can be termed the Hobbesian answer, after the seventeenth-century English philosopher Thomas Hobbes. This answer says that for 'science' to progress in this perplexing area, we need to find a way of showing, once and for all, what is the best way to get organized. The sort of administrative doctrines which our street philosophers put to us in the last chapter, need to be put to the proof. A proof which would satisfy the orthodox canons of science would demand an extensive programme of systematic investigation.

9

There would need to be carefully selected test and control groups, extensive monitoring and observation of changes over time, and a large array of cases.[1] But once the hard work was done and the winning formula was established, the argument could be closed.

The other stock response can be termed the Aristotelian response. Discussing constitution-making, the Greek philosopher Aristotle argued that there was no *single* best way to get organized. A constitution had to be fitted to the particular geography and character of a people. This answer became the reigning orthodoxy in administrative science in the 1960s and 1970s. It says that 'science' means finding ways of discovering *under what circumstances* each of a set of rival doctrines best fits the facts. Perhaps our military-minded philosopher's doctrines may be the best way to get organized in some circumstances, but in other conditions the doctrines offered by the other two philosophers might be better applied. To adopt an Aristotelian view means treating each set of doctrines as potentially applicable in some circumstances but not others.

These two approaches make up the orthodox agenda for the 'science' of administration, particularly as it has developed since the 1940s. Do they exhaust the possibilities?

There is a third way. Rather than focus exclusively on the link between *design* and *performance*, we can also look at the link between *argument* and *acceptance*. Rather than looking only at the objective truth or falsity of administrative doctrines as recipes for better performance, we can treat them as objects of study *in themselves*, deserving to be carefully mapped and catalogued as a set of available ideas.

To look at administrative argument in this third way is to start from the proposition that the impact of an administrative doctrine is a function of its credibility, not necessarily of its truth. If it is believed, an administrative doctrine 'wins', whether or not it is true. In deciding winners and losers, truth claims are a part – not the whole – of the story. To look at administrative argument in this way is to engage in a rhetorical analysis. Such an approach underlies this book's analysis of administrative argument.

Persuasive arguments in other areas of social science have already been viewed through similar analytic spectacles. Ricca Edmondson (1984) has identified the rhetorical features of sociology, exploring areas such as the persuasive power of citations and the use of 'epitomes' of telling quotations drawn from interview material. Sociology might perhaps seem an especially soft target for such an approach, since popular prejudice often dismisses sociology's claims to 'scientific' status. So it is interesting that Donald McCloskey (1985) has employed a similar approach for a harder and much more prestigious target in his analysis of the rhetorical aspects of argument in modern economics. Lindblom and Cohen (1979) and Giandomenico Majone (1989) have looked at persuasive processes in the policy sciences more generally. All of these authors have argued that what makes ideas stand or fall in the fields which they examined is something other than the ability of the proponents of those ideas to close the argument in a strictly Hobbesian way by proving their claims on the basis of irrefragable evidence. That 'something' is the persuasive power with which the ideas are argued. And persuasive power typically comes from the creative use of metaphor and analogy. Often the most effective metaphors are those which are not readily recognizable as such, such as statistical significance tests.

It is a short step to extend this analysis to administrative argument. Winning administrative ideas, when we strip them down to their essentials, are rarely very profound. Often they are repackaged and relabelled versions of an idea which has been advanced many times before. Frequently their premises come down to some banal notion of 'human nature' coupled with a contestable view about links between cause and effect. 'Proof' typically consists of no more than a few colourful examples. These features were easy to see in the arguments offered by the consultants who gave us their views in the last chapter. But, as we will show later, such features are just as commonly seen in how-to-get organized doctrines drawn from the prestigious science of economics, with its massed ranks of Nobel laureates and its 'econocrats' in high places. What makes for winning administrative doctrines is *rhetorical power*: the standing of the proponent and the packaging of the argument.

Some readers may equate rhetoric with 'hot air' or 'sound without meaning'. It cannot be denied that there is plenty of that in debate about how to get organized. But it is far from true that all administrative argument is 'empty rhetoric' in this disparaging sense. We are certainly not saying that all discussion of how to get organized is a self-conscious hawking of quack cures by opportunists with a cynical eye on the main chance. The field is rich in serious scholars who could never be justly accused of that – even if they are usually outnumbered by the instant fix-it quacks. We use the term rhetoric in a neutral sense to denote the careful selection and fashioning of argument in particular circumstances. Rhetoric as a phenomenon has been likened to a combination which opens a lock.[2] The 'lock' is a complex situation - a particular issue, a particular person or group, a particular time and place. The combination is that form of discourse which will convince a particular audience as to how to act over an issue. The conviction may come through skilful manipulation, though some students of persuasive argument go so far as to argue that rhetoricians must actually speak as their audience before they can successfully convince (Burke 1950, 19-24).

Can this third approach - the analysis of argument and persuasion - have any useful payoff in administrative 'science'? This book argues that it can, and this chapter rehearses the argument. In the next section, we return to our starting point, administrative doctrines, and explore their properties a little more closely, building on our observations in the last chapter. In the following section (III), we look at the orthodox approach to administrative science developed by the Nobel laureate Herbert Simon, and discuss the limitations of that approach. Finally, in section IV, we sketch out a different approach which builds on Simon's own insights and particularly on the work of one of his disciples, David Braybrooke. Our conclusion is that the exploration of doctrines and persuasion in administrative argument, a phenomenon which was discovered but not fully explored by Simon, merits some attention in administrative science.

II ADMINISTRATIVE DOCTRINES

As we saw in the last chapter, administrative doctrines are ideas that win arguments in disputes about how to get organized. They offer authoritative answers to the what-to-do questions of administration. They are prescriptions for action in one way rather than another (cf. Dunn 1981, 41–3).[3]

Doctrines, Philosophies and Justifications in Administrative Argument

Here, for the sake of clarity, we need to elaborate the terminology a little by distinguishing *doctrines*, *philosophies* and *justifications* in administrative argument. We summarize the difference between these three items in Figure 2.1 (p. 13).

We use the term *doctrine* to denote specific ideas about what should be done in administration. (They correspond to what William Dunn (1981, 65) terms 'advocative claims' in policy analysis.) The number of doctrines available in administrative argument is large, but it is finite, and we shall present a collection of common doctrines in Part II of this book, arranged under the headings of who-type doctrines, what-type doctrines and how-type doctrines. As we indicate in Figure 2.1, there are significant areas of overlap between these headings.

An example of a doctrine is the idea that all members of a particular organization or group (school, occupational group, political or religious movement) ought to wear uniform clothing. Doctrines, as quasi-imperative statements about a single aspect of how to get organized, have no necessary relation to broader political views as ordinarily categorized. For instance, the doctrine of uniform clothing can be espoused by groups as apparently different as the bosses of today's McDonald's hamburger restaurants, the Chinese Cultural Revolutionaries of the 1960s, and those nineteenth-century utilitarians who thought that paupers ought to be made to wear uniform (to signify their dependence on public charity). Same doctrine: different context, ideology, argument.

We use the term *justification* to denote the reasons which are given for following a particular doctrine, before or after the event. (Justifications

PHILOSOPHIES
(sets of doctrines with relatively
coherent justifications)
Number: small

Examples: cameralism, utilitarianism
' new public management'

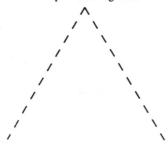

DOCTRINES

(specific maxims about administrative
whos, hows and whats)

Number: large

Examples: promotion by seniority,
decision by fixed rules

JUSTIFICATIONS

(reasons for adopting doctrines)

Number: medium

Examples: equity, efficiency
adaptivity

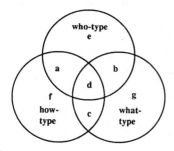

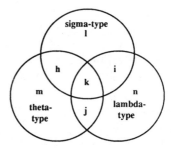

<u>**who-type**</u>: doctrines relating to
people

<u>**what-type**</u>: doctrines relating to
organizational
structure

<u>**how-type**</u>: doctrines relating to
procedure

<u>**sigma-type**</u>: justifications relating to
matching of resources to
tasks

<u>**theta-type**</u>: justifications relating to
fairness, neutrality and
accountability

<u>**lambda-type**</u>: justifications relating
to adaptivity, learning
and resilience

**Figure 2.1   The DNA of administrative argument?
Philosophies, doctrines and justifications**

correspond to what Dunn (Ibid) terms 'designative' and 'evaluative' claims – i.e. claims about facts and norms.) When we look at our collection of doctrines in Part II of this book, we will see that the number of typical justifications is much smaller than the number of available administrative doctrines. Most justifications of administrative doctrines are couched in terms of ideas such as efficiency, effectiveness, equity, fairness, honesty, reliability, adaptivity, robustness.

To simplify, we can fit most justifications of administrative doctrines into three generic types. One, which we can term for convenience as 'sigma-type' justifications, are based on precepts about matching resources to tasks for particular and defined circumstances. Justifications relating to the limitation of waste, the pursuit of efficiency, the avoidance of muddle and confusion come into the 'sigma' family of justifications.

A second common class of justifications, which we can term for convenience as 'theta-type' justifications, are based on precepts about how to ensure fairness, mutuality, the proper discharge of duties. Justifications relating to fair treatment, the avoidance of bias, the pursuit of accountability, the avoidance of abuse of office (through dishonesty, self-servingness, carelessness or rapacity) come into the 'theta' family.

A third class of justifications, which we can term for convenience as 'lambda-type' justifications, are based on precepts about how to ensure resilience, even in adverse conditions. Justifications relating to considerations of reliability, adaptivity, robustness come into the 'lambda' family.

To take the example of the doctrine of uniform clothing which was introduced earlier, a 'sigma-type' justification might be constructed in terms of a claim that getting a job done properly requires the wearing of clothing which is specifically designed for a particular task, and which simplifies the task of establishing identities. A 'theta-type' justification might be constructed in terms of a claim that the pursuit of equality requires the specification of clothing which avoids distinctions of wealth or social background from making themselves felt, or that uniform clothing may make it harder for people to escape their duties or obligations. A 'lambda-type' justification might be constructed in terms of a claim that uniformity of clothing makes it easier for parts to be interchanged or roles reallocated in a crisis.

Some administrative doctrines, as we will see in Part II, are closely related to only one type of justification. But, as in this example, the same doctrine is often advanced on the basis of justifications from different families. And the justifications themselves frequently overlap in places, as all families do. Hence the overlapping circles in Figure 2.1.

We use the term *philosophy* to denote a constellation of doctrines which is relatively coherent in terms of the justifications offered for them. It will be recalled that we used the term 'philosophers' to describe the three lay consultants who gave us their instant opinions on how to get organized in the last chapter. This usage was not simply ironic. Such people might not think of themselves as philosophers, but they count as philosophers in our terms because they offered us a set of doctrines based on a relatively coherent set of precepts.

We stress 'relatively', in that most real-life administrative philosophies embody some contradictions. A philosophy, in the terms of this book, is thus a combination of doctrinal 'whos', 'whats' and 'hows', linked with a combination of justificatory 'sigmas', 'thetas' and 'lambdas'. 'Coherence' means that a set of doctrines are not a random grouping, but belong together as a set which is compatible with a particular set of values.

Fully-fledged philosophies of administration in this sense are few in number. Examples of administrative philosophies include 'consociationalism' (a combination of doctrines about how to avoid domination of one social group by another); 'cameralism' (a combination of doctrines about how the state may lead economic growth), 'utilitarianism' (a combination of doctrines about how to make 'interest' and 'duty' run together in the provision of collective goods), 'managerialism' (a combination of doctrines about how to promote efficiency through the activities of a professional class of managers). These are all cases of ideas embodying bundles of doctrines which are informed by a relatively consistent set of justifications.

Administrative philosophies need to be understood in the same way as philosophies of war, as discussed by Anatol Rapoport (1968, 11)

> ... to understand a philosophy means to see its logical structure, that is, the way its concepts and ideas relate to each other and how they are derived from other concepts or ideas. In order to understand a philosophy ... it is often necessary to compare it with other philosophies.

We follow Rapoport's precept in an examination of two key administrative philosophies in Part IV of this book.

These three phenomena in administrative argument are relatively distinct. There are 'degrees of freedom' among them. As we saw above, the same doctrine can be defended by very different justifications. Equally, different doctrines can be based on the same justification. Different philosophies may include the same doctrines as part of their portfolio of ideas, while similar philosophies may include different doctrines. You cannot necessarily extrapolate from one item to another. A full discussion of administrative argument would give equal attention to each of the three components, in terms of labelling, tracing genealogy and variants. In this book, we look mainly at administrative doctrines, giving subsidiary attention to the other two features of administrative argument.

Doctrines and Theories

The essence of administrative doctrines has been elegantly captured by Andrew Dunsire (1973b, 39). Dunsire describes doctrines as

> ...a set of ideas that lies half-way between 'theory' and 'policy' – where 'theory' means an attempt to explain some part of the environment, so as to make all observations about it consistent with one another, with the sole purpose of approaching 'truth' or understanding; and 'policy' means a statement of intention towards some part of the environment, designed to initiate and guide actions in it so as to make all actions in it consistent with one another, with the purpose of furthering or preventing change. A 'doctrine', then, looks both ways; it makes plain, but in the manner of 'revealed truth' rather than the tentative hypothesizing of theory: it shows what must be done, but as if it were from necessity rather than the mere instrumentalism of policy. The doctrines of actors are derived from theories that are not questioned; policies are derived from doctrines that purpose to be 'fact'.

Table 2.1   Administrative doctrine and administrative theory

	Doctrine	Theory
Primary Object or Focus	Influence	Understanding
Key Test	Prescriptive Persuasiveness	Explanatory Power
'Problematic'	Link between Administrative **Argument** and **Acceptance**	Link between Administrative **Design** and **Performance**
Method of 'Proof'	*Creative Ambiguity *Symmetry *Metaphor *Private Interest Presented as Public Good *Selective Example *Suspension of Disbelief	Systematic Analysis of Cases ('Hard Data')

We summarize the distinction between doctrines and theories in Table 2.1 above. We emphasize this point because, in spite of the insights of writers such as Dunsire, many discussions of administrative 'theory', organization 'theory' and even 'theories' of the state treat explanatory theories and prescriptive doctrines as interchangeable. This often creates confusion.

Each of the three answers to the how-to-get-organized question which our street philosophers offered us – the military discipline recipe, the business efficiency recipe, the spiritual commitment recipe – involve a set of doctrines in Dunsire's meaning. The doctrines imply some underlying theory of cause and effect – the idea that if you do x, y will follow. But the connection is not fully demonstrated, either by including the full chain of reasoning which would be needed to make the proposition coherent in formal logic, or by amassing a systematic array of evidence to substantiate the case.

Administrative doctrines have their cousins and counterparts in other fields. David Henderson's (1986) case of the doctrines of 'home-made economics', which he encountered in Whitehall in the 1950s, is a very close relation. Other near kin include international-strategy doctrines such as 'massive retaliation' and 'first strike', industrial policy doctrines such as 'transparency' and 'a level playing field', doctrines of social policy such as 'workfare' and 'less eligibility'. These doctrines, too, are based less on incontrovertible proof than on the prestige of their proponents, the way that they seem to be 'in tune with the times', the power of the examples which are used to support the case.

We noted some of the features of administrative doctrines in the last chapter. As we explore administrative doctrines in the later parts of the book, we will find six recurrent features.

1   Administrative doctrines are ubiquitous. For better or worse, they are part of the human condition. Wherever there is organization, there are doctrines of how to 'do' it successfully.
2   Administrative doctrines usually rest on soft data and soft logic. Soft data means casually or selectively drawn examples rather than hard data drawn from systematic survey. Soft logic means argument with key premises left out, by 'proofs' based on authority symbols or by appeal to a persuasive example or analogy, such as a machine or a human body, rather than argument on the basis of rigorous syllogism.
3   Administrative doctrines 'win' over potential rivals by a social process which labels them as the received view, accords them prominence and ignores competing doctrines or treats them as heresies or outdated ideas. Conviction is achieved mainly by timing, packaging, presentation, not by objective, conclusive demonstration of the superiority of one doctrine over its rivals. When one doctrine replaces another in a radical reversal, the process must usually be explained by something other than a crucial experiment or definitive head-to-head comparison.

4   Administrative doctrines are often contradictory. For each doctrine
suggesting that we should do x rather than y, there tends to be another
doctrine arguing that we should do y rather than x. This feature of administrative argument has often been commented upon. It is satirized in
Cornford's (1908) classic account of the contradictory *clichés* of argument which endlessly recur in the debates of academic governing bodies,
such as the stereotyped 'window of opportunity' argument versus the
equally hackneyed contrary doctrine of 'unripe time'. It appears in
Mackenzie and Grove's (1957, 366–7) classic account of the repertoire
of convenient stock arguments about how to design and reorganize
government departments:

> The debates in these cases follow patterns which tend to recur. A shake-up
> of the organization will give a chance to get rid of dead wood and to make a
> fresh start.... But it is a pity to dislocate existing relations, familiar to all
> concerned, and it will take time for a new organization to find its feet. It is
> desirable to group similar functions together, for instance functions of
> research and production.... But it is dangerous to divide producer from user.
> If they are separated, the user gets into the habit of stating impracticable
> requirements, the producer ceases to respond quickly to need. It is desirable
> to get rid of small Departments because they are expensive in overheads and
> make coordination difficult. But large Departments are slow and cumber-
> some ... And so on: in isolation, each of the conflicting 'proverbs' makes
> good sense, but they cancel out ...

5   Administrative doctrines are often unstable. Like clothing and automobiles, administrative doctrines are subject to the ever-present search for
new styles, fashions and fads. The search is to replace the dated style of
'yesterday's management' by a new-look doctrine, with accompanying
special argot. Nor is this turnover of doctrines entirely a process driven
by consumer fickleness. Producers have a stake in it too. If doctrines
never turned over, there would be much less scope for consultancy
services, executive development seminars, degree courses, popular literature on successful management. As Richard Spann (1981, 14) put it:

> As in fashion, skirts go up and down, ties narrow and widen, so in Public
> Administration there are alternations – the economies of large-scale are
> preached at one time, to be succeeded by the gospel that 'small is beautiful';
> periods of administrative pluralism are followed by ones of integration when
> semi-independent bodies become suspect...; there is oscillation between the
> demand for functional rationality and for a holistic approach to clienteles;
> between the desire to politicize and to depoliticize public administration.
> Sometimes tendency and counter-tendency are present simultaneously.

6   Administrative doctrines tend to rotate. Genuinely new doctrines are far
less commonly invented than it might appear. Today's ruling doctrine –

whether it be privatization, performance pay, self-management – is often no more than a resurrection of something that has had its day, or days, before. Large bureaucracies are often said to be elephantine, in capacity for memory as well as in bulk and immoveability. But the world of public administration as well as private corporate management often seems to be positively programmed to forget yesterday's ideas.[4] As Downs and Larkey (1986, 3) put it:

> The same strategies, usually renamed, are tried again and again with limited success. Rarely do proponents ask why previous attempts achieved only modest success and what this implies for their proposals ... For example, if all that was needed to improve the performance of government was to give control to a group of hard-charging, tough-minded business executives committed to remaking government in the image of the private sector, government's problems would have been solved when that strategy was first attempted some 100 years ago in city governments.

All of these six points about administrative doctrines will be illustrated in the cases which we consider later.

III ESCAPING FROM DOCTRINE: HERBERT SIMON'S AGENDA

We owe to the Nobel laureate Herbert Simon a clear recognition of administrative argument as rhetorical and of the proverb-like character of received administrative doctrines. In a famous article published nearly fifty years ago, Simon (1946) weighed conventional administrative science in the balance and – as academics usually do when reviewing a literature to which they are about to contribute – found it to be wanting. He showed that what were claimed to be principles of good administration were more like proverbs than they were like the laws established by natural science.

Simon argued that this situation was neither necessary nor desirable. What was needed, he argued, was the replacement of argument based on ordinary knowledge by argument based on a positivist style of 'professional social inquiry', in the terms used by Lindblom and Cohen (1979). In short, Simon argued that the sole basis for administrative argument should be 'grounded theory' linking design to performance on the basis of systematic experiments as nearly as possible resembling the laboratory tests of natural science. Only that way would it be possible to realize what we earlier termed the 'Hobbesian' or 'Aristotelian' answers to the question of how administrative science should relate to administrative argument.

This agenda was deeply influential in the post-World War II development of administrative science. It ran with the current of positivism which was flowing strongly in the social sciences in the USA at that time. A huge investment of research dollars and intellectual effort went into the attempt to realize this agenda, by careful measurement of organizational properties and 'scientific' objectivity. The tone of articles in prestigious journals such as *Administrative Science Quarterly* in the 1960s and 1970s was strongly related to Simon's programme. The Aristotelian answer to the administrative science problem was rediscovered and dubbed as 'contingency' theory, the quantitative testing of the contingencies that influence the link between structure and performance.[5]

After nearly fifty years, what fruit has Simon's positivist research agenda borne? It must be said that the harvest has been somewhat disappointing. At least three things seem to have gone wrong for that agenda.

First, very few of the old proverbs seem to have been decisively laid to rest by the positivist administrative science advocated by Simon. We seem to be little nearer to 'scientific' answers about when to use contradictory principles of administration than was Aristotle two thousand years ago.[6] Within the community of scholars, no commonly accepted paradigm of 'normal science' (Kuhn 1962) has developed. The 'contingency approach' has tended to run into the sand. Good administrative practice remains deeply contestable.

Second, fifty years of administrative 'science' in the Simonian mould seems to have had remarkably little effect on the way that administrative argument is conducted in practice. For better or worse, the proverbial approach to administrative doctrine that Simon complained about in 1946 is still alive and well. Undoubtedly, styles change, with changing idioms and fads. Today's management cookery books have more business buzzwords and anecdotes, more economics-based jargon, and fewer quotations from religious texts, of the kind that were once common. But underneath, not very much seems to have changed since 1946 in the conduct of administrative argument. Simon himself, in the introduction to the second edition of his classic *Administrative Behavior* (1957, xxxiii) noted that, eleven years after his famous attack on the 'proverbs', proverbial arguments still featured strongly in writing on public administration and business management. Over thirty years later, he could not avoid coming to the same conclusion.

For example, Christopher Pollitt's (1984) account of the way that 'machinery of government' questions were handled in UK central government over twenty years demonstrates a process of administrative argument which is no different from the exchange of proverbs noted by Mackenzie and Grove nearly thirty years earlier. Pollitt shows that the arguments were invariably proverbial in character, in Simon's sense. Such debate as there was consisted of swapping of contradictory first principles, rather than of careful and systematic analysis of data-sets enabling cumulation of knowledge and steady development of better machinery.

Does this finding simply reflect what is often said to be a peculiarly British amateurism and dilettantism about administration? Not if we believe Downs and Larkey's (1986) account of recurrent American arguments for improving the efficiency of government bureaucracy by the use of private business people and methods. Like Pollitt, Downs and Larkey show that the arguments are almost always proverbial in character. Preference is for simple, uncomplicated maxims that chime with stereotypical views of government bureaucracy ('Don't confuse me with the facts'). 'Evidence' comes in the form of selective example, committing the familiar logical fallacy of taking illustration for proof (Price 1968, 10). It seems that Simon's attack on the proverbial approach to administration might never have existed, for all the practical influence it has had on administrative argument.

This outcome in administrative science is consistent with Lindblom and Cohen's (1979) more general argument that 'professional social inquiry' often does not have the decisive impact on problem-solving in public policy that is expected of it, and in some cases is actually obstructive to social problem-solving. Lindblom and Cohen (ibid, 65) argue that professional social inquiry is rarely conclusive, and that an interactive process of argument or social learning is often superior as a method of problem-solving. Continuing reliance on arguments built on ordinary knowledge rather than 'scientific data' is not a 'pathology', nor should we expect it to be ultimately replaced by professional social inquiry *a la* Simon. In similar vein, Giandomenico Majone (1989, 21ff) argues that the basic skills of policy analysis are closer to the argumentative skills of a lawyer or a judge than to those of an engineer or scientist. He argues that 'decisionism' (the idea that policy debates can be settled once and for all by authoritative analysis or inquiry) is an inherently flawed approach to policy analysis in most cases, and that a process of 'dialectic' is often preferable.

Third, positivism itself as a research methodology commands much less universal respect even in US social science than it did when Simon was writing over four decades ago. The shortcomings of positivism as a strategy for social inquiry have been too often pointed out to need detailed rehearsal here. One common criticism relates to the difficulty of accommodating the analysis of value, as in traditional political philosophy, within a positivist framework. Another relates to various aspects of the observer paradox, namely the tendency of causal knowledge in human affairs to be self-negating or self-fulfilling (Bobrow and Dryzek 1986, 128–35), such that positivism cannot in practice live up to its claims to authoritativeness.

Accordingly, a variety of non-positivist social science methodologies have come back into favour, particularly in work focusing on the 'construction of social reality' through linguistic interaction. At the very least, it has to be recognized that this kind of argument is much more fashionable and more powerfully entrenched than it was in US academia after World War II. Scholars working in these epistemological mines have sought and found theories of knowledge that reject the Cartesian and Baconian assumptions that underly the sort of positivism that Simon was advocating in 1946, and in particular the assumption that there can be an absolute basis for knowledge.

They have discovered philosophers such as Wittgenstein, Dilthey and Husserl who conceive formal knowledge to be embedded in shared experience, meaning that scientific theories emerge from intersubjective symbolic and political action in just the same way as works of art and literature (Brown 1983, 129–30).

Taken together, these alternative methodologies can be labelled as post-positivism. Though the approaches are disparate, the varieties of post-positivism are unified by an emphasis on the location of truth in time and space, coupled with a rejection of the positivist goal of a transcendental truth. The emphasis is on context, with a common assumption that claims to truth such as those made by positivists are only made by repression of the rhetorical character of science and philosophy (Feyerabend 1978; Rorty 1979; Norris 1985).

How seriously do these three problems disable the research agenda which Simon set for students of administration in the 1940s? Do we have to come down on one side or the other? Or is it possible to conceive of an approach to administrative science which would both meet Simon's concerns for systematic analysis rather than top-of-the-head judgements and the concerns of the post-positivists with the analysis of 'discourse'?

IV   A DIFFERENT APPROACH?

Probably it is impossible to propose an agenda for administrative science which would simultaneously satisfy the most extreme wings of each epistomological camp – the purists of positivism and post-positivism respectively. But we suggest that a two-point agenda would have the capacity to integrate at least the 'moderate' wings of each movement.

First, we should look carefully at the 'bunch of keys' in administrative argument. That is, the array of administrative doctrines, justifications and philosophies (in our terminology) would deserve systematic study *as a set*, without necessarily focusing on the universal validity of their 'truth claims'. Second, instead of focusing exclusively on the relation between administrative design and administrative 'performance', we should systematically study the process by which one key out of the bunch comes to fit the lock – i.e. how a subset of the larger set of administrative doctrines become(s) the received ideas.[7]

Taking Administrative Doctrines Seriously

We saw above that Simon did not develop his perception of administrative argument as proverbial in character. He took his insight just far enough to use it as a launching-pad for a positivist research agenda to explore the relationship between administrative design and administrative performance. Simon could have developed his observation in a different way. Instead of instantly discarding the proverbs, he might have argued that there could be no meaningful administrative science until there was a reasonably complete catalogue or dictionary of all the rival proverbs (and justifications and philosophies, in our terminology) that come into play in administrative argument. To take that course would be to follow the classical analysis of rhetoric, with its preoccupation with categorizing all the available forms of argument.[8] Instead of trying to replace administrative doctrines by scientific laws, we could take the doctrines themselves as a proper object of study, collecting together and juxtaposing as many of them as possible. It is from this matrix that each generation draws its supply of doctrines.

It is curious that such a programme has never been undertaken. Administrative science often seems to neglect its heartland while spending its energies on boundary issues. And a careful labelling of the doctrines, philosophies and justifications which appear in administrative argument can be justified from both sides of the epistemological street. For the Simonian positivist camp, it is the sort of systematic data-set which that camp holds to be an essential precondition for 'hard science'. For the post-positivist army, it is a logical approach to laying out administrative ideas as the cultural artifacts which those ideas are claimed to be. Cataloguing of forms is a traditional starting point for the analysis of culture in the humanities. So why not treat administrative doctrines in just the same way as the cultural analyst treats clichés, hieroglyphs, fertility rites, folk songs? If administrative argument is really to be treated as 'text', as the post-positivists would have it, we need a dictionary.

If this justification seems a little abstract and scholastic, consider the more practical and down-to-earth benefits of cataloguing administrative ideas systematically. At present, those who engage in administrative argument are in the position of the student of French law before the *Code Napoleon* or of the users of the Library of Babel in Jorge Luis Borges' famous (1974) allegorical story of that title. The story was about a library containing everything which had ever been written or which could be written. But the library had no central catalogue, so the only way to find anything in this treasure-house was by serendipity, personal memory or years of trial and error.

Without a catalogue to the 'Library of Babel', the scales of administrative argument are loaded in at least two ways. First, the absence of such a catalogue gives an advantage to the well-educated articulate people in positions of power who assert administrative doctrines so confidently. It lends their (often banal, usually contestable, sometimes contradictory) thoughts on administration an appearance of special and arcane knowledge denied to the laity whom we consulted in Chapter One. Second, it aids the social forgetting process that Mary Douglas (1987) has written about. In that sense it makes us slaves to the meretricities of the administrative fashion trade of consultocracy and pop management.

Herbert Simon did not include the production of a comprehensive 'book of proverbs' in his research agenda. Even from his austere, positivist standpoint he might have argued that such a collection could serve the same sort of pedagogic purpose as (say) Bentham's catalogue of political fallacies. It would be a systematic inventory of the mistaken maxims that are adopted as a result of human folly, weakness or power.

Indeed, one of Simon's most distinguished disciples, David Braybrooke, has developed a methodology for compiling such a book of proverbs. Braybrooke's method was anticipated by Richard Spann (1966, 9) in a classic article on clichés in political science. Spann argued that it would be better to use alphanumeric symbols to denote standard or hackneyed elements of argument, than for those elements to be described afresh each time that they were introduced into a debate.

> There are ... various **Standard Lines of Argument**, which I should like to see collected into a single reference book, a sort of Encyclopaedia of Received Ideas like that planned by Bouvard and Pecuchet. Each would be allocated a number; and instead of repeating them we would say or write A2 or M4. The reader would then consult the Encyclopaedia, or might even learn the arguments by heart. Either would save a great deal of time.

This is, of course, much easier said than done. We would need separate notation and classificatory apparatus for doctrines, justifications and philosophies as the components of administrative argument. And how could Spann's encyclopaedia actually be arranged? Should the doctrines be arranged chronologically? Should they be laid out by country or region? Or should they be presented in alphabetical order of key names or authors, following the conventional arrangement of a dictionary or encyclopaedia?

Each of these possible methods of carrying out Spann's idea would have its advantages and disadvantages. But in this age of computerized databases we do not need to make an irrevocable either-or choice between such possibilities.

In Part II, we present some of the more common doctrines of administration, arranged around three key interrogatives – *who, what* and *how*. As indicated in Figure 2.1, the whos, whats and hows of administration are better seen as spheres having areas of overlap rather than strict mutual exclusivity. But looking at doctrines in terms of interrogatives both fits the subject-matter, in so far as doctrines are advocative ideas which purport to offer *answers* to the action questions of administration, and helps to bring out the essentially contestable nature of administrative doctrines.[9]

This method is built on David Braybrooke's (1974) ideas. Braybrooke, a disciple of Herbert Simon, worked out this approach in order to develop a systematic language for exploring how political systems operate as 'machines' for processing issues. Issues are defined as sets of alternative policy proposals. Processing occurs by 'testing' the various proposals in play. Braybrooke demonstrated the method by labelling the rival arguments which are available to answer the familiar public policy problem of what to do about road traffic congestion in big cities. For example, you can adopt measures to reduce traffic or measures to increase road capacity. You can ration by price or by direction, reflecting some judgement or policy on 'need to drive' or 'need to park'. You can concentrate on parking capacity or on traffic flow. You can look at it from the viewpoint of pedestrians or of drivers...and so on. By labelling each of these familiar proposals relating to the congestion problem by a symbol, it is possible systematically to chart successive rounds of policy debate, in terms of the order in which particular proposals are advanced, who advances them, which proposals are selected and which are ignored or defeated.

A complete encyclopaedia of administrative argument would need to apply such principles to philosophies and justifications as well as doctrines. Database presentation would enable the encyclopaedia to be accessed through alphabetical, chronological, territorial, or topic-based gateways, according to the preferences of the user. That is ultimately the only way to tame the administrative Library of Babel. But all that is for the future. This book tries to explore how it could be done by applying Braybrooke's method to the commonest doctrines about administrative whos, hows and whats. This appears in Part Two.

Focusing on the Acceptance Factor

We suggested earlier that a focus on the 'acceptance factor' is a second line of inquiry which could potentially accommodate both the post-positivists and the Simonian tradition of administrative science. If the orthodox approach to administrative science focuses on the link between administrative design and administrative performance, a rhetorical approach focuses on the link between doctrines and acceptance. If the set of available administrative doctrines are a bunch of keys, how do we explain which of the keys fits the lock in any particular time and place? The issue at stake here is what makes a doctrine acceptable as the received view, while others are ignored or treated as heresies, not which doctrine leads to objectively superior administrative performance.

It also opens up the question as to why doctrines or arguments drawn from some intellectual sources seem to be more persuasive than arguments drawn from other sources. Why is it, in this case, that economics, accounting and corporate management tend to be the sources of winning doctrines in administration today rather than (say) philosophy, history or traditional Public Administration? Where are the massed ranks of 'philosocrats', 'histocrats' and 'adminocrats' to match the 'econocrats' and 'accountocrats'? (Self 1975.)

Again, this is a question which Simon's observations on administrative argument could have led him to ask, and its exploration could be fitted within his preferred method of inquiry. His own observation showed that administrative argument is typically not a process of validation and disproof using hard data, but rather a process of persuasion through doctrines having the six characteristics which we identified earlier.

Explaining the 'acceptance factor' is the traditional concern of the study of rhetoric, one of the oldest areas of analysis in the humanities. In the ancient world, the study of persuasion was regarded as just as central to public affairs as the study of (say) economics today. Major treatises on the subject were written in classical Greek and Roman times, and rhetoric remained important as a field of study in medieval and Renaissance Europe. But the subject gradually declined in importance in the modern world as it was excluded from 'science' and modern literary analysis alike. Only over the past few decades has there been a degree of rebirth of interest in the field, among sociologists and students of language (cf. Edmondson 1984, 5–8).

Much of the concern of the classical students of rhetoric lay in identifying the available keys in the bunch, in setting out the various forms and styles available for persuasion. But they were concerned with explaining the 'acceptance factor' too. Six ideas about this can be noted here.

First, one answer to the 'acceptance' question is the idea of *symmetry* as essential for persuasion.[10] According to Aristotle (1932), in the classic treatise on the subject, the mark of the rhetorician's skill is to produce linguistic 'solutions' which are exactly symmetrical to the social 'problems' experienced by the audience. Brown (1978, 1983) has applied this basic idea to administrative analysis. According to him, successful administrative analysis, and successful social science more generally, lies in the construction of a reality symmetrical with the perceived 'problem'. As an example, Brown shows (1983, 150–3) how the success of Emile Durkheim's classic treatise *Suicide* can be interpreted in this light as providing a legitimating principle for a secular morality at a crucial point in French educational history. Herbert Simon's own analysis is clearly capable of being interpreted in much the same light, in that positivism can seem to garb students of administration in the authoritative dress of natural science, and distance them from associations with alchemy and fortune-telling.

Second, a related aspect of the 'acceptance factor' was seen to lie in the successful use of *metaphor* to tap into or build on shared modes of thinking. Where final proof is impossible, persuasion needs to be achieved by the correct choice of metaphor. Brown (1978, 377) touches on this in a discussion of 'reality broking' as the key to cognitive control over organizations. From a broader perspective, Mary Douglas (1987) argues that all successful institutions need to be cognitive paradigms grounded in analogies that appeal to 'reason and nature' – the head and the hands, the sun and the planets, the parent and the child, the male and the female.

Third, a key to acceptance was held to be *ambiguity*, the ability to speak simultaneously to persons or groups with different views and interests (cf. Pocock 1971, 17). Thus in discussing what we now call democracy, Aristotle observed that a vital precondition for successful leadership was the ability to speak simultaneously in tongues. To be successful, the rhetorician must communicate the same idea to different constituencies in ways each constituency finds congenial.

Fourth, successful persuasion demands that private benefit must be justified in terms of *public good*. A proposal must not be presented in terms of the private or special benefits that may accrue to the rhetorician, or even to the group of people to whom s/he belongs, if the argument is accepted. For example, when MPs argue the case for higher parliamentary salaries and perquisites, the case is usually based on theta-type justifications – for instance, in terms of the need to recruit the best talent for parliamentary service or of 'enhancing democracy' by increasing Parliament's capacity for analysis and scrutiny. The private benefits to existing MPs of adopting such a course are never mentioned. The same point applies when managers argue for the doctrine of 'management's right to manage', which is usually based on sigma-type justifications (efficiency), not in terms of the personal power of managers.

Fifth, to be successful, a rhetorical argument needs to be highly *selective* in its choice of maxims and arguments to fit the desired conclusion. Those which go against the conclusion must be left out or downplayed. To pursue the parliamentary-pay example, when MPs argue for higher salaries and perquisites, comparisons are typically drawn with other countries where MPs receive higher pay or with professions (such as managers or lawyers) whose members are higher paid than MPs. No reference is made to countries where MPs receive lower pay, to comparable professions (such as teachers or social workers) whose members are lower paid than MPs, or to the fact that 'comparability' arguments are often rejected when put forward by other social groups.

Sixth, successful persuasion requires *suspension of disbelief* by those to whom the argument is addressed – rather as suspension of disbelief is needed for a successful theatrical performance. One of the commonest strategies for this purpose is to appeal to urgency of time in order to cut the debate short. The audience must be convinced that it is the eleventh hour for action, pressing deadlines imposed by other considerations must be met, vital opportunities will be lost unless immediate action is taken.

These six features of 'acceptance' drawn from writings on rhetoric are tentative, not definitive. But they can serve as a starting point for an inquiry as to why some doctrinal and disciplinary keys fit the lock of administrative argument in particular times and places, while others fail to do so. The starting point is the hypothesis that the combination of the six features is the way to open the lock. We will apply these ideas to three key reform documents in Part III and to two administrative philosophies in Part IV.

V   CONCLUSION

In this chapter we have sketched out an agenda for administrative science which has the potential to reconcile the orthodox neo-positivist approach, traditionally focused on the link between design and performance, and the rival post-positivist approach, with its concern with language and persuasion.

Our minimal programme consists of a systematic examination of the various components of administrative argument – namely, doctrines, justifications and philosophies – and of an exploration of the way in which particular keys fit the lock of acceptance as received doctrine.

We think that it is curious that the study of administration, perhaps because it has been so intent on being a respectable and relevant 'science', has neglected such an obvious way of looking at its basic stock-in-trade.

In fact, Herbert Simon could himself be regarded as the 'father' of this approach (albeit unintentionally), in so far as he forcefully exposed the rhetorical character of administrative argument. He thus opened up a path for administrative analysis which has not yet been fully trodden.

Simon himself chose to go down another path. But this path has proved to be a difficult one. It has yet fully to yield the sort of promise that Simon held out for it. Traditional administrative doctrines and modes of argument have not been replaced, as Simon hoped in the 1940s, by administrative design principles validated by the traditional methods of natural science. After forty years the prospect of quick results seems decidedly slim.

The alternative path to administrative analysis – the path that Simon found, but chose not to follow – remains to be properly explored. At the least, administrative science can start to do a more systematic job of mapping out its own heartland while we are waiting for Simon's preferred route to yield its promise of an administrative 'science' modelled on physics or chemistry. But that, as in the old (and now perhaps outmoded) Eastern European joke about waiting for the coming of socialism, may be a job for life.[11]

Beyond that, it may even be ventured that adding a concern with doctrine and persuasion to administrative science has the potential to improve the intellectual vitality and power of administrative analysis. This is, we recognize, a bold claim. A sceptic's response to the intellectual agenda sketched out in section IV might be that it could be no more than an apparatus of commentary on 'real' administrative theory, and a means of sensitizing writers about administration to the importance of style and presentation. It might be argued that, since rhetorical analysis presupposes the prior existence of statements to be worked upon, such analysis must be more like the role of the armchair sports critic than that of the athlete proper. As such, the sceptic might argue, such an approach could never amount to more than a marginal contribution to administrative analysis.

There are two answers to that, which can be put briefly. First, there is no reason why this illegitimate child of the Simonian revolution in administrative science should not be nurtured as rigorously and systematically as its acknowledged and official offspring. Second, the understanding of persuasiveness is not necessarily something that bobs along in the wake of real science. Persuasiveness and new thinking are in large part fed from the same source, namely metaphor, fiction and figure of speech. Focusing on such items is a way of putting more attention on the springs of evolution in administrative science.

NOTES

1   That is, 'hard data', in the terms used by Atkin (1977, 1).
2   An analogy to which we were introduced by Professor William Mackenzie.
3   Such features are common to all political thought, according to the ideas of Michael Oakeshott (1964, 292) and his followers.
4   Mary Douglas (1987) sees this phenomenon as built in to the world of natural science as well as to a range of other institutions.
5   Using the method of multiple regression to analyze large data sets in a way that the development of computers in the 1960s had made possible.
6   Aristotle (1984, 2063–4) was in fact well aware of the problem, as is shown in his discussion of the alternative possible maxims for structuring the Athenian magistracy.
7   There is a parallel here with alternative approaches to the study of public policy. One approach seeks to explain and evaluate policy outcomes (such as levels of economic growth, unemployment, inflation, etc.) in relation to government activity. Another approach focuses on explaining why government takes up the policy positions that it does, without reference to the relation between government 'outputs' and final policy 'outcomes'.
8   A preoccupation which, it is true, ultimately became futile and scholastic, and is satirized by Sterne in the epigraph to this chapter.
9   For this reason, analysis by interrogatives is a traditional method for exploring a topic. Aristotle used it to arrange his discussion of the alternatives for organizing government (see Aristotle 1984, 2064). Roman lawyers traditionally analysed cases by using the interrogatives *'quis, quid, ubi, quibus auxiliis, quomodo, quando, quanto'* (who, what, where, with whose help, how, when, how much) as the basis of ordering information (cf. Kassem and Hofstede 1976, 136).
10 This is, of course, potentially tautological.
11 See Larsen 1980.

PART II
WHOS, HOWS AND WHATS OF ADMINISTRATION: 99 DOCTRINES

Introduction

After the scene was set in Part I, a platoon of researchers got to work. We told them to comb through the major textbooks in administration, plus a set of well-known reform documents and historical works and gave them five main instructions

1   Record administrative doctrines which actually exist or have existed at one time. Do not include doctrines which are logically possible but never existed.
2   Find *examples*, but not necessarily the *first use* of each doctrine.
3   Prefer over-inclusion to under-inclusion.
4   Arrange the specimens found under the broad headings of administrative whos, hows and whats.
5   Stop when 99 separate specimens have been identified.

Table II.1 summarizes what our research squad produced. The left-hand column is simply a tally number; the second column is an alphanumeric identifier for each doctrine, following David Braybrooke's method. The centre columns give a brief verbal description of each doctrine and its variants. To the right of the descriptions is a column giving a keyword for each doctrine, and then a column showing the heading under which our researchers placed each doctrine (the whos, hows and whats, and overlapping areas labelled in Figure 2.1 of Chapter 2), followed by a column giving a page number for the discussion of each doctrine.

This collection, we stress, is illustrative. We have collected the 99 doctrines in the same way that you might collect 99 Hungarian folk songs – not

Table II.1   99 Doctrines of administration

#	Doctrine Label	Main Doctrine	Variants/Subtypes	Keyword		Area/Sphere	Page
1	A1	Use classic public bureaucracy		AGENCY	g	WHAT	88
2	A2	Use independent public bureaucracy		AGENCY	g	WHAT	89
	A3	Use private/independent organization		AGENCY	g	WHAT	91
3	A3.1	Use pte/ind org'n	/For profit	AGENCY	g	WHAT	91
4	A3.2	Use pte/ind org'n	/Non profit	AGENCY	g	WHAT	92
5	B1	Prefer large-scale organization		SCALE	g	WHAT	72
6	B2	Prefer small-scale organization		SCALE	g	WHAT	73
7	C1	Put unlikes together		DIVISION	g	WHAT	95
	C2	Put like with like		DIVISION	g	WHAT	96
8	C2.1	Put like with like	/By purpose	DIVISION	g	WHAT	97
9	C2.2	Put like with like	/By process	DIVISION	g	WHAT	97
10	C2.3	Put like with like	/By clients	DIVISION	g	WHAT	98
11	C2.4	Put like with like	/By area	DIVISION	g	WHAT	98
12	D1	Prefer continuity in service		DEPLOYMENT	a	WHO/HOW	61
13	D2	Prefer discontinuity in service		DEPLOYMENT	a	WHO/HOW	62
14	D3	Mix continuity and discontinuity		DEPLOYMENT	a	WHO/HOW	62
15	E1	Prefer experienced hands		EXPERIENCE	e	WHO	38
16	E2	Prefer raw recruits		EXPERIENCE	e	WHO	38
17	F1	Compel consumption		PROVISION	c	WHAT/HOW	94
	F2	Allow choice		PROVISION	c	WHAT/HOW	94
18	F2.1	Allow choice	/To opt out	PROVISION	c	WHAT/HOW	95
19	F2.2	Allow choice	/Of supplier	PROVISION	c	WHAT/HOW	95
20	G1	Select by congenital qualities		SELECTION	a	WHO/HOW	43
21	G2	Select by purchase		SELECTION	a	WHO/HOW	44
	G3	Elect to office		SELECTION	a	WHO/HOW	45
22	G3.1	Elect to office	/At large	SELECTION	a	WHO/HOW	45
	G3.2	Elect to office	/Sp. group	SELECTION	a	WHO/HOW	46
23	G3.2A	Elect to office	/Sp. group/Peers	SELECTION	a	WHO/HOW	46
24	G3.2B	Elect to office	/Sp. group/Consumers	SELECTION	a	WHO/HOW	46
25	G4	Select by lot		SELECTION	a	WHO/HOW	46
26	G5	Conscript to service		SELECTION	a	WHO/HOW	47
27	G6	Select by connections		SELECTION	a	WHO/HOW	48
28	G7	Select by objective test		SELECTION	a	WHO/HOW	49
	H1	Equalize authority		AUTHORITY	c	HOW/WHAT	102
29	H1.1	Equalize authority	/By indiv conscience	AUTHORITY	c	HOW/WHAT	102
30	H1.2	Equalize authority	/To vote	AUTHORITY	c	HOW/WHAT	103
	H2	Use differentiated ranks		AUTHORITY	c	HOW/WHAT	105
	H2.1	Use diff. ranks	/One boss	AUTHORITY	c	HOW/WHAT	106
31	H2.1A	Use diff. ranks	/One boss /With staff	AUTHORITY	c	HOW/WHAT	107
32	H2.1B	Use diff. ranks	/One boss /Delegation	AUTHORITY	c	HOW/WHAT	107
	H2.2	Use diff. ranks	/Grp boss	AUTHORITY	c	HOW/WHAT	108
33	H2.2A	Use diff. ranks	/Grp boss /Board	AUTHORITY	c	HOW/WHAT	108
34	H2.2B	Use diff. ranks	/Grp boss /Functional	AUTHORITY	c	HOW/WHAT	109
35	I1	Prefer secrecy		INFORMATION	f	HOW	117
36	I2	Inform those who need to know		INFORMATION	f	HOW	118
37	I3	Prefer openness		INFORMATION	f	HOW	118
	J1	Specialize work		SPECIALISM	c	HOW/WHAT	114
38	J1.1	Specialize by size of clientele		SPECIALISM	c	HOW/WHAT	114
39	J1.2	Separate 'policy' and 'admin' specialism		SPECIALISM	c	HOW/WHAT	115
40	J2	Consolidate work		SPECIALISM	c	HOW/WHAT	116
41	K1	Decide by rule & rote		DISCRETION	f	HOW	120
	K2	Decide by discretion		DISCRETION	f	HOW	120
42	K2.1	Decide by discretion	/Active	DISCRETION	f	HOW	120
43	K2.2	Decide by discretion	/Passive	DISCRETION	f	HOW	121
	L1	Give leaders the best		LEADERSHIP	f	HOW	110
44	L1.1	Give ldrs the best	/Conditions	LEADERSHIP	f	HOW	111
45	L1.2	Give ldrs the best	/Work behind lines	LEADERSHIP	f	HOW	111
46	L2	Give leaders normal work		LEADERSHIP	f	HOW	112
	L3	Give leaders the worst		LEADERSHIP	f	HOW	112
47	L3.1	Give ldrs the worst	/Client conditions	LEADERSHIP	f	HOW	113
48	L3.2	Give ldrs the worst	/Front-line work	LEADERSHIP	f	HOW	113
49	M1	Single-source supply		SOURCING	g	WHAT	80
	M2	Multi-source supply		SOURCING	g	WHAT	81
50	M2.1	Multi-source supply	/Between orgns	SOURCING	g	WHAT	81
51	M2.2	Multi-source supply	/Within orgns	SOURCING	g	WHAT	81
52	M2.3	Multi-source supply	/Metaphytic comp.	SOURCING	g	WHAT	82

Table II.1   cont'd

#	Doctrine Label	Main Doctrine	Variants/Subtypes	Keyword	Area/	Sphere	Page
53	N1	Prefer technical skills		SELECTION	e	WHO	41
54	N2	Prefer admin/managerial skills		SELECTION	e	WHO	41
55	N3	Prefer general/cultural skills		SELECTION	e	WHO	42
	O1	Contract out		PROVISION	c	HOW/WHAT	83
56	O1.1	Contract out	/For the field	PROVISION	c	HOW/WHAT	84
57	O1.2	Contract out	/Rival supply	PROVISION	c	HOW/WHAT	84
58	O2	Do it yourself		PROVISION	c	HOW/WHAT	85
59	P1	Promote from all comers		PROMOTION	a	WHO/HOW	63
	P2	Fill higher positions from lower ones		PROMOTION	a	WHO/HOW	63
60	P2.1	Promote by seniority		PROMOTION	a	WHO/HOW	64
	P2.2	Promote on merit		PROMOTION	a	WHO/HOW	64
61	P2.2A	Promote on merit	/Objective	PROMOTION	a	WHO/HOW	64
62	P2.2B	Promote on merit	/Bosses' judgement	PROMOTION	a	WHO/HOW	65
63	Q1	Pick the best and the brightest		QUALITY	e	WHO	39
64	Q2	Pick the average or second-rate		QUALITY	e	WHO	39
65	R1	Prefer unpaid or low-paid work		REWARD	a	WHO/HOW	54
	R2	Prefer paid to unpaid work		REWARD	a	WHO/HOW	55
	R2.1	Prefer paid work	/Fixed pay	REWARD	a	WHO/HOW	56
66	R2.1A	Prefer paid work	/Fixed pay/Lead market	REWARD	a	WHO/HOW	56
67	R2.1B	Prefer paid work	/Fixed pay/Follow Market	REWARD	a	WHO/HOW	57
68	R2.1C	Prefer paid work	/Fixed pay/Exploit mkt niche	REWARD	a	WHO/HOW	57
69	R2.1D	Prefer paid work	/Fixed pay/Link pay to trust	REWARD	a	WHO/HOW	58
	R2.2	Prefer paid work	/Variable	REWARD	a	WHO/HOW	58
70	R2.2A	Prefer paid work	/Variable /Pay by time	REWARD	a	WHO/HOW	59
71	R2.2B	Prefer paid work	/Variable /Pay by piece	REWARD	a	WHO/HOW	59
72	R2.2C	Prefer paid work	/Variable /Pay by outcome	REWARD	a	WHO/HOW	60
73	S1	Pick an unrepresentative group		SELECTION	e	WHO	50
	S2	Pick a representative group		SELECTION	e	WHO	51
74	S2.1	Pick a rep. group	/Of whole society	SELECTION	e	WHO	51
75	S2.2	Pick a rep. group	/Of client group	SELECTION	e	WHO	51
	T1	Give lifetime career tenure		TENURE	a	WHO/HOW	66
76	T1.1	Give career tenure	/Without loss	TENURE	a	WHO/HOW	66
77	T1.2	Give career tenure	/With 'fallback'	TENURE	a	WHO/HOW	67
78	T1.3	Give career tenure	/After probation	TENURE	a	WHO/HOW	67
	T2	Limit tenure		TENURE	a	WHO/HOW	67
	T2.1	Limit tenure	/Fixed terms	TENURE	a	WHO/HOW	67
79	T2.1A	Limit tenure	/Fixed t. /No renewal	TENURE	a	WHO/HOW	68
80	T2.1B	Limit tenure	/Fixed t. /With renewal	TENURE	a	WHO/HOW	68
	T2.2	Limit tenure	/By recall	TENURE	a	WHO/HOW	68
81	T2.2A	Limit tenure	/By recall/Hirer fires	TENURE	a	WHO/HOW	69
82	T2.2B	Limit tenure	/By recall/Others fire	TENURE	a	WHO/HOW	69
83	U1	Have uniform units of orgn		UNIFORMITY	g	WHAT	75
84	U2	Have a pluriform structure		UNIFORMITY	g	WHAT	76
	V1	Have inclusive responsibility		INCLUSION	g	WHAT	76
85	V1.1	Have incl. resp.	/horizontal	INCLUSION	g	WHAT	77
86	V1.2	Have incl. resp.	/vertical	INCLUSION	g	WHAT	78
	V2	Have divided responsibility		INCLUSION	g	WHAT	78
87	V2.1	Have div. resp.	/varied	INCLUSION	g	WHAT	78
88	V2.2	Have div. resp.	/concurrent power	INCLUSION	g	WHAT	79
89	W1	Treat like cases alike		CASEWORK	f	HOW	122
	W2	Treat unlike cases alike		CASEWORK	f	HOW	122
90	X1	Control by input		PROCEDURE	f	HOW	123
	X2	Control by process		PROCEDURE	f	HOW	124
91	X2.1	Control by open adversarial processes		PROCEDURE	f	HOW	124
92	X2.2	Control through standards of prof. practice		PROCEDURE	f	HOW	125
	X2.3	Control through 'business methods'		PROCEDURE	f	HOW	125
	X3	Control by output		PROCEDURE	f	HOW	126
93	X3.1	Control by output measures		PROCEDURE	f	HOW	126
94	X3.2	Control by outcome measures		PROCEDURE	f	HOW	126
95	Y1	Use long hierarchies		RANKING	c	WHAT/HOW	99
96	Y2	Use short hierarchies		RANKING	c	WHAT/HOW	99
97	Z1	Pick stakeholders for office		SELECTION	b	WHO/WHAT	52
98	Z2	Pick non-stakeholders for office		SELECTION	b	WHO/WHAT	52
99	Z3	Mix stakeholders and non-stakeholders		SELECTION	b	WHO/WHAT	53

because there are only 99, but because 99 is enough to demonstrate the variety of the phenomenon. We do not claim that there is any special significance about the number 99 or about the letters of the alphabet assigned to each doctrine. We do not claim that the categories are jointly exhaustive or mutually exclusive, though we have tried to classify broadly *per genus et differentiam*. The purpose of the collection is to show what a 'book of proverbs' might look like. It explores how Braybrooke's method could be applied to pin down the proverbs of administration which Herbert Simon began to identify in the 1940s. The method could thus contribute to the Benthamite programme for making the social world knowable by systematically marking out and identifying its objects (Bahmueller 1981, 44).

This part of the book is accordingly set out like a mini-encyclopaedia or a computer manual, expanding on the summary of the 99 doctrines which is given in Table II.1. And like an encyclopaedia or a computer manual, it is not designed – nor is very appropriate – for reading linearly from end to end like the chapters of a novel. It is best used as a resource and read selectively, using the cross-references given in Table II.1.

Though the specimens are arranged below under the headings of 'whos', 'hows' and 'whats' of administration, many are hybrid. Not much more than half of the 99 specimens found by our researchers fitted into the pure areas of 'who', 'how' and 'what' (the areas e, g and f in Figure 2.1) and the rest were classed as hybrids, belonging in the overlapping areas labelled as a, b and c in Figure 2.1. In order to make the discussion more comprehensible, each interrogative is broken up into subheadings and each of the doctrines discussed under each subheading is flagged for the reader in a box at the beginning of that section, along the lines of a computer manual. The doctrines listed in the boxes have the same alphanumeric identifiers as those given in Table II.1, so readers who want to refer to only one of them can refer back to the table for the page reference for that particular doctrine.

3   Who-type Doctrines

What shall their [office-holders] number be? Over what shall they preside, and what shall be their duration? ... Shall they be for life or for a large term of years; or, if for a short term only, shall the same person hold them over and over again, or once only? Also about the appointment to them – for whom are they to be chosen, by whom, and how? (Aristotle 1984, 2062)

I   INTRODUCTION

Getting 'the best sort of person' in office raises a host of doctrinal issues. Many of the issues were posed by Aristotle in his inquiry into appointments to public office, as indicated by the epigraph. Jeremy Bentham, in his analysis of offices, added the crucial questions of remuneration, attendance and relations with other offices and authorities (see Hume 1981, 4).

For each of these 'who-type' questions, there are doctrines purporting to tell us what is the best way to do it – and, as Simon said, the doctrines often come in contradictory pairs.

II   DOCTRINES OF SELECTION

Under 'selection', we review doctrines relating to experience, quality, expertise, mode of selection, social representativeness and interest.

Experience

E1: PREFER EXPERIENCED HANDS
E2: PREFER RAW RECRUITS

E1: Prefer Experienced Hands

E1 holds that it is best to pick people with relevant experience. A veteran is often counted to be worth far more than a raw recruit, and preference for experience is often made a formal requirement in hiring.

Justification for E1 comes in all of the three basic forms identified in the last chapter. The normal sigma-type justification of E1 is that costs can be cut by 'free-riding' on training expenses, leaving others to pay for the acquisition of experience and knowledge. (Hence the common observation that employers collectively will tend to 'underinvest' in training in the absence of regulation.)

However, there are also theta- and lambda-type justifications for E1. A common theta-type claim is that reformed poachers make the best gamekeepers, or vice-versa. A lambda-type justification holds that it is desirable to pick people with experience in fields quite *unrelated* to the current task, on the grounds that breadth of experience widens the perspective of a group. Preference for that kind of experience is often expressed for selection into some of the 'caring' professions and for elected representatives. An example of such preference is the frequent disparagement of MPs or councillors who have known no profession other than party politics (Weller and Fraser, 1987).

E2: Prefer Raw Recruits

Contrary to E1, E2 holds that it is best to 'pick them green and train them yourself'. Conventionally, E2 is defended by sigma-type justifications, on the grounds that it leads to lower costs and better corporate control than E1.

This justification has a long history. As we shall see later, it was advanced by the German cameralists who offered the first coherent philosophy of public management in modern Europe. They argued that public offices should be filled by raw recruits trained in special college classes. Similar claims were made in the 1854 Northcote–Trevelyan Report on the British civil service, at which we will be looking more closely in Chapter 6 (C 1713, 1854). The Report argued (ibid., 8) that the civil service should follow E2:

> A young man who has not made trial of any other profession will be induced to enter that of the civil service on much more moderate remuneration than would suffice to attract him a few years later (ibid).

Apart from cheapness, the other conventional sigma-type justification for E2 is that it produces staff who are more docile and malleable to fit an established corporate culture and power-structure than experienced staff are likely to be. This claim was also made by the Northcote–Trevelyan Report and it was also often used to justify the 'lifetime employment' system of private corporate employment which was a distinctive feature of big corporations in Japan during its industrialization stage (Dore 1973, 413).

Quality

Q1: PICK THE BEST AND THE BRIGHTEST
Q2: PICK THE AVERAGE OR THE SECOND-RATE

Q1: Pick the Best and the Brightest

Q1 advocates picking the best and brightest that society has to offer. (Conventionally 'best and brightest' are lumped together, as in the ironic title of David Halberstrom's book *The Best and the Brightest* (1972), although intellectual and moral qualities are sometimes distinguished.) Q1 goes back to Aristotle, who justified it by drawing a famous analogy between the allocation of public offices and the distribution of flutes among players of differing standards. The justification was that, just as the best flutes ought to go to the best players, so offices of responsibility ought to be given to those of greatest ability (Aristotle 1984, 2034–5). Those of the greatest ability would make the most use of the opportunity afforded by office, and this would be of common benefit to society.

Many since Aristotle have argued that Q1 is a recipe for good public administration. Both the German cameralists and John Stuart Mill held that 'the administration of public affairs should be in the most competent hands' (Mill 1854, 92). Q1 has typically been used to attack particular modes of selection (such as those emphasizing noble birth or party-political connections), on the grounds that they conflict with the principle of taking 'the best' for public service.

Q2: Pick the Average or the Second-rate

Opposed to Q1, Q2 is a 'mediocrity doctrine' which opposes the idea of picking the best and brightest. Q2 is common in private business, where the 'best and brightest' are often seen as likely to be a disruptive force within an organization, or as likely to move quickly to greener pastures, leaving a gap and perhaps taking skills, valuable information and even other staff with them to strengthen the competition. Hence the very frequent preference in practice for dull, steady plodders who stay put and do not 'make waves'.

In public administration, Q2 typically rests on one or both of two justifications. One is the theta-type claim that public bureaucracies ought to be
representative of the electorate and that therefore public officials should be
average – mediocre – people. This is a view of public office made famous by
a Senator Roman L. Hruska from Nebraska, who declared that US Supreme
Court justices should be mediocre, like the rest of us (*New York Times*
16.3.70, 21).

The other main justification for Q2 is a hybrid of sigma and theta-type
claims. It holds that government should not pre-empt the best talent in the
workforce. Hence the 'best and brightest' should be discouraged from public
employment and encouraged to work in the private 'wealth creating' sector,
leaving those of only average ability to work in government administration.
Such a view has parallels with the doctrine of 'less eligibility' in welfare
provision or with the economic doctrine that government borrowing should
not 'crowd out' potentially profitable private sector investment, by pre-
empting available investment funds. A recent statement of this justification
for Q2 comes from Terry Culler, former Associate Director of the US Office
of Personnel Management:

> [The government] should be content to hire competent people, not the best and
> most talented people'. (Quoted by Levine 1988, 128)

Whatever he may have thought, Culler was not the first to express this
view. Exactly similar ideas were voiced by critics of the 1854 Northcote–
Trevelyan report, on the grounds that hiring first-class people for government
service was as inappropriate as 'putting racehorses to the plough' (Sir James
Stephen, quoted in Chapman and Greenaway 1980, 27). The same view was
echoed almost a century later by the 1949 Pakistan Pay Commission:

> We do not think it to be a right policy for the State to...attract the best available
> material. The correct place for our men of genius is in private enterprise and not
> in the humdrum career of Public Service, where character and a desire to serve
> honestly for a living is more essential than outstanding intellect. (Quoted in
> Wilenski 1977, 87)

Expertise

N1: PREFER TECHNICAL SKILLS
N2: PREFER ADMINISTRATIVE OR MANAGERIAL SKILLS
N3: PREFER GENERAL, CULTURAL SKILLS

N1: Prefer Technical Skills

N1 holds that office-holders should be skilled in the technical aspects of the field in which they work. The implication is that hospitals should be run by people with medical qualifications, nuclear power plants by physicists, education departments by qualified teachers, art galleries by artists, computer units by computer specialists. Whenever an outsider is appointed to head an organization of specialists, N1 is usually advanced in protest.

A classic application of N1 is the traditional Grands Corps system in the French civil service, and N1 is often advocated by critics of the 'amateur' tradition in the top ranks of the UK civil service. Perhaps the most forceful exponent of this view was Sir Edwin Chadwick. He argued, on sigma-type grounds, that technical skill in the relevant field, attested by specialist examination and certification of ability to *practise*, was the key to competence and effectiveness. Ridiculing the Northcote–Trevelyan scheme for selecting top civil servants on the basis of (mainly) general examinations, Chadwick (1854, 161, fn) held that N1 was the typical selection principle in private business and should also be followed in public service:

> No merchant or banker would require his clerk to undergo an initiatory examination in the Antigone of Sophocles or in De Morgan's Differential and Integral Calculus, nor would he think that such qualifications, however interesting in themselves, would be of more use in his business than the power of copying a painting of Turner's or a statue of Canova's.

He developed this claim with carefully selected examples of specialists who had attained great eminence but who would have been barred from high office on the basis of a general academic examination. General qualifications, he concluded (ibid., 166):

> ... would have given preference for the Poor Law Service to a gentleman who could tell me the names of Actaeon's hounds, but who could not tell me the names of the chief statutes to be dealt with ...

N2: Prefer Administrative or Managerial Skills

Contrary to N1, N2 holds that administrators should possess generic management or administrative skills, not a detailed knowledge of the technical processes of particular activities. Skills such as law, economics, accounting and management are held to be 'portable' throughout the world of administration, irrespective of its specific subject-matter.

N2 is usually based on sigma-type justifications, and it has figured in several administrative philosophies. As we will see in Part IV, German cameralists held that public officials should be drawn from those who had studied the cameralistic sciences (originally focused on fiscal management, but later including natural resource management and economic regulation). A similar idea figured in Jeremy Bentham's claims for 'chrestomathic knowledge', – that is, knowledge directly relevant to the engineering of public policy (see Ogden 1932, xcii). N2 was also central to the doctrines of the 'scientific management' movement, as it developed from the late nineteenth century (see Merkle 1980, 2-3), with its gospel that all purposeful human activity needs professional 'managers' to oversee it, and that professional management skills can readily be taken from one context to another. It figures as part of the early development of Public Administration in the USA. It appears in the rise of 'econocracy' after World War II, with the idea that all resource allocation decisions should be made on the basis of a training in economics (cf. Self 1975). It figures large in the 'New Public Management' which we will consider in Chapter 8.

N3: Prefer General, Cultural Skills

N3 is the doctrine of the 'cultured all-rounder', the view that the best background for administrators is a broad general education, with particular attention to the study of culture and the humanities. N3 often relates to the idea that some degree of nobleness of character and developed ethical sense is more important than specific technical skills, and that these qualities are best developed on the basis of a literary and cultural training. The justification tends to be based on a mixture of theta-type and lambda-type claims – the idea that cultural or literary study sharpens social sensitivity, capacity for detached analysis, ethical awareness and the capacity for resilence in situations of crisis and disaster.

N3 has few explicit champions today, but it was long established as a dominant doctrine in Imperial China, with the tradition of selecting civil servants according to proficiency in literary scholarship. It developed as part of the reform programme for the civil service in nineteenth-century Britain, buttressing the liberal education programmes of the leading private schools and the reformed universities. And it is not uncommon today to find high-level appointments which implicitly follow N3.

Method of selection

G1: SELECT BY CONGENITAL QUALITIES
G2: SELECT BY PURCHASE
G3: ELECT TO OFFICE
G3.1: ELECT TO OFFICE BY A GENERAL FRANCHISE
G3.2: ELECT TO OFFICE THROUGH A SPECIAL GROUP
G3.2A: ELECT TO OFFICE THROUGH A SPECIAL PEER GROUP
G3.2B: ELECT TO OFFICE BY A SPECIAL CONSUMER GROUP
G4: SELECT BY LOT

| G5: CONSCRIPT TO SERVICE |
| G6: SELECT BY CONNECTIONS |
| G7: SELECT BY OBJECTIVE TEST |

G1: Select by Congenital Qualities

G1 holds that office-holders should be selected on the basis of characteristics which they acquire at birth, such as parentage, social class, race, sex. (The possibility of sex-change operations admittedly raises questions about the 'congenitality' of that item.) G1 is outlawed for some types of selection by anti-discrimination legislation, but hereditary monarchies still have their passionate defenders. So do family dynasties in private business.

Traditionally, G1 was equated with picking those who are privileged by birth – the *jus indigenatus* approach to filling public office. A form of G1 was advocated by Frederick the Great of Prussia for military officers and by the redoubtable Captain O'Brien (editor of the British *Quarterly Review* and prominent among the conservative critics of the Northcote–Trevelyan Report) for civilian public service. O'Brien made the theta-type claim that fidelity and trustworthiness could only be achieved by taking administrators from the ranks of the social elite.

> I believe...that the high character for moral worth enjoyed by the civil service ... results from their having been selected generally by the high officers of state who naturally nominate the sons of their relations, friends and acquaintances. In short, I would have gentlemen in the public offices... (Quoted in Mueller 1984, 202)

The form of G1 favoured by Frederick the Great and Captain O'Brien has been out of favour as a doctrine for filling the ranks of mainstream public bureaucrats since the eighteenth century, when cameralists such as Bielfeld attacked the principle of noble birth as a criterion for selection to bureaucratic office (Hume 1981, 52), and the Napoleonic regime in France created the slogan of the career open to the talents. More favour (in public, at least) is nowadays shown to the opposite form of G1, which calls for 'affirmative action' – that is, the selection of those who are disadvantaged rather than privileged by birth. This variant of G1 also normally rests on a theta-type justification - the idea that selection, particularly for public office, should be designed to *reverse* traditional patterns of social domination rather than to reflect them. This applied to the Bolshevik preference for 'workers and peasants' over the middle class in recruitment after the Russian Revolution of 1917, and for modern affirmative action precepts of preference for female or racial minority candidates as part of a broader programme of social change.

However, the case for G1 is not solely made in terms of theta-type justifications. There are also lambda-type justifications for the doctrine, as building resilience into organization by buttressing the established ruling class. Leadership of armies by aristocrats and gentry was traditionally seen as a way of combining interest with duty, since the defence of the country was thereby entrusted to those who had the most to lose from defeat and invasion (a version of doctrine Z1, to be discussed later). Similarly, the reservation of top military or administrative office to the propertied and high-born might be held to minimize the risk of such officials seeking to subvert the state on behalf of a revolutionary underclass.

The sigma-type case for G1 holds that there can be efficiency advantages in the family dynasty approach to selection. The claim is that damaging effects of jockeying for power can be avoided, no loss of face is involved for outsiders in losing to the predestined winner, and that the arrangement serves to link family pride and interest with the faithful performance of a service, insofar as it gives each incumbent an interest in preserving the family's claim on it and passing it on in good shape to the next generation – an incentive which cannot apply to non-hereditary offices.

G2: Select by Purchase

Like the aristocratic variant of G1, G2 is rarely advocated explicitly today. The practice, however, was once widespread in the concept of government offices as 'incorporeal hereditaments' (Finer 1952a). It has survived until modern times in the corrupt purchase of office, for instance in Voslensky's (1984, 189) assertion that venality of office was widespread in parts of the USSR in the Brezhnev era. The purchase of positions (such as apprenticeships and medical practices) is quite common in the private sector. The practice of 'honesty bonding' (for instance for police, tax officials, delivery people) comes close to it.

The two classic defenders of G2 are Montesquieu and Bentham. Montesquieu (1977, 150) argued that venality was desirable in monarchies, though it would not be acceptable in despotic governments, where the prince demanded instant hire-and-fire power for all public officials. Venality was, however, desirable in monarchies because (1) 'chance will furnish better subjects than the prince's choice'; (2) opening up prestigious public offices to purchase would stimulate entrepreneurship and wealth-creation; and (somewhat contradictorily) (3) 'it renders that a family employment which would never be undertaken through a motive of virtue; it fixes likewise everyone to his duty and renders the several orders of the kingdom more solid and permanent'.

Bentham's case for G2, as advanced in his essay on reward and in his plans for a 'patriotic auction' of offices in the French judiciary, is more substantial. As he put it (1962, Book II, 246):

> If it be desirable that the public servants should be contented with small salaries, it is more desirable that they should be willing to serve gratuitously, and more

desirable that they should be willing to pay for the liberty of serving, instead of being paid for their services. Such is the simple but conclusive train of argument in favour of the venality of offices ...

Bentham's case for G2 rested on three main assumptions. First, he assumed that G2 should be linked to an effective system of performance appraisal, and that those who failed to perform the duties of their offices effectively would be removed from them without compensation (see Hume 1981, 106).

Second, he assumed that under these circumstances no-one would purchase an office the duties of which they were unable to perform, and indeed that purchase of an office would necessarily reflect a liking for carrying out the necessary duties and skill in performing them.

Third, he assumed that people who had invested their own capital to buy positions would in general have a greater interest in retaining those positions than someone who had merely been appointed to a position. His argument here was that the ending of a 'gain' (a salary paid by the public) is less severely felt in general than the 'loss' of a corresponding amount of capital which the individual has actually possessed (Bentham did not discuss how this principle related to capital obtained by loan or mortgage).

Montesquieu and Bentham are, however, almost alone in offering a reasoned defence of G2. Though many of their other doctrines, for instance Bentham's principles of punishment, performance pay, contracting out, have been taken up or reinvented by today's 'New Right', G2 for some reason remains unrediscovered. (This is curious, because it would be easy to extend orthodox 'theta-type' arguments as applied to bureaucratic provision to the franchising of administrative office.)

G3: Elect to Office

G3 holds that 'democratic administration' means that the route to (and from) office should be through election. Its variants differ according to who is to do the electing, but are all normally based on theta-type justifications.

G3.1: Elect to office by a general franchise   Like N3, G3.1 is exotic today, and was never very widespread. The doctrine that all administrators ought to be elected by the whole population is perhaps most closely associated with the 1871 Paris Commune. In this famous but short-lived experiment in radical government, one of the basic principles of the Commune as laid out in its (only) official programme of April 1871 was:

...the choice by election or competition, with the responsibility and permanent right of control and revocation, of the Communal magistrates and officials of all classes. (Edwards 1973, 82)

G3.1 survives in the American practice of direct election of many public officials, from judges to sheriffs (rural police chiefs), and to quite low-level officials such as rat-catchers or fence post inspectors.

G3.2: Elect to office through a special group   Less radical than G3.1, G3.2 holds that selection for office ought to be made by a special electorate, not by the society as a whole. G3.2 is widely applied in practice, from the election of the Pope by the College of Cardinals to the election of company directors by owners of voting stock in a corporation.

G3.2A: Elect to office through a special peer group   G3.2A is the variant of G3.2 which holds that office-holders should be elected by the relevant peer or producer group. The justification goes that selection in this way helps to ensure that the office-holder commands reasonably wide support and confidence among the group's members, in order to speak credibly for them in negotiations, and that the office-holder is thereby obliged to be sensitive to the feelings of colleagues or fellow-producers. Traditional applications of G3.2A are the election of officers in traditional collegiate institutions (abbots, deans, etc.) and the French Revolutionary tradition that the officers of the National Guard were elected directly by the soldier-citizens of each *arrondissement*, rather than holding office by royal commission, as in the traditional European armies (Rihs 1973, 37). Officers were also elected in the opening months of the American civil war.

G3.2B: Elect to office by a special consumer group   This variant of G3.2 aims to achieve responsiveness to customers or to clients rather than to colleagues or fellow-producers (see for instance Ostrom 1974). The justification goes that an official who is elected by a specific customer or client group will be directly motivated to respond to the needs of those clients, and will not be able to obscure poor performance by 'linkage' tactics to the same extent as is possible for an official elected on a general franchise to provide a range of services. Directly elected US school boards are a traditional application of G3.2B. Other applications include agricultural cooperative/producer boards, port authorities, and sporting bodies in some countries.

G4: Select by Lot

G4 is another doctrine which is little advocated or applied today, in spite of occasional academic enthusiasm for the idea of representation by lot (cf. Burnheim 1985). Its main contemporary application is in the selection of jurors – officials who have administrative as well as more narrowly judicial functions in the operation of the Grand Jury system of the USA (see Clark 1975).

However, G4 was dominant in the administration of classical Greece (for example in the choice of the Athenian public auditors). For Aristotle (1984, 2276), the *only* two valid principles of selection for public office were lot and vote:

> In democratic states legislation ought to provide for appointment by lot to the less important and the majority of offices (for thus faction will be avoided).... In oligarchical states the laws ought to distribute the magistracies impartially to all who possess the rights of citizenship; most of them should be bestowed by lot....

It is interesting that William Niskanen (1971), in a pioneer economics-based 'New Right' treatise on public bureaucracy, proposes a version of the old Athenian principle of picking public auditors by lot in arguing that the oversight of public bureaucracies should be randomly assigned to legislative committees, to avoid biases from self-selection. However, he does not go on to argue that administrators *themselves* should be chosen by lot, even though that would be consistent with his assumptions about how to check the self-servingness and power-hunger of public bureaucrats.

G5: Conscript to Service

G5 holds that selection for office should be by compulsion, in which anyone (or everyone) may be obliged to perform a particular service.

There are two standard justifications for G5, both of which come into the 'theta' family of justifications. One of them relates to the sort of paradoxes embodied in Joseph Heller's (1964, 54) famous *Catch-22* principle (that anyone trying to get out of combat duty on grounds of insanity is thereby proved to be sane) or Groucho Marx's quip that he would not want to be a member of any club prepared to accept him as a member. The idea of conscription as a means of getting out of such difficulties goes back at least as far as Thomas More's (1965, 106) *Utopia*, where it is declared that 'anyone who deliberately tries to get himself elected to a public office is permanently disqualified from holding one'. In consequence, those who have *not* expressed a willingness to serve need to be conscripted to the task.

The other standard justification for G5 is the idea of compulsion to serve as reducing the risk of tyranny. The standard justification for compulsory military service is that it decreases the probability of military *coups d'état* by preventing the development of a military profession divorced from civil society. Machiavelli (1961, 77ff) used this reasoning for preferring citizen armies to mercenaries.

The classic expression of G5 is the Swiss tradition of a citizen militia, the foundation of the Swiss state. Every male citizen is obliged to perform military service for the whole of his active life, a system imitated by Sweden in the nineteenth century and by Israel in 1948. Similarly, and drawing from the same tradition, G5 is central to the political theory lying behind the famous Second Amendment to the US Constitution, namely that 'a militia of the body of the people is necessary to guarantee a free state' (Halbrook 1984, 8).

G5 was also applied to the organization of police in the administrative doctrines of the Paris Commune, and was in turn taken up as the model of Soviet police administration by the early Lenin (Leggett 1985). Indeed, Lenin's general 'solution' to the public administration problem before the Russian Revolution was to propose that all the essential functions of the state should be reduced to tasks of accounting and control so simple that they would be performed on a rotational basis by all citizens, at workmen's wages (cf. Merkle 1980, 109).

G6: Select by Connections

G6 holds that persons should be selected for office primarily on the basis of personal or political connections and recommendations rather than on any other basis. This is how most of us go about acquiring a lawyer, a doctor or a plumber in private life; and G6 applies the same principle to business and government generally. Usually it is justified by some mix of sigma-type and theta-type claims, in the idea that selection by connections is a way of maximizing the chances of selecting loyal, trustworthy, politically reliable people with a known track record, particularly for positions where those qualities are especially important.

G6 can take many forms. The 'proper sort of person' may be defined by social status, as for example in the paramount importance of a private school and Oxbridge background in Britain. This is a preoccupation which was satirized by John Galsworthy in the 1920s but was still said to have influenced the investigation of Kim Philby in the 1960s and the treatment of Sir Anthony Blunt in the 1980s.

Another variant of G6 is the principle of political spoils, which gives elected officials the right to appoint and dismiss administrators according to their political connections. This version of G6 is associated with American and German traditions of administration, though a weak version of it gained some ground in some of the 'Westminster' type public bureaucracies from the 1960s onwards, with the argument that more control by elected representatives over selection of officials was necessary in order to ensure that the bureaucracy was responsive to the demands of elected politicians.

The classic exponent of this variant of G6 is the early nineteenth-century US President Andrew Jackson. Jackson opposed the idea of a permanent cadre of professional administrators, which he considered to be a recipe for elitism rather than democracy. He argued that turnover of administrative offices through appointment and dismissal by politicians was a means of promoting equality of opportunity. Simon, Smithburg and Thompson (1950,

321–2) quote from Jackson's first State of the Union message in 1829, when he defended this principle, as follows:

> Office is considered as a species of property, and government rather as a means of promoting individual interests than as an instrument created solely for the service of the people.... The duties of all public officers are, or at least admit of being made, so plain and simple that men of intelligence may readily qualify themselves for their performance, and I cannot but believe that more is lost by the long continuance of men in office than is generally to be gained by their experience.

> In a country where offices are created solely for the benefit of the people no one man has any more intrinsic right to official station than another. Offices were not established to give support to particular men at the public expense.

Jackson's original case for G6 was couched mainly in terms of egalitarianism. Today G6 is more commonly justified in terms of political accountability — as a means of guaranteeing the responsiveness of administrators to their political superiors, by making them dependent for their office on political chiefs. Such dependence means that the fortunes of the agent are inextricably tied to the rise or fall of the principal.

G7: Select by Objective test

G7 holds that selection for office should be based on an objective test of ability or skills, not on connections, parentage, political support, wealth or chance. An early and famous application of G7 was the traditional system of selecting officials in Imperial China by means of competitive examination. For a time the same system was applied to the Imperial Japanese bureaucracy too (see Reischauer 1977, 45). Much later, G7 came into favour in Europe, as part of the revolution in government which took power away from the hereditary aristocracy.

Normally, the case for G7 is made in terms of sigma-type justifications. Sigma-type claims were the main grounds on which the German cameralists (and, to some extent, the utilitarians) based their case for G7. Though Jeremy Bentham generally argued (on theta-type grounds) that election was the best way of requiring government to act in the interest of the governed, he became enthusiastic about competitive examinations for public service after 1802 (Hume 1981, 201). His utilitarian successor John Stuart Mill was even more unequivocally in favour of G7. He argued

> A most important principle of good government in a popular constitution is that no executive functionaries should be appointed by popular election: neither by the

votes of the people themselves, nor by those of their representatives (Mill 1910, Ch XIV, 335).

Mill applied the same precept to the judiciary, arguing that the qualities needed for success in elections are very different from those needed for fair and considered judicial work – namely, calmness and impartiality.

Such claims for G7 were later made by the Progressives in the late-nineteenth century USA, in alliance with the 'scientific managers', to attack the patronage power of party machine bosses in the big cities. This attack linked with Woodrow Wilson's famous idea that administration is, or can be, a technical middle-class profession and that it should be separated from electoral politics (Wilson 1887). On the eve of World War I, Max Weber produced perhaps the most well–known sigma-type claim for G7. According to Weber, G7 is most likely to result in the selection of people with technical expertise and to make organizations run smoothly and precisely (Weber in Gerth and Mills 1948, 201). Like Mill before him, Weber believed that the appointment of judges and civil servants ought to follow similar principles.

Social Representativeness

S1: PICK AN UNREPRESENTATIVE GROUP
S2: PICK A REPRESENTATIVE GROUP
S2.1: PICK A GROUP REPRESENTATIVE OF THE WHOLE SOCIETY
S2.2: PICK A GROUP REPRESENTATIVE OF CLIENTS

S1: Pick an Unrepresentative group

S1 holds that disproportionate preference in appointments should be given to some special group in society – for example, veterans, the disabled, the intelligentsia. S1 differs from G1 in that the special group is not necessarily selected by *congenital* qualities. Justifications of S1 come in sigma-type, theta-type and lambda-type forms.

A lambda-type justification puts the case for S1 in terms of enhanced reliability or resilience in crisis. This is the case for picking eunuchs to guard the harem or foreigners to form the bodyguard of an unpopular leader.

A theta-type justification usually puts the case for S1 in terms of the special deservingness of particular groups, as in the idea of preference for hiring veterans after a war. A sigma-type justification puts the case in terms of simple effectiveness or problem-solving. An example is the idea that picking people of high status and connections may bring lustre and attention to the organization which they serve. This idea goes back at least to Machiavelli (1961, Part XXII, 124), who thought that princes should choose advisers who are respected throughout society, because the reputation of advisers is the basis on which observers judge the sagacity of the prince. Likewise, the justification for the 'Lord on the board' principle (often applied to high positions in banking, financial regulation, diplomacy and the like) goes that selecting from the ranks of an elite helps office-holders to deal with other people of high status in negotiating or customer-client relationships. They may also be able to draw on their social network as a resource for 'backdoor' problem-solving.

S2: Pick a Representative Group

S2.1: Pick a group representative of the whole society   S2.1 is commonly known as the doctrine of 'representative bureaucracy', although it advocates only one out of many possible senses of representation (see Kingsley 1944; Subranamian 1967). It holds that office-holders should reflect the distribution of racial, linguistic, gender or social class characteristics in society at large. Office-holders at every level should be an exact microcosm of the wider society. S2.1 is a central feature of a broader philosophy of consociational administration, as applied in countries such as Lebanon, Belgium or the EC (cf. O'Leary 1989).

Obviously, there are practical and logical limits to the application of S2.1. For example, it would hardly be possible even in principle to make the workers in every organization exactly representative of the age structure of society. Representation of some groups – the criminally insane, for instance – is infeasible for different reasons. In practice, it is rare for more than one or two types of representation to be on the agenda at once – as for example with the representation of different national groups in the UN or EC bureaucracy.

S2.2: Pick a group representative of clients   Contrary to S2.1, S2.2 holds that it is representativeness of specific *clients* or *customers* which counts. S2.2 is advanced by Martin Shubik (1986, 247) on theta-type grounds, as a means of reflecting the 'golden rule' in moral philosophy (do unto others as you would wish them do to you). The golden rule is, of course, hard to apply for social interactions across groupings which cannot readily experience each other's feelings (the young for the old, whites for blacks, men for women and vice versa). To cope with such divisions, office-holders should be representative of the specific groups they serve, not just of society in general. Applications of S2.2 include the hiring of disabled staff by disability organizations, the institution of 'lady cabs' (mini-cabs driven by women for women, to minimize risks of sexual assault), the hiring of muslim teachers in schools with predominantly muslim children. Shubik (ibid) puts it like this:

> ... a society supplying social services has a better chance of success if the social workers and managers are roughly of the same age structure and are of the same

sex as their clients. For example, a requirement that the personal attendants and managers at an old age home be older than 50 might help ...

Interest

Z1: PICK STAKEHOLDERS FOR OFFICE
Z2: PICK NON-STAKEHOLDERS FOR OFFICE
Z3: MIX STAKEHOLDERS AND NON-STAKEHOLDERS

Z1 : Pick Stakeholders for Office

Z1 is closely related to S2.2. It holds that the oversight or performance of a task should be done by those who have a clear interest in it. Perhaps the commonest application, usually based on a theta-type justification, is the principle of drawing the governing body of an institution from representatives of the major stakeholders.

A different theta-type justification for Z1 rests on the idea of sheeting home the consequences of their actions to decision-makers. An example is the idea that architects should have to live in the houses they design, as in the current doctrine of 'community architecture', which requires that the 'community architect' must sign a contract undertaking to live in the community served.

Sometimes this idea is extended into lambda-type justifications too, in cases where reliability in the face of life-and-death risks is said to be guaranteed by giving the job to those with a sufficiently strong personal stake in the outcome to make it worth their while to work conscientiously. An example is the notion that those administering air safety regulations should themselves be frequent air travellers (see Perrow 1984, 127); that those who carry out security checks on aircraft baggage and passengers should themselves be aircrew in the relevant aircraft (since they will be the first on the scene of any accident, they will have the clearest interest in the accuracy of their work).

Z2 : Pick Non-stakeholders for Office

Contrary to Z1, Z2 holds that particular tasks should be done by persons who have no personal interest or connection with the subject-matter, in order to achieve impartiality or to avoid the colouring of judgements by personal interest or experience. Plato and Thomas More argued that the best rulers were those with no personal interest at stake.

Today this doctrine is usually applied to judicial-type work and to other fields where the ability to distance oneself emotionally from work is held to be a condition of effectiveness. A case in point is the determination of salaries of company chairmen and directors, which in many UK companies is decided by remuneration committees composed of non-executive directors. A public administration example is the US Securities and Exchange Commission. SEC members are obliged to give up their jobs in the securities industry, whereas most of the UK equivalent, members of the Securities and Investments Board, are currently working within the financial industry that SIB regulates (Reid 1988, 250). The case for Z1 in the British case is that regulators have a close 'feel' for the industry as a result of their stake in it, whereas the case for Z2 in the US case is that impartiality can only be achieved by occupational disinterest.

Z3: Mix Stakeholders and Non-stakeholders

Z3 is the intermediate doctrine that best results are obtained by selecting a mix of stakeholders and non-stakeholders. Z3 is also commonly applied to the governing bodies of public and private corporations. An example is the efforts of some large corporations to provide channels for expression of dissent within the organization by combining non-stakeholders with stakeholders in the government of the corporation. One application of this idea, as applied for instance by the Westpac banking corporation in Australia, is the creation of corporate ombudsmen to receive and evaluate independently complaints made by employees or customers. Another application, used for example by the US General Motors corporation, is to appoint a public interest advocate to the board of directors, to sit alongside the various private stakeholder interests. Such 'angels' advocates' are charged with making sure that the interest of the wider community is recognized in corporate decision-making. Part of the purpose of such a move is to satisfy corporate employees who might be worried about the ill effects of corporate decision-making on the community that the public interest will be well represented at the highest level.

III DOCTRINES OF REWARD

R1: PREFER UNPAID OR LOW-PAID WORK
R2: PREFER PAID TO UNPAID WORK
R2.1: GIVE FIXED REWARDS
R2.1A: LEAD THE MARKET
R2.1B: FOLLOW THE MARKET
R2.1C: PAY ONLY WHAT IS NEEDED TO RETAIN OR HIRE STAFF
R2.1D: PROPORTION LEVEL OF REWARD TO DEGREE OF TRUST
R2.2: PREFER VARIABLE REWARD

| R2.2A: PROPORTION REWARD TO TIME SPENT ON THE JOB |
| R2.2B: PROPORTION REWARD TO OUTPUT |
| R2.2C: PROPORTION REWARD TO OUTCOMES |

R1: Prefer Unpaid or Low-paid Work

R1 holds that it is best to use unpaid or low-paid labour. The normal justification for R1 is that people who offer their labour at no or low cost will perform a task out of a real vocation for the work, rather than out of mere desire for sustenance or for self-enrichment.

A common application of R1 is in social services and 'caring' activities. The claim is that such services are best and/or most cheaply provided on the basis of R1. (Hatch and Mocroft 1979). The greater effectiveness is held to come from the solidarity of non-hierarchical moral communities. The lower costs are held to arise from the use of voluntary or low-paid workers who are motivated, by religious views or other convictions, to work harder for less money than the conventional *homo economicus* in the labour market.

R1 is also commonly applied to leadership roles. It is a recurring idea that the people at the top ought to be motivated by an ethical ideal of service to the community rather than by material rewards. The Confucian code of ethics holds that those in authority should be first in worrying about the world's troubles and last in enjoying its pleasures. Similar doctrines were asserted in classical Greece, and echoed in Thomas More's *Utopia*. The most extreme statement is Plato's argument that the state's high officials (the philosopher-monarchs) should live a life of extremest austerity, with no private property or family life, and with sex strictly rationed to what was needed to maintain their numbers. Less drastically, Aristotle asserted (1984, 2078) that: '...every state should be so administered and so regulated by law that its magistrates cannot possibly make money...'. Benedict de Spinoza (1951), the seventeenth-century Dutch philosopher, argued that the rulers of the state should only have their food and other physical necessities provided, rather than receiving a money salary. For all of these thinkers, those in high office should derive their satisfaction from service alone. If they do not, they are unfit for such office.

R1 was also advocated by the early twentieth century British philosophers of Public Administration such as Beveridge and Haldane (see Thomas 1978, 42 and 158). Explicit comparisons were drawn with the vows of poverty taken by monastic orders such as the Order of St Francis. R1 is epitomized in Sir Arthur Helps's dictum that 'There should be men in office who love the state as priests love the church' (Schaffer 1973, 39), and in Lenin's (1933, 35) view that the rulers and administrators of the state should be paid no more than the wages of an ordinary worker:

All officials, without exception, elected and subject to recall at any time, their salaries reduced to 'workingmen's wages' – these simple and 'self-evident' democratic measures, which, completely uniting the interests of the workers and the majority of peasants, at the same time serve as a bridge leading from capitalism to socialism.

The theta-type claim for R1 is that rulers will only identify with the plight of ordinary people by sharing their conditions. Equally, it is held that if rulers receive only an honorarium and not a salary adequate to live upon, they will need to continue their occupation while in office. Without being kept in touch, by direct personal experience, with the problems encountered by ordinary people in making a living, they are liable to turn into a remote, self-serving elite. This is the case for amateur legislators and administrators.

R2: Prefer Paid to Unpaid work

Contrary to R1, R2 holds that paid work is the key to realizing administrative efficiency or other broader 'system' values. There are three common justifications for R2.

First is the lambda-type claim that properly paid work is more *reliable* than unpaid or low-paid work. It is held to be more reliable because it offers clear, targetable and variable sanctions against irregular attendance, lack of discipline or poor-quality work. The classic source of this idea is Max Weber's claim that

> ... as far as complicated tasks are concerned, paid bureaucratic work is not only more precise but, in the last analysis, it is often cheaper than even formally-unremunerated honorific service. (Gerth and Mills 1948, 214)

Weber's statement includes a second, sigma-type justification for R2, namely the claim that payment for work makes it possible to select workers from a broader pool of talent than would be available for unpaid work, and hence leads to better quality and even to lower costs.

Third is the theta-type claim that regular payment for work provides a basis for *disinterested* service. For instance, Georg Hegel argued for a comfortable level of payment to public servants, on the grounds that such payment would free the officials from worldly cares and make them act in the altruistic pursuit of the collective interests of the state (cf. Avineri 1972, 159–60). An important variant of the theta-type case for R1 is Alexis de Tocqueville's (1946, 143-4) claim that payment of public officers and representatives was essential for effective democracy:

...if public officers are not uniformly remunerated by the State, the public charges must be intrusted to men of opulence and independence, who constitute the basis of an aristocracy....

But payment, of course, can be made in several different ways, and hence there are many variants of R2.

R2.1: Give Fixed Rewards

R2.1 is that variant of R2 which advocates that payment be *fixed* and regular. R2.1 holds that payment fixed according to status ultimately produces better results than rewards narrowly linked to time or results.

There are four common justifications for R2.1. One is a sigma-type claim for administrative simplicity. Fixed payment avoids the difficulty, cost and conflict of measuring work. Second is the theta-type claim that R2.1 minimizes the scope for corrupt favouritism by bosses and makes a system 'transparent' to outside scrutiny. Third is the sigma-type claim that fixed salaries, linked with classification of work, enable an organization to use labour efficiently by moving workers from one position to another, like soldiers, according to where the 'hot spots' develop (see Dunsire 1973a, 18-9) rather than laboriously negotiating new contract terms every time that circumstances change.

The fourth justification is the lambda-type idea that motivating workers by status rather than by trying to count work done produces greater loyalty and commitment in the long run. Max Weber put this view in extreme terms (Gerth and Mills 1948, 208), arguing:

> A strong status element among officials not only agrees with the official's readiness to subordinate himself to the chief without any will of his own, but – just as is the case with the officer – status sentiments are the consequence of such subordination, for internally they balance the official's self-feeling.

Weber's claim reflects a long line of idealistic thought about bureaucracy, stretching back to Confucius and Plato. It probably echoes Georg Hegel's early argument (in his *Jenenser Realphilosophie*) that the high bureaucracy of the modern state is the moral equivalent of the aristocracy of ancient times.

R2.1A: Lead the market   R2.1A is a variant of R2.1 which applies mainly to public administration and non-business organizations such as churches, trade unions and charitable organizations. It holds that payment should not be set by slavishly following the market. Rather, the aim should be to lead, buck or ignore the market. Often this implies an aspiration to set salary and work conditions as a model for society at large, and an example to other employers.

Sometimes R2.1A is held to mean offering lower rewards than those to be found in the general labour market – for instance, pay restraint in public bureaucracies in order to inspire private employers to hold back. Conversely, R2.1A sometimes means offering pay and conditions well above the market price of labour of a particular type. Examples include pay and conditions designed to improve the conditions of disabled people or women (equal pay, childcare facilities, maternity leave) by a 'pathfinder' approach in the public sector. University student unions have often been known to aspire to be 'model employers', as part of a strategy to fight social injustice.

R2.1B: Follow the market R2.1B, the 'fair relativity' doctrine, is a variant of R2.1 which holds that salaries ought to be fixed by comparison to pay levels for similar work in other organizations or walks of life. R2.1B was first adopted in the UK civil service in 1910, endorsed by several official reports on public sector pay, and only formally abandoned in 1981. It has been used in many other countries, such as the USA, Canada, Australia and New Zealand (see Rodger 1986).

R2.1B is usually justified on theta-type grounds of 'fairness', as argued for instance by the UK 'Priestley' Commission Report of 1955 (Cmd 9613 1955, 23ff):

> ... the State is under a categorical obligation to remunerate its employees fairly .... We think that a correct balance will be achieved only if the primary principle of civil service pay is fair comparison with the current remuneration of outside staffs employed on broadly comparable work, taking account of differences in other conditions of service.

R2.1C: Pay only what is needed to retain or hire staff R2.1C superseded R2.1B as a pay principle for the UK civil service in 1981, and the same has happened in New Zealand (see Rodger 1986). R2.1C is a variant of R2.1B, but is significantly different in some cases, in that it is more 'opportunistic'. The aim is not to secure pay comparability as an end in itself (theta-type claims of fairness), but to pay whatever is needed to attract and retain staff (sigma-type claims of matching resources to task). For example, if politicians' pay were based on R2.1B, pay would go up if wage rates rise in what are considered to be roughly comparable occupations – such as journalists, teachers, used-car dealers. But if legislators' pay is to be based on R2.1C, pay should be raised only if the supply of people offering themselves for election starts to dry up. (Needless to say, politicians who advocate R2.1C for the public service generally tend to argue for R2.1B when it comes to their own pay.)

R2.1C thus produces different results from R2.1B if staff are in practice 'locked in' to employment in a particular organization. The same goes if there are intangible factors which enable an organization to attract staff at lower pay levels than other organizations of the same kind – for example to organizations with high prestige or to public organizations which can provide their employees with a springboard for a remunerative private sector career and thus can attract able and ambitious people contemplating an 'up and out' career (legislatures, tax bureaucracies, central banks, central finance departments).

R2.1D: Proportion level of reward to degree of trust   R2.1D is perhaps a hybrid of R2.1A and R2.1B, but it deserves separate mention because it offers a rather special criterion for fixing levels of payment. It holds that especially high payments should be made to people occupying offices of trust, in order to ensure that they have more to lose by dishonesty than by remaining honest.

Classic advocates of R2.1D were Adam Smith and Jeremy Bentham. They held that high pay was one of the best ways to avoid malfeasance and corruption. Smith's argument in *The Wealth of Nations* (1937, 105) ran as follows:

> Such confidence could not safely be reposed in people of a very mean or low condition. Their reward must be such, therefore, as may give them that rank in society which so important a trust requires.

Jeremy Bentham (1931, 396) went further than Adam Smith in developing Smith's own principles:

> The more of fortune and honour those [in public employment]...have to lose, the stronger hold we have upon them. Their salary is a means of responsibility. In case of misconduct, the loss of this salary is a punishment which they cannot escape, though they may avoid every other.... If you cannot insure the honesty of a cashier in any other way, make his appointments rise something above the interest of the greatest sum which is intrusted to him. This excess of salary is like a premium paid for an insurance against his dishonesty. He has more to lose by becoming a rogue than by remaining honest.

R2.2: Prefer Variable Reward

Contrary to the fixed salary doctrine in its various forms, R2.2 holds that reward should be *variable*, so as to provide incentives for diligence and effectiveness. Adam Smith (1937, 678) provided what is perhaps the classic statement:

> Public services are never better performed ... than when their [public officials'] reward comes only in consequence of their being performed, and is proportional to the diligence employed in performing them.

Many later authors (such as Niskanen 1983) have also advocated R2.2. But Smith's precept is very general, and there are at least three different ways in which reward can be proportioned to diligence.

R2.2A: Proportion reward to time spent on the job   R2.2A holds that the best way of proportioning reward to diligence is to relate payment to time spent at work. Jeremy Bentham (generally an advocate of the piece-work approach to reward) offered a sigma-type justification for R2.2A for cases where salaries needed to be paid. Using the example of payment to the members of the French Academy and the Academy of Sciences, he argued that the best way to ensure that salaried office-holders performed their office was to pay them on a daily basis, conditional on attendance. As he put it (1962, Book 2, 238):

> ...of all duties, *assiduous attendance* is the first, the most simple, and the most universal. In many cases, to ensure the performance of this duty ...is to ensure the performance of every other duty ... In the highest offices, an individual, if paid by his time, should, like the day-labourer, and for the same reason, be paid rather by the day than by the year.... When the officer is paid separately for each day's attendance, each particle of service has its reward: there is for each particle of service an inducement to perform it.... And who are the individuals, how low or how high soever, who cannot, and who ought not, to be paid in this manner?

R2.2B: Proportion reward to output   R2.2B is the doctrine of piece-work payment. It comes in many variants, notably in collective and individual forms, and in different formulae for fixing the rate. All depend on some way of measuring work done. Bentham argued that payment by the piece was a cardinal principle of good administration, and his follower Sir Edwin Chadwick (1854, 193) offered a graphic defence of R2.2B:

> By accounting [measurement of work], or by the principle of piece-work, an interest is given to the operative in every blow he strikes, for he feels that the blow is struck for himself as well as for his employer....

As 'evidence' for R2.2B, Chadwick cited his own administrative experience in the Poor Law Commission (ibid, 200). Instead of using clerks paid at a fixed salary to do the Commission's copying work, he paid a per-folio rate for the job. The result, he claimed, was that he had the Commission's copying work done by 35 rather than 70 clerks, and that the income of the 35 remaining clerks rose by more than 30 per cent.

Another advocate of R2.2B was Alexis de Tocqueville (1954, I, 215). On his famous visit to America in 1830, de Tocqueville was impressed with the service given by public officials. Their enthusiasm was induced, de Tocqueville thought, because they were not paid a salary. Rather, they were paid piecework on the revenue raised by their efforts. The analogy here is the American practice of tipping a waiter for service in a restaurant.

Better known than Bentham, Tocqueville or Chadwick for his part in the development of R2.2B is Frederick Winslow Taylor, the American engineer who turned piece work payment into a 'science' in the 1890s. Taylor's system differed from other schemes for incentive pay in that it applied to the individual, not the work group. It separated the individual worker from the group for the purposes of payment, measured work input and time, and set payment rates by a formula which had a punitive effect for below-speed work while rewarding above-speed work at rates well below the value of the additional output. This fairly complex incentive formula demanded highly accurate written records of work performed, careful determination of unit values and central control of machine operations (Merkle 1980, 2, 13, 30). Resisted in the US federal government service as a result of labour union pressures, the Taylor system became world-famous and turned into the centrepiece of factory management in the Soviet Union.

R2.2C: Proportion reward to outcomes   A third way to proportion reward to diligence is to relate it to results in a wider sense. The obvious potential drawback of R2.2A is that it encourages workers to 'spin out the job', by spending longer on it than is necessary, while the drawback of R2.2B is that it tends to make a fetish of raw output, rather than 'working smart', quality of work and care and maintenance of equipment. It can lead to the outcome satirized by Dickens (1910, 536) in *Little Dorrit*:

> ... the more the Circumlocution Office did, the less was done, and...the greatest benefit it could confer on an unhappy public would be to do nothing.

R2.2C seeks to proportion rewards to the effects produced in society, rather than to the production of intermediate outputs. Hence the argument for 'health maintenance' payments to health care workers (meaning that reward is inversely proportioned to the extent of medical treatment, so that doctors have the maximum incentive to keep their patients in good health).

Like R2.2A, R2.2C is normally linked with utilitarianism, though it certainly has earlier roots. Spinoza, writing in the 1670s, argued that military leaders should have no gain to expect from war except the booty they can win from the enemy (Spinoza 1958, 331). Spinoza presaged the later argument of Bentham (1962, Book 2, 239–40) that:

> Instead of appointing a fixed salary...it would be well to make the emolument of such persons [as are responsible for running prisons, hospitals or other 'total' residential establishments] depend upon the care with which their duties have been performed, as evidenced by their success.

The method which Bentham advocated for that purpose was to reward the directors of such establishments by a fixed sum for each person under their charge, on condition that an equal sum be deducted from the director's reward for each person who died. He noted that the system of payment to military commanders which was common at the time when he was writing, of paying commanders according to the size of the corps 'establishment' rather than by the number of soldiers actually serving, had the very opposite effect from that which he aimed to produce, since it was 'a reward offered, if not for murder, at least for negligence' (ibid, 240).

Bentham thought that the general principle was capable of many other applications, for example in the reward of military commanders (as with the traditional system of 'prize money' for naval commanders). In general he wanted to link rewards to objectively-observable results. But in today's 'New Public Management', R2.2C is commonly applied in relation to the 'results' perceived by bosses, so that 'merit pay' is within the gift of the superordinate.

IV DOCTRINES OF DEPLOYMENT, PROMOTION AND TENURE

The next group of doctrines relate to the kind of career structure that is held to lead to the best performance. Contested issues in this group of doctrines relate to the way that office-holders are *deployed*, the way that they are *promoted*, and the kind of *tenure* that they should possess.

Deployment

D1: PREFER CONTINUITY IN SERVICE
D2: PREFER DISCONTINUITY IN SERVICE
D3: MIX CONTINUITY AND DISCONTINUITY

D1: Prefer Continuity in Service

D1 holds that administration works most smoothly when it retains the same people in the same job permanently. This is the Platonic doctrine that once the appropriate people are in office they should be left in place to do the job. D1 need not necessarily imply a doctrine of formal career tenure. Nor need it necessarily imply advocacy of career service in the sense of a lifetime ladder of promotion system. In fact it may be incompatible with that system in so far as it demands continuity of service in the same position.

D1 can be applied to different senses of 'continuity' and dimensions of administration. A highly schizophrenic form of D1 was argued by the UK Fulton Committee Report on the Civil Service (Cmnd 3638 1968) which advocated D1 as a general principle for administrative positions, while simultaneously arguing that it was desirable for civil servants to switch jobs between government and business and between specialist and administrative positions (see Schaffer 1973).

Common justifications for D1 are the sigma-type claim that it is the best way to build up cumulative expertise and the theta-type claim that it makes an organization accessible and comprehensible to clients. Certainly, much of the frustration and error associated with large administrative structures (truncated memory, endless learning curves, clients or customers who never encounter the same person twice in their dealings with an organization) is associated with rapid turnover in office.

D2: Prefer Discontinuity in Service

D1 is commonly advocated by those who like to see the same face behind the counter or hear the same voice on the telephone when they deal with an organization. But it has its opposite, the doctrine D2, which holds that there are positive advantages to be gained from discontinuity in service. D2 is more commonly advanced by managers and directors rather than by clients, and the case for it conventionally rests on three main justifications.

First is the sigma-type claim that people who stay for too long in the same job tend to 'go native', to be 'captured' by their clients, and that such an attitude may conflict with the organization's goals. D2 was traditionally applied to functionaries such as priests, diplomats and colonial administrators, but it is also commonly applied within today's multinational companies, and for the same reasons. By preventing office holders from becoming too closely known to, or identified with, their local clients, it is held to ensure that those office holders put general goals (profit, the interest of the state) before 'parochial' ones and that a degree of respect, mystery or fear, is retained.

The second justification is the lambda-type claim that D2 helps to avoid staleness and burnout in stressful situations – ensuring that a fresh mind periodically comes to bear on a problem or providing variety and a sense of perspective. Such is the argument for an 'in-and-outer' approach to deployment. The third justification is the theta-type claim that D2 is a way of avoiding corruption, in the sense of the desire and ability to subvert the formal goals and procedures of the organization for personal self-interest. Hence the frequent application of D2 to officials such as auditors, tax-collectors and bank managers.

D3: Mix Continuity and Discontinuity

D3 is a hybrid doctrine which is designed to secure the advantages claimed for D1 and D2 simultaneously. One of its commonest variants is the renewal of governing bodies by rotation. The idea is that where a group of people holds office as a unit, it is best to renew its membership in a staggered process, leaving some members to remain in office while others are replaced. The sigma-cum-lambda case for D3 is that it minimizes 'tired blood' in an organization without losing the benefits of experience, while the theta-type case is that it provides a degree of mutual checking, damping the effects of the mood of the moment.

This form of D3 is often applied to political institutions, and is also commonly applied to company boards and governing bodies of other institutions such as clubs and associations. D3 was used in the composition of the governing board of the British East India Company, which was taken by Jeremy Bentham (1931, 452) as a model for other institutions. Its most famous application lies in the US Senate, a third of whose members come up for election every two years, but the same principle is applied in many other contexts.

Promotion

P1: PROMOTE FROM ALL COMERS
P2: FILL HIGHER POSITIONS FROM LOWER ONES
P2.1: PROMOTE BY SENIORITY
P2.2: PROMOTE ON MERIT
P2.2A: PROMOTE BY 'OBJECTIVE' MERIT
P2.2B: LET SUPERIORS DECIDE ON MERIT FOR PROMOTION

P1: Promote from all Comers

P1 holds that promotion should be no different from selection, and that higher positions in an organization should be open to applications from all comers. Hence the case for filling senior positions in academia, the public bureaucracy, private firms, by public advertisement and entertaining applications from all comers.

P1 tends to be justified either in theta-type terms of intrinsic fairness, as a means of removing all artificial barriers to the advancement of talent, or in sigma-type terms, in ensuring that organizations draw from the largest possible field of talent at all levels. 'Lateral entry' in promotion is a crucial administrative battleground, and P1 is often advanced by reformers who wish to take away established 'career service' entitlements in promotion as part of a process of political change – for example, to put more women into top jobs, to bring business experience into public bureaucracy, to bring managerial experts into senior police positions.

P2: Fill Higher Positions from Lower Ones

P2 is a key doctrine of career service – the view that organizations work best when they concentrate their recruitment at bottom entry-level grades and pick their senior staff mainly from those who have come in from the bottom. P2 is common in public and private management alike, and has frequently been applied to political positions. Committee chairmanships in the US Congress were once allocated on the basis of seniority, and the British parliamentary tradition also used to require a long period of back-bench service from those who aspired to positions of leadership, so that they could learn the conventions of the House of Commons.

The five commonest justifications used for P2 mostly come from the sigma family. One is that P2 encourages loyal service rather than a fly-by-night, job-hopping approach to employment at the lower organizational levels. Second is that P2 brings in better-quality people as recruits to junior entry-level grades than would happen under a P1 regime. Third is that P2 helps to strengthen an organization's distinct ethos or culture among its senior staff. Fourth is that P2 makes possible a more *reliable* rating of applicants for promotion than can be applied to external applicants, since the latter can more easily conceal their strengths and weaknesses. Fifth is that P2 ensures that leaders are well informed about their organization. They will know where the bodies are buried and will have personal hands-on experience of the basic, front-line or 'coal-face' activities.

P2.1: Promote by seniority   A variant of P2, P2.1 holds that promotion should rest on length of service in an organization. Less commonly professed than doctrines of 'merit' promotion, P2.1 plays at least a subsidiary part in many promotion systems, and it is often claimed to be particularly appropriate to routine work. For example, John Stuart Mill argued that promotion in the public service should be according to seniority for routine-type duties and according to merit for other, less easily programmed, duties (Mill 1910, 345).

P2.1 is conventionally defended by lambda- or theta-type claims. One is the idea that P2.1 serves to cement solidarity within working groups, thus avoiding the damage that can be done to collective effort (mistrust, information distortion) by intensive rivalry and jockeying for position. Another is the theta-type claim that P2.1 avoids the risk of favouritism and corruption which other approaches to promotion can engender. A third is the claim that P2.1 is a *robust* method of selecting senior staff for senior positions, in that determination of 'merit' is at best an inexact science.

P2.2: Promote on merit   P2.2 is the doctrine of promotion on 'merit', but within a career service rather than a lateral entry system. There are two general justifications for P2.2. One is the theta-type claim that promotion on merit is intrinsically just, since it rewards both faithful service and intrinsic ability. The other is the sigma-type claim that promotion on merit is the only means of encouraging people in junior positions to work hard and effectively. There are two main variants of P2.2.

P2.2A: PROMOTE BY 'OBJECTIVE' MERIT   P2.2A holds that merit should be determined by means such as examination, automatic qualification criteria, or by resolution of some body which is to some degree detached from the influence of a potential promotee's boss. P2.2A is a doctrine which is applied in systems of promotion by examinations in fields such as nursing, the police, the merchant navy. It is conventionally justified on a mixture of theta- and sigma-type claims – namely the view that promotion on merit will in practice degenerate into favouritism and corruption, which may be highly corrosive of performance, unless 'merit' can be demonstrated in a clear, unambiguous way.

P2.2B: LET SUPERIORS DECIDE ON MERIT FOR PROMOTION   If P2.2A is a doctrine traditionally associated with public service practices in promotion, P2.2B is the doctrine which tends to be associated with promotion in private business. Those who argue for P2.2B in public organizations tend to use (selective) examples of the successful private businesses which use P2.2B in order to 'prove' that the doctrine should be applied to public bureaucracies.

The justification for P2.2B is normally twofold. First is the sigma-type view that effective leadership depends on being able to motivate subordinates to follow the leader's line, and that such motivation demands that staff depend on their immediate bosses for promotion. The argument goes that 'freedom to manage' requires that supervisors directly control this vital aspect of the incentive structure of their staff.

Second is the lambda-type claim that P2.2B is a more *flexible* basis for promotion than P2.2A, in that it allows the definition of 'merit' to be varied according to changing circumstances or to the specifics of particular jobs, in a way that would be impossible to lay down in advance in a set of objective rules for promotion. Such a system is held to permit a more rapid process of organizational adaptation than P2.2A.

Tenure and Dismissal

T1: GIVE LIFETIME CAREER TENURE
T1.1: GIVE CAREER TENURE ON A 'NO-LOSS' BASIS
T1.2: GIVE TENURE ONLY AT BASIC 'FALLBACK' LEVEL
T1.3: GIVE TENURE SUBJECT TO RIGOROUS PROBATION
T2: LIMIT TENURE
T2.1: APPOINT FOR FIXED TERMS
T2.1A: APPOINT FOR FIXED TERMS WITHOUT RENEWAL
T2.1B: MAKE FIXED-TERM APPOINTMENTS RENEWABLE
T2.2: LIMIT TENURE BY SUBJECTION TO RECALL
T2.2A: THOSE WHO HIRE OFFICE-HOLDERS SHOULD ALSO BE ABLE TO DISMISS THEM
T2.2B: THOSE WHO DISMISS OFFICE-HOLDERS SHOULD BE DIFFERENT FROM THOSE WHO APPOINT THEM

T1: Give Lifetime Career Tenure

T1 holds that it is best to appoint persons to office for life, or until retirement. The doctrine is not identical with D1, in that tenured appointment is not the same as continuous service in the same job. T1 is most commonly applied to judicial, administrative and academic appointments. There are four conventional justifications for T1.

Two of them are sigma-type claims. One is the idea that adopting T1 is ultimately cheaper to the employer than temporary tenure, and this overlaps with the conventional case for E2 mentioned earlier. The other is the idea that T1 encourages close specialization at an early age, of a kind that would not occur under a regime of instant hire-and-fire management.

The other two common justifications for T1 are theta-type claims. One is that T1 is the only reliable basis for objective judgement and candid expression of opinion in circumstances where people expressing such judgement or opinions might otherwise need to fear for their jobs. The other is the claim that T1 is an antidote to corruption. The argument is that if office-holders have an expectation of a permanent career, they will find it less necessary to divert energy away from the task in hand in order to provide for the 'downside risk' of loss of position, with the risk of corruption that this implies. A classic statement of this justification for T1 came from Max Weber (in Gerth and Mills 1948, 202):

> When legal guarantees against arbitrary dismissal and transfer are developed, they merely serve to guarantee a strictly objective discharge of specific office duties free from all personal considerations.

There are three main variants of T1.

T1.1: Give career tenure on a 'no-loss' basis   T1.1 is the strongest variant of T1, in that it holds that career service should apply without any loss of promotion except for gross misbehaviour or incompetence. One of its earliest applications is the American and British constitutional doctrine that in order to preserve the independence of the judiciary from other branches of government, pay and conditions of service should not be worsened during a judge's tenure in office, and pay is taken from a fund upon which Parliament does not vote. T1.1 later became extended, though with less explicit justification, to public service occupations. Indeed, some successful athletes negotiate no-cut contracts in which they are guaranteed not only a salary but also a place on the team, regardless of the quality of their performance; and film and TV stars sometimes secure even more favourable conditions of employment. Rumour has it that such arrangements have been known in academia, but we have no personal knowledge of them.

T1.2: Give tenure only at basic 'fallback' level   T1.2 is a significant modification of T1.1. It holds that career tenure should only mean guaranteed employment at some basic career grade, but that continuance in promoted positions should be dependent on continuing merit or suitability.

T1.2 was traditionally applied to the German public service, to staff appointments in the British army and to brevet ranks in the American civil war. It was advocated by John Stuart Mill for public service generally (1910, Ch XIV, 334) and it has been adopted more recently by some contemporary 'New Right' critics of public bureaucracy (notably Niskanen 1983). Mill's case for T1.2 was the sigma-type claim that permanent tenure was most likely to secure the best candidates at entry-level appointments, but that it was unsuitable for those who hold 'high offices'. He held that the latter should hold their promoted posts only for a fixed term unless reappointed. He argued that such a system makes it possible to move people on without affront and to bring younger people on.

T1.3: Give tenure subject to rigorous probation   It is comparatively rare for T1.1, the absolute doctrine of tenure, to be applied in unalloyed form, though it does appear in some contexts, such as high judicial appointments in the Anglo-American tradition or their equivalents (for instance, the Comptroller and Auditor-General in countries such as the UK, Australia and New Zealand). Much more common is the doctrine that career tenure should be subject to the satisfactory completion of a more or less rigorous period of probationary service. For example, Sir Edwin Chadwick (1854, 190–1) held that:

> Success in...examination should in no case ensure permanent appointment, but only admission to a preliminary appointment, generally of a year's duration, to be renewed by a distinct act and with additional securities against the probation being made a mere formality.

The model of T1.3 is monastic life, with the rule that the novice cannot be admitted to lifetime service before being subjected to a period of rigorous testing, both by the candidate and by others. It has been generally applied to professions and public bureaucracies, though the degree of severity of the probationary process is far from uniform.

T2: Limit Tenure

Ranged against T1 in its variant forms is a set of rival doctrines which hold that tenure should be restricted or limited in order to guarantee effective or honest administration.

T2.1: Appoint for fixed terms   T2.1, a common variant of T2, holds that appointments should be limited to fixed terms. Sometimes the justification for

T2.1 is the sigma-type claim that a fixed term of office can make it easier to draw able candidates for a position that is not especially attractive. More commonly, T2.1 is justified by theta-type claims about accountability and attention to duties, but there are two distinct variants of such claims. One is the claim that T2.1 makes it easier to hold office-holders to account, and encourages good performance, in the hope of having the term renewed. Another is the rather different idea that a fixed term of office, *without* the possibility of renewal, prevents corruption and other distortions that may result from attempts to curry favour to gain a further term.

T2.1A: APPOINT TO FIXED TERMS WITHOUT RENEWAL   T2.1A is the strongest doctrine of fixed-term appointment. It is reflected in such institutions as the Mexican president, who is elected for a single, seven-year term. The claim is that barring reappointment will serve to prevent office-holders from the sort of 'political' behaviour associated with seeking another term of office. An office-holder who cannot be reappointed, it is held, will be more likely to take a 'long' view, to be willing to take hard or unpopular decisions, to be less tempted to compromises or meretricities designed to curry favour, than one who can hope for reappointment. Similarly, restrictions on employment after leaving government service – revolving door legislation – is meant to discourage trading on government service.

T2.1B: MAKE FIXED-TERM APPOINTMENTS RENEWABLE   T2.1B is the direct opposite of T2.1A, holding that a fixed term of office should be linked with the possibility of reappointment for one or more terms. Conventionally, the case for T2.1B is twofold, and rests on a mix of sigma, theta and lambda-type justifications. One claim relates to the 'learning curve' advantages of securing administrative experience and continuity. The other is that the possibility of renewal creates incentives to serve satisfactorily. Contrary to T2.1A, the case for T2.1B holds that barring reappointment tends to encourage irresponsible behaviour on the part of office-holders. That is, the risk that those who cannot be reappointed to office may be driven to actions which are designed to secure a good job or a comfortable independence after their single term, or to activities which give no thought for the morrow – as in the well-known tradition of Mexican Presidents spending all the money in the public treasury, because they only got one chance.

T2.2: Limit tenure by subjection to recall   T2.2 holds that it should be possible to dismiss office-holders other than by the expiry of their term. The case for T2.2 goes that the only way to make office-holders perform effectively and give constant attention to their duties is to make it possible to dismiss them *at any time*, not just at the end of a stipulated term. Such dismissal may be achieved by exercise of powers of 'instant hire and fire management', the typical private sector approach to the problem. In the public sector, it may also be in the form of 'recall' by popular vote.

Recall in this sense refers to the legal ability of a specified number of voters to require a ballot to decide whether a named public official should be removed from office. In the later nineteenth century, recall was part of the recipe advocated by the US Progressive movement for limiting political corruption, and T2.2 was applied in a number of states to judges, state and local officials (see Walker 1986, Chapter 6). T2.2 was also built, at least formally, into the administrative architecture of the USSR. It is a monument to Lenin's early fascination with the administrative doctrines of the 1871 Paris Commune, for which the subjection of officials to recall at any time was a fundamental design principle (Edwards 1973, 82).

T2.2A: THOSE WHO HIRE OFFICE-HOLDERS SHOULD ALSO BE ABLE TO DISMISS THEM T2.2A holds that dismissal from office should be a mirror-image of appointment, in that it should be undertaken by the same people. If an electorate appoints, the same electorate should have the power to recall; to do otherwise is somehow undemocratic. So, at least, it appeared to the architects of the Paris Commune and late nineteenth century US Progressivism. Likewise, if management appoints, the same management should be able to dismiss. So at least argue those who believe that efficient administration is best achieved by giving management the 'freedom to manage'. Such a principle, it can be held, keeps lines of responsibility clear, makes it most likely that consistent criteria or judgements will be applied and allows mistakes in appointment to be quickly rectified.

T2.2B: THOSE WHO DISMISS OFFICE-HOLDERS SHOULD BE DIFFERENT FROM THOSE WHO APPOINT THEM Contrary to T2.2A, T2.2B holds that the procedures and people to be used in dismissal from office should not be the same as those used for appointment. T2.2B as a general doctrine was advocated by Jeremy Bentham (1931, 452), on the grounds that it made for more rational judgements about dismissal than can be achieved under T2.2A. Since 'our pride is interested in not condemning a man of our own choice', Bentham believed, the power of removal should be put into quite different hands from the power of appointment.

High-level applications of T2.2B are the procedures for dismissing judges in the Anglo-American tradition or the procedures for impeaching a US President (Congress plays the decisive role in impeachment, though the President is elected popularly). But the same principle is often applied to disciplinary dismissal procedures in public bureaucracy.

V   CONCLUSION

It is no coincidence that nearly half out of the 99 doctrines identified by our researchers are closely related to 'who-type' questions. To many, the question of 'getting the best person for the job' is all-important, and everything else is secondary. 'The best person for the job' can, of course, be defined in many different ways. It may relate to birth, background, or skills. Or it may relate to inherent qualities of character, as in apocryphal maxim once applied to the US Congress (before the days of sexual equality); 'Any man who can't take their [the vested interests'] money, drink their booze, screw their women, and still vote against them, doesn't belong in this legislature'. It is a commonplace that if we concentrate on the 'whos' of administration, the 'hows' and the 'whats' will take care of themselves.

In practice, these three things are not so easily separated. After all, who holds office depends on the criteria according to which office-holders are appointed; the conditions of their appointment; the way that they are rewarded, deployed and promoted. Many of the doctrines explored here belong in the intersecting areas of 'whos', 'whats' and 'hows' – the areas marked a, b, c and d in Figure 2.1 earlier. 'Men not measures' (Sennett 1977, 104–5) – or 'women not measures', in its feminist counterpart – is a beguiling slogan; but in practice 'men' and 'measures' intersect.

4   What-type Doctrines

...it is essential to the working of every one of these improvements that the administration...should be entrusted...to one central authority with extensive powers....(Chadwick, quoted by Finer 1952, 48)

I   INTRODUCTION

'What-type' doctrines here denote ideas relating mainly to *organizational form* – that is, doctrines which turn on what type of organization to choose for a particular task and how to arrange its component parts. 'What-type' doctrines turn on at least seven what-to-do issues. How *inclusive* should responsibilities be? Should *single* or *multiple* sources be used? What should be the degree of *internal capacity* in provision – 'make' or 'buy'? How *uniform* should units of organization be? What *scale* is best? What *corporate form* should be used? How should *internal* units of organization be arranged?

II   DOCTRINES OF SCALE, UNIFORMITY AND INCLUSIVENESS

Scale

B1: PREFER LARGE SCALE ORGANIZATION
B2: PREFER SMALL-SCALE ORGANIZATION

Scale is distinct from inclusiveness and uniformity, though doctrines of scale in practice often relate closely to inclusiveness and uniformity. Doctrines of large scale disparage 'Lilliputian administration', and usually build on sigma-type claims that small scale means high overhead costs, lack of scope for specialization, and absolute lack of resources. Conversely, doctrines of small scale disparage 'giantism', and usually build on stereotyped arguments that large organizations are uncontrollable and tend to generate *anomie*.

B1: Prefer Large-scale Organization

B1, the idea that 'big is beautiful', is one of the most venerable of all administrative doctrines and is defended by justifications from the sigma, theta and lambda families.

The lambda-type claim for B1 was made by Jeremy Bentham and was echoed by John Kenneth Galbraith (1967). It holds that B1 is linked to ability to innovate and learn. Bentham argued that big organizations are better fitted for systematic learning than small ones because they can more easily keep formal records of its operations and hence have access to a reliable laboratory of data.

Theta-type claims for B1 come in two main variants. One is the broad political argument that there is a 'national will' in democracy which requires large-scale organization to override more parochial interests. This idea belongs to the French revolutionary tradition of democratic national administration and the British utilitarian tradition of impatience with local democracy (cf. Hill 1974, 26). The other variant is Jeremy Bentham's claim that large-scale organization lends itself more easily to functioning according to predictable written rules, and hence to the observance of the 'rule of law' in administration (see Hume 1981, 134).

The commonest justifications for B1 are sigma-type claims, of which there are three main varieties. One is the claim that significant collective power can be achieved by an *absolute* massing of resources, for example in defence, insurance, labour unions. A second is the idea that B1 is a condition for effective forward planning. It is claimed that large-scale units are better able to co-ordinate activities and order priorities across a range of related activities than would be the case if the activities were in the hands of a diverse set of organizations needing to negotiate with one another in areas where their interests or activities overlap. This claim is the standard case for 'metropolitan reform' and 'super-departmentalism' in public administration.

The third, and commonest, sigma-type justification for B1 is the claim that larger scale means lower unit costs. The argument goes that the greater the scale on which operations are conducted, the greater is the scope for specialization in the use of staff and equipment. Specialization through scale, it is held, allows a single large unit to provide more varied services at a lower cost than would be possible if the service were provided by a number of separate smaller units.

The *locus classicus* for this claim is Adam Smith's *Wealth of Nations*, in which Smith uses the famous example of a pin-factory to argue that unit costs of production can be lower for a large unit than for a small all-purpose unit as a result of specialization. The same idea has been applied to public services, for instance in road-making and education (see Dunsire 1973a, 186ff). It is held that resources will be most efficiently used if organization is on a sufficiently large scale to keep specialized persons or equipment busy, and as technological development increases specialization, so the efficient scale of organization tends to increase.

Interestingly, the existence of production economies of scale is often very hard to demonstrate 'scientifically', even for manufacturing industry (see Stigler 1958; Hannah 1976, 180), and still more for public enterprise. (Hannah (1976, 75 and 183) has suggested that *financial* economies of scale, in terms of the transactions costs of raising funds, may be more important than managerial economies of scale, and the same might well apply to public bureaucracies.) But lack of evidence has not stopped B1 from gaining acceptance as a reigning administrative doctrine. A case in point is the passion for business 'rationalization' in the UK in the 1920s and 1930s and again in the 1960s and 1970s. These movements extolled the virtues of B1, and they were built on a classic rhetorical basis – an hypnotic slogan, plus an apparently 'scientific' principle, coupled with selective appeals to the manufacturing success of the USA and Germany (see Hannah 1976, 32–44). Likewise, public administration is periodically gripped by a fever for 'Brobidnagian administration', for example in the moves for amalgamating local authorities into larger units which swept Europe in the 1960s, and in super-departmentalism at national-government level (Britain in the early 1970s, Australia in the late 1980s).

B2: Prefer Small-scale Organization

Contrary to B1, B2 holds that smaller scale units of organization are preferable to larger units. B2 often appears as a reaction against B1, for example with the late 1970s wave of disillusion against elephantiasis in public and private organization. Like B1, its defenders use sigma-type, theta-type and lambda-type claims to justify it.

A common sigma-type justification for B2 holds that size brings diseconomies. If the efficiency case for B1 tends to rest on arguments about affordable specialization and absolute resource levels, the efficiency case for B2 tends to rest on arguments about motivation and capacity for oversight.

For instance, those who use Adam Smith's ideas as authority for B1 can be countered by advocates of B2 by reference to Adam Smith's deep distrust of large joint-stock companies, his belief that politicians and public officials could much more easily enrich themselves at public expense in big countries than in small ones, and his belief that wherever possible public administration through smaller (local) governments is to be preferred to that of larger, national units (see Rosenberg 1960, 565-6).

This idea was given a harder edge by public choice arguments developing since the late 1960s. Two important ones are William Niskanen's (1980, 171) view that efficiency is a negative function of the size of a public bureau (with size measured in terms of area and population covered) and Mancur Olson's (1982) argument that long-term stability allows special interests to capture public bureaucracies. The public choice school tends to argue that decentralization brings general social benefits (see Jackson 1983, 206), partly on the grounds that contestability in supply is more likely to be achieved in this way. That is, more options for consumer choice are offered by the ability of individuals and organizations to choose their location or service outlet.

The claim that oversight is easier to exercise over small-scale units of administration mixes sigma and theta-type justifications. It is based on what are held to be the inherent limits to communications channels and span of control. Hence Lammenais' famous dictum that centralization produces 'apoplexy at the centre and paralysis at the extremities' (quoted in Legendre 1968, 136). Gordon Tullock (1965) puts this idea in terms of the span of control which voters can effectively exercise in a democracy. Using Switzerland as a key case, he argues that the greater the number of levels of government, the less is the span of control which the voter is called upon to exercise, and therefore the more effective democratic oversight can be. (In effect, Tullock is arguing for more levels of government, more politicians and more elections – an unconventional recipe for 'efficiency'.)

A purer 'theta-type' claim is the idea that organization should be on a 'human scale' for maximum access and responsiveness. The communitarian ideas which came back into vogue in the 1970s, notably Ernst Schumacher's (1973) well-known thesis that 'small is beautiful', gave new life to this traditional case for B2.

A third justification for B2, which is a hybrid of theta- and lambda-type claims, points to three potential advantages of undertaking major projects on the basis of confederative arrangements among multiple small organizations rather than of a single all-purpose organization. One of the advantages is the requirement that major projects be grounded in a *broad basis of consent* before they can be undertaken (advocates of B1, of course, stress the dangers of deadlock). A second, according to Vincent Ostrom (1974) is the technical advantages that B2 can bring to the management of common-pool resources. He claims that common-pool resources (such as rivers and lakes) are more likely to be degraded as a result of incompatible uses when responsibility for managing such resources is taken out of the hands of the immediate community of beneficiaries for the relevant services. The third, lambda-type, advantage claimed for confederation (and for small scale units of organization more generally) is that it leads to greater adaptivity by allowing the constituent parts to innovate individually and to borrow ideas from one another – the classic case for federalism as a learning system.

Uniformity

U1: USE UNIFORM ORGANIZATION
U2: HAVE A PLURIFORM STRUCTURE

U1: Use Uniform Organization

U1 is a 'Lego-brick' doctrine which says that administrative structure should be uniform, in matters such as scale, conditions of employment, operating procedures, and even the dress of staff ('uniform' in the common-speech sense). It represents the 'pluralization' approach to administrative design (Kochen and Deutsch 1980), as in the uniform 'steel frame' of yesterday's colonial administration or the standard format of today's McDonald hamburger franchisees.

There are two main justifications for U1. One is a theta-type concern with predictability and uniformity both for customers (as in the McDonald hamburger case) and for outside monitoring and control. The underlying idea is that administration should be simple to understand, for consumers and controllers. Uniformity of dress – for instance for priests, police officers, corporate employees – makes functionaries easier to identify and may make it harder for them to avoid their duties in a crisis. A classic advocate of uniform in this sense is Spinoza (1951, 369), who argued that rulers of a state should wear a special distinguishing garment at all times so that they could always be marked out for public scrutiny. We doubt if many of today's politicians would be enthusiastic about such an idea.

Uniformity in a structural sense also makes exact comparison possible. Bentham, for example, argued that effective central control could only operate on the basis of uniform management, so that ready comparisons could be made between the units in the league (Hume 1981, 160).

The other conventional justification for U1 is based on the potential efficiency advantages of building administrative structures from standardized parts. That is, like the uniform system of military ranks, it offers the advantages of uniform and replaceable parts and fewer bargaining points for pay and conditions. The claim is that such a structure gives maximum scope for redeployment of people and equipment, and that it raises labour efficiency by creating a large promotion pool. The idea is that a large promotion pool motivates staff to work better in aiming for promotion and that it enables the organization to pick staff for top positions from a broad range of talent.

U2: Have a Pluriform Structure

U2 is the rival doctrine of diversity and pluriformity. It holds that individual units and organizations should be allowed to develop in their own way, rather than organizing everything along the lines of a single blueprint. Such ideas were prominent in the resistance to a uniform structure in the British civil service in the nineteenth century (see Wright 1969; Parris 1969) and are often used by line managers to resist schemes for uniformity or 'cloning' put forward by a central controller.

It is possible to defend U2 on a lambda-type 'gene pool' claim. The idea is that different forms of organization ought to be encouraged, just as a variety of plant or animal genes ought to be preserved, because even if one can be shown to be most efficient *at any one time*, the others may be needed in a crisis or when circumstances change in an unforeseen way.

This justification for U2, however, is exotic. The standard justification for U2 is the sigma-type claim that there is no single uniform best way of organization irrespective of time and context. This Aristotelian view was developed by the well-known 'contingency school' of organization theory, which developed in the 1960s and 1970s. According to this school, optimum size and structure depends on the particular context and task in hand, and therefore each service unit may need to be organized in a distinctive way in order to gain maximum efficiency or responsiveness. This idea came into strong favour in the 'new public management' era of the 1980s, with the corporatization of formerly monolithic public services and the partial breakdown of the uniform pay and grading systems so laboriously built up over a century or so.

Inclusiveness

V1: HAVE INCLUSIVE RESPONSIBILITY
V1.1: HAVE INCLUSIVE RESPONSIBILITY BY HORIZONTAL INTEGRATION
V1.2: HAVE INCLUSIVE RESPONSIBILITY BY VERTICAL INTEGRATION
V2: HAVE DIVIDED RESPONSIBILITY
V2.1: HAVE ADMINISTRATIVE PLURALISM
V2.2: HAVE CONCURRENT POWER

V1: Have Inclusive Responsibility

Doctrines of inclusiveness point to the advantages of integrating diverse processes or services under single responsibility. There are two major forms of V1, relating to horizontal and vertical integration.

V1.1: Have inclusive responsibility by horizontal integration   V1 holds that administration works best when a range of different but related services are provided under a single roof. That single roof may be literal, as in Bentham's argument in his *Constitutional Code* for putting all government Ministries into one building (Hume 1981, 234), the traditional 'town hall' location of local government or Corbusier's famous *Unité d'Habitation* apartments in Marseilles. Just as commonly, the 'single roof' is metaphorical, in the sense of single authority. Conventionally, there are three main justifications for V1.1.

One is a sigma-type productive efficiency justification. It holds that horizontal integration lowers production costs. The claim is that V1.1 affords the greatest scope for flexible deployment of staff, space and equipment, creating conditions for the topmost directorate to move resources around when political priorities or circumstances change.

A second is a theta-type, democratic-theory argument. It says that representative democracy, to be effective, requires unified political responsibility. This idea was one of the central tenets of the British nineteenth-century reformers of local government. According to Dilys Hill (1974, 28), this concept of local democratic administration derives from the ideas of John Stuart Mill, the Fabians and the early socialists. Hence (ibid):

> The movement...was for uniform and inclusive administration, that is, local bodies which would provide services to a minimum standard and bring these together under one comprehensive roof. This meant a unified political responsibility – one body of elected representatives to control and guide services.

A third justification for V1.1 is a theta-type claim resting on the potential advantages of horizontal integration for *consumer* convenience. Consumer convenience is served by offering 'one-stop shopping' for customers who may wish or need to draw on a number of services or units simultaneously or who do not know in advance which out of several services they need. This is the rationale for the department store in retailing and of the 'financial supermarket' in the financial services industry, even the marketing services industry (as practised by Saatchi and Saatchi in the 1980s under the slogan of 'integrated service marketing'). In the public sector, it comes in advocacy of one-stop agencies for employment services, health care, official information and other all-in-one administrative packages (for instance to provide potential overseas investors with tax advice, financial assistance, accommodation and zoning matters at a single service point). Advocacy of 'one stop shop' public administration figured in the Report of the Royal Commission on Australian Government Administration (1976, 161-2 and 340). The aim is to avoid the costs and vexation involved in the need to go to a number of offices or outlets in different places in order to deal with different aspects of the same problem.

V1.2: Have inclusive responsibility by vertical integration　V1.2, a different doctrine of inclusiveness, holds that different temporal stages of a chain of production should be brought under single responsibility. For example, there should be integration of manufacture and distribution, of research and production, of policy-making and execution.

V1.2 is unfashionable in public administration today. The reigning doctrines of 'new public management' favour instead an uncoupling of provision and production. But V1.2 was once a winning doctrine both in private and public administration, and indeed it is still often applied in practice. At the time of writing, the UK government is defending V1.2 for the bracketing of responsibilities for agricultural support and food safety regulation, against consumerist demands for a split in responsibilities in order to avoid conflicts of interest.

There are two conventional justifications for V1.2. One is the lambda-type claim that it makes for security of supply, avoiding deadlocks and transactional difficulties which would otherwise arise in project-by-project deals between separated units. A classic example is the difficulty of handling the sale of innovative ideas within an open market structure. The purchaser is not in a position fully to evaluate the worth of the innovative idea unless the seller provides sufficient information so that the customer no longer needs to pay for the idea at all, leading to under-investment in innovation.

The other justification for V1.2 is the claim that it results in better quality decisions than would arise in an 'uncoupled' administrative structure, because it promotes informal information exchange and limits the incentives for withholding and distorting information that would arise if the units in the vertical chain were separated. For example, it is commonly argued that 'policy' issues can only be fully worked out in detailed 'execution', so that better policy will result if there is no rigid separation of 'advice', 'policy' and 'management' functions, or that better procurement decisions will be made if knowledgeable providers can help ignorant procurement units to specify needs on the basis of feasibility and the state of technological art.

V2: Have Divided Responsibility

V2 holds that responsibilities in administration are better divided up. One form of the doctrine advocates administrative pluralism; the other advocates concurrent powers.

V2.1: Have administrative pluralism　V2.1 is a general doctrine of polycentric administration, in opposition to 'single-roof' doctrines of a horizontal or vertical type.

One standard justification for V2.1 is a theta-type claim about 'democracy'. Whereas the 'democratic' claims for V1.1 are based on ideas of *representative* democracy, the corresponding 'democratic' case for V2.2 is built on ideas of *direct* or *consociational* democracy. Direct-democracy ideas can be linked with the idea that each unit of administration should be directly accountable to its particular community of users rather than to a general legislature or council. The idea of 'consociational' democracy implies that in a divided society there should be separate administrative institutions serving each community and controlled by that community (cf. O'Leary 1989).

A second justification for V2.1 is a mixture of theta- and sigma-type claims. It is Montesquieu's (1977) case for compound organization , advanced in *L'Esprit des Lois*, first published in 1748 (see Ostrom, 1987). Montesquieu claimed that developing compound organization from a polycentric structure produces a system which can simultaneously reap the benefits of small- and large-scale organization alike.

Basing himself on classical Greece and Rome and on the cases of the Netherlands, Germany and Switzerland, Montesquieu argued that the republican form of government could only match the military strength of the monarchical form by federal arrangements. Montesquieu argued that military strength was proportionate to scale, yet, like many of today's Public Choice theorists, he also held that political degeneration was linked to scale in the republican form of government. Confederate arrangements, according to him, combined the military advantages of large scale with the politically corrosion-resistant qualities of small republics (see Montesquieu 1977, 183). He further argued (ibid., 184) that an organization of this type is more resistant to 'disease' than a system organized on only one level of scale. The argument went that, if abuses develop in one part of the system, they can be reformed by those parts that remain sound.

V2.2: Have concurrent power   V2.2 is the strongest form of 'divided responsibilities' doctrine. Rather than a simple advocacy of pluriformity and 'each pig in its own pen', it advocates an administrative structure designed in such a way that the consent of several authorities or units must be obtained before a valid decision can be made.

V2.2 is usually justified in theta-type terms. Like V2.1, its classic source is also usually taken to be Montesquieu's *L'Esprit des Lois*. The argument goes that the risks of abuse of power are greatest when responsibilities are centralized, and therefore there should be some structure of deliberately engineered 'checks and balances'.

V2.2 is not confined to high constitutional engineering. Even at quite low levels of organization, it is commonly claimed that only multiple veto power can limit risks of bias (for instance in the use of multiple independent testers or examiners) or of corruption (for example by multiple-key systems or multi-person police patrols in order to make it necessary for several police officers to collude in shirking, extortion or bribery).

III   SOURCING AND 'MAKE OR BUY' DOCTRINES

Sourcing structure

M1: SINGLE-SOURCE SUPPLY
M2: MULTI-SOURCE SUPPLY
M2.1: MULTI-SOURCE SUPPLY BETWEEN ORGANIZATIONS
M2.2: MULTI-SOURCE SUPPLY WITHIN ORGANIZATIONS
M2.3: MULTI-SOURCE SUPPLY BY METAPHYTIC COMPETITION

Very closely related to doctrines of inclusiveness of responsibilities are doctrines about sourcing of products. Is it better to have a single source or multiple sources, and how can that be achieved?

M1: Single-source Supply

M1 holds that good administration means avoiding rivalry and overlap in drawing up the boundaries of the producer units for any particular service. For instance, John Stuart Mill in his *Considerations on Representative Government* of 1861 (Mill 1910, 331) argued:

> Where the object to be attained is single (such as that of having an efficient army), the authority commissioned to attend to it should likewise be single.

Many later writers on administration have echoed this maxim. Max Weber saw the technical superiority of bureaucracy over other organizations as lying in part on its monocratic nature. That is, one part is not permitted to tear down what another part builds, meaning that 'the organization does not ride off in all directions' (Thompson 1976, 85).

There are two main justifications for M1, both of the sigma family. One is the claim that single-sourcing is the best way to make services effective, and to avoid the potential confusion, underlaps and deadlocks which can arise where service provision is fragmented among many separate organizations. A case in point is the current debate over air traffic control in Europe, where it is commonly argued that the variety of technical systems in use is inefficient and that the deadlocks introduced into the system by strikes in the individual national units is an infallible formula for chaos and frustration.

The other standard justification for M1 is that single-sourcing is often the cheapest form of supply. The argument goes that such a structure may make it easier fully to realize the advantages of specialization and scale economies, and may avoid the 'waste' of resources that competitive activity may involve (for example, in promotional costs which would be saved if all the activities were under a single producer). There is a parallel here with the common argument that advertising between rival oligopolists offering an essentially similar product in a mature market (such as tobacco or soap powder) is 'wasteful' and dysfunctional.

M2: Multi-source Supply

Contrary to M1, M2 is the doctrine of 'contestability' – the view that competition and rivalry should be preferred in administration wherever it is possible to introduce it. Sacred texts for this approach include the writings of Adam Smith and Jeremy Bentham, and of the more recently canonized saints of the public choice approach, such as Gordon Tullock (1965) and William Niskanen (1971).

M2.1: Multi-source supply between organizations This variant of M2 holds that rivalry between competing suppliers should be a cardinal principle of administrative design. It is normally justified by a mix of sigma and theta-type claims to the effect that competition serves to reduce the arrogance of office and sets up pressures to minimize costs and prices. Jeremy Bentham (1931, 361) thought that M2 had its place in some unconventional contexts:

> All modern historians have remarked how much the abuses of the Catholic Church have diminished since the establishment of the Protestant religion. What Popes and Councils could not do by their decrees, a fortunate rivalry has accomplished without difficulty.

William Niskanen (1980, 173) argues that M2 produces better quality decisions quite apart from pressure to minimize costs and keep close to the clients:

> Competition among bureaus may reduce the probability that the expected task is accomplished, but it increases the probability that the right task will be accomplished, often in unexpected ways.

This doctrine is by no means the exclusive property of the 'New Right'. During the 1930s the Roosevelt administration initiated a number of competing institutions like the PWA and the WPA, and President Roosevelt also made a practice of surrounding himself with competing advisors.

M2.2: Multi-source supply within organizations M2.2 is a variant of M2.1 which advocates competition within an enterprise as well as within an industry of separate enterprises. Its best-known form is the 'M-form' approach to organization, in which a large enterprise is divided up into quasi-separate divisions, competing as profit centres and as areas for corporate investment by the central board. The practice of 'multi-sourcing', which is now a commonplace of strategy in large corporations, is an extension of the same doctrine. M2.2 is currently coming to be emulated quite explicitly in public sector management, with the cabinet or political chief intendedly in the role of the central board of directors, and the various 'corporatized' units buying and selling services from one another along 'M-form' lines.

The 'M-form' structure was adopted by DuPont and General Motors in the 1920s, but it was not generally adopted by large corporations in the USA and the UK until after World War II (Hannah 1976, 96). Its academic recognition did not appear until later than that, in Chandler's (1962) historical study and Williamson's (1975) theoretical justification in terms of transactions costs. Williamson (1975, 159) described the M-form structure of organization as 'capitalism's creative response' to the problems of large-scale organization.

The normal justification of M2.2 is the sigma-type claim that it combines the transactional advantages of large scale organization (in matters such as PR and financial market dealings) and of the efficiency properties of competition in capital and product markets. The argument is that it lessens the load otherwise carried by the top directorate of an organization, while retaining their strategic role as allocators of capital and system designers, and thus enables the size of effectively managed organizations to increase.

M2.3: Multi-source supply by metaphytic competition   M2.3 holds that competition should be deliberately engineered between the public and private sector. The term 'metaphytic competition' was coined by Corbett (1965, 117) to denote a system of (regulated) competition between public and private enterprises, each having a substantial share of the relevant industry's market.

M2.3 is a doctrine which has been adopted in many countries for broadcasting services, banking services and air transportation. It is particularly strong in the Canadian and Australian administrative traditions – the background from which Corbett was writing.

The normal justification for M2.3 is the sigma/theta type claim that it keeps the private sector honest and the public sector competitive. As Corbett (ibid., 117–18) puts it:

> Hypothetically, metaphytic competition should bring out the best qualities of both public enterprise management and private enterprise management. By putting one against the other, it should give Cabinet, Parliament and the citizen a yardstick by which to measure the success of the public enterprise. It should also check any tendency of the private enterprise to put profits ahead of service, or of the public enterprise to become smug and bureaucratic.
>
> Hypothetically, too, metaphytic competition should keep the peace politically between doctrinaires of the left and right. If consumers have strong preferences for either public enterprise or private enterprise, they will value the opportunity to patronize enterprises with whose 'politics' they agree. Even if such preferences are held by only small fractions of the public, they may be held with intense feeling. And since those who have such prejudices are likely to be politically

active, it is important that they should arrive at terms of economic truce to which they will both agree.

Make or buy doctrines

O1: CONTRACT OUT IF YOU CAN
O1.1: PROMOTE COMPETITION FOR THE FIELD
O1.2: PROMOTE SIMULTANEOUS COMPETITION
O2: DO IT YOURSELF

O1: Contract Out if You Can

O1 holds that performance contracts should in general be preferred to direct provision. Currently in high fashion with the 'new public management', the idea has a long history. Johann von Justi took it as a cardinal principle of cameralism that the state should avoid direct management of trading activities or complex transactions (see Small 1909, 379). Jeremy Bentham (1962, 250) and his follower Sir Edwin Chadwick believed that contracting out of public services was generally superior to direct performance, although Bentham noted that public opinion was easily excited against the shortcomings of contractors.

O1 is usually defended by sigma-type claims to the effect that it limits costs, for three or four reasons.

One is the claim that contractors, out of self-interest, will be more concerned to conduct their affairs at least cost (for instance, in hiring and supervision of staff) than permanent internal providers can be. Second is the claim that O1 cuts costs because it brings some element of competition into the provision of public services, whereas direct provision is associated with monopoly. Third, even without competition, it is claimed that O1 forces decision-makers to specify some *standard of performance* which can later be used for evaluation of whether, or how well, the contract is performed. Fourth, O1 forces a *term* to be set to the contract period, when review and evaluation must take place, and this again applies even without competition.

However, there are also lambda-type and theta-type justifications for O1. The lambda-type claim is that O1 allows greater flexibility than in-house provision, specifically in 'putting the activity where the talent is' (Hague, Mackenzie and Barker 1975, 362). The flexibility claim typically applies less to routine-type work, such as cleaning and catering, than to non-routine work, for instance by hiring people as consultants who would not be available as regular employees.

The theta-type claim is linked with liberal and even a strain of socialist ideas, and it deserves mention, if only because a bias towards contracting is so often associated today with 'New Right' conservatism. The liberal and socialist case for O1 rests on its potential for limitation of arbitrary power at the centre.

In the socialist version, O1 is a method of regulating relationships between different public or co-operative bodies, as an alternative to command relationships. Such was the argument of Pierre-Joseph Proudhon. Proudhon held that contract relationships ought to be an important device for retaining the independence of lower-level units in a socialist state in their relationships with the centre and with each other. In this view, contracts are important precisely because they are terminable and limit the use of arbitrary authority, since the conditions of the contract need to be clearly specified in advance (see Vincent 1984, 214–15).

O1.1: Promote competition for the field   O1.1 holds that rival contractors should be periodically allowed to bid for the exclusive entitlement to supply a good or service over a fixed period. The franchising principle is old in practice, going back to the almost universal system of tax-farming in pre-eighteenth century Europe and the old oriental empires. Later, after tax-farming had been abandoned throughout Europe, the doctrine was reinvented and championed by Sir Edwin Chadwick, who formulated the idea of 'competition for the field' in 1859.

Chadwick advocated O1.1 using the sigma-type claim that:

> Government is utterly incapable of any direct management of manufactures, or of anything else of an administrative character (quoted in Crain and Ekelund 1976, 154).

He argued that O1.1 is often preferable to simultaneous competition (even where the latter is feasible), because O1.1 produces less waste, more continuity, more responsibility and lower prices (ibid, 152). Chadwick thought that this argument extended far beyond 'natural monopolies' as conventionally defined by economists. He held that O1.1 should be applied anywhere where consumers faced high costs of information and search, such as funeral services. Chadwick's arguments have been partially resuscitated and taken up by modern public choice economists such as Demsetz (1968).

O1.2: Promote simultaneous competition   O1.2 holds that public services ought as far as possible to be provided by rival producers engaged in *simultaneous* competition rather than by applying O1.1. For example, instead of periodically farming taxes, rival tax-collecting firms could operate, collecting a share of the taxes which they collected. An important modern variant of this idea is the doctrine of *voucher schemes* as a method of ensuring simultaneous competition to supply a service which citizens are legally obliged to consume for some reason – for instance, education up to a statutory school leaving age or garbage collection services (in those comparatively rare

American cases where householders have the chance to choose among a range of approved suppliers).

Though doctrines of contracting are often used as a justification for private sector entitlements to the public administration market, we can note that neither O1.1 nor O1.2 in fact imply any necessary preference for private sector contractors over public sector ones, and in that sense one can (like Proudhon) favour contracting without necessarily opposing public ownership. Both in the case of competition for the field and of simultaneous competition, the rivalry built into the contract system can involve competition between different public suppliers, between different private suppliers, or between public and private suppliers.

O2: Do It Yourself

O2 holds that direct management or self-provision is preferable to contracting out, for up to three reasons.

One standard justification for O2 is the sigma-type claim that direct management is cheaper (at least in the long run) than contract provision. Such claims involve some or all of the following three assumptions:

1   That direct management cuts costs by 'cutting out the middleman' – i.e. by operating on a non-profit basis. (This assumption usually applies to profit-making organization only.)
2   That collusion among contractors will force up the price of contract provision above the cost of direct management
3   That contracting, even if it is at first cheaper than direct management, will later become more expensive. This comes about as a result of the destruction of the possibility of 'metaphytic competition' or of the giving of 'first mover' advantages to whoever secures the contract – such that subsequent competition will be impossible and substantial monopoly rents will then be extracted.

Interestingly, no less an authority than Adam Smith used these ideas to justify O2 in tax law enforcement. This is surprising, in view of Smith's generally low opinion of public bureaucracy. Smith (1978, 534) argued that the eighteenth-century British system of direct provision was more than twice as efficient as the eighteenth-century French system of competition for the field. He thought that the contracting system was inherently deficient in such a case because

> ... in an auction of this kind, there are very few bidders, as none are capable of undertaking the office but those who are brought up to business, and are possessed both of a great stock and credit, and can produce good security. When there are

few bidders, they can easily enter into association among themselves and have the whole at a very easy rate ...

It is interesting to speculate whether Smith's own personal and family interests in the tax bureaucracy played any part in his enthusiasm for O2 in this case. We will be suggesting later that propounders of administrative doctrines tend to put forward those doctrines which will benefit people like themselves. Certainly, Smith had a family connection with tax bureaucracy in that he was the son, by a second marriage, of the Comptroller of Customs for the Scottish town of Kirkcaldy. He advised the British government on tax matters and was appointed Commissioner of Customs for Scotland and also a commissioner of the salt duties, less than two years after the publication of *The Wealth of Nations* – lucrative bureaucratic positions which he held until his death.

Certainly, this passage is little quoted by those who commonly invoke Adam Smith's name in inveighing against 'bureaucracy'. In fact, Bentham (1962, 250–1) argued that Smith

...forgot in this instance to apply the principle...of which he had elsewhere made such beautiful applications.

Bentham argued that, if Adam Smith's own normal motivational assumptions about the working of institutions were applied to the case, it was difficult to conclude that the state would be able to make as much profit as the tax farmers in collecting the taxes directly. That is, even if it is true that a tax farmer collects no more revenue than a public bureaucracy would do, the former has a personal interest in keeping the administrative operation 'lean' that the latter does not, and hence will collect the taxes at lower cost.

A second justification for O2 is the lambda-type claim that direct provision is more *flexible* than contracting, even though a lambda-type justification is also often used for O1, as noted earlier. Here the argument goes that direct provision avoids the need to specify all the contingencies in advance, as must be done for a contract. Williamson (1975, 25) argues that O2 allows for greater flexibility, because informal evidence can be used, a quasi-moral element can be introduced into relationships among producers, nuances of direction can be developed which it would be impossible to put into a written contract, and otherwise costly litigation can be avoided. In short:

...internal organization often has attractive properties in that it permits the parties to deal with uncertainty/complexity in an adaptive, sequential fashion without incurring the same types of opportunism hazards that market contracting would pose. Such adaptive, sequential decision processes economize greatly on bounded rationality. Rather than specifying the decision tree exhaustively in advance, and deriving the corresponding contingent prices, events are permitted to unfold and attention is restricted to only the actual rather than all possible outcomes.

The third standard justification for O2 is the lambda-type claim that direct provision is more reliable than contracting. Here the argument is that it is easier to ensure that standards (of safety, thoroughness, etc.) are complied with when such tasks are undertaken by direct provision. A well-known example of the application of this doctrine is the famous Venetian Arsenal, which was founded in 1104 on a Byzantine model and stayed in existence for nearly seven centuries. The institution reflected the view that only direct state construction of warships could guarantee a dependable product and provide capacity for expansion in a crisis – items which were crucial to the establishment and maintenance of a maritime empire. As McNeill (1974, 6) remarks:

> ...the efficiency and predictability associated with modern factory assembly lines were, to some extent, realized by the Venetian Arsenal. In its heyday, the Arsenal was capable of assembling a completely equipped galley in less than an hour.

Some other products too, such as the manufacture of cordage and bow-strings, were held to be too important to the interests of the state to allow their quality to depend on private enterprise, and concerns for reliability also led to direct organization of the provision of those products. This was achieved by the famous state rope factory (the so-called *Tana*) which operated from 1303 to the late eighteenth century. As Lane (1966, 269) puts it:

> The safety of the cargoes of wealth, for which the Venetian merchants 'held the gorgeous East in fee,' might in some storm depend on the strength of a single anchor line... The state had not faith enough in human nature to let this rope maker go unwatched. For the sake of supervising him, it became involved in a manufacturing venture....

The doctrine of direct provision in order to ensure a reliable product was quite explicit, as Lane (ibid., 270) shows:

> The manufacture of cordage in our house of the Tana...' declared the Venetian Senate, 'is the security of our galleys and ships and similarly of our sailors and capital.

The lambda-type claim for O2 is still frequently used today, for instance in arguments about security checks by police or troops as against the use of private security firms, about the transport of dangerous substances or the handling of dangerous materials, as in the case of the stripping of asbestos out of surplus public buildings before they are sold (an example given by Dunleavy 1986, 26).

IV   DOCTRINES OF AGENCY TYPE

A1: USE CLASSIC PUBLIC BUREAUCRACY
A2: USE INDEPENDENT PUBLIC BUREAUCRACY
A3: PREFER PRIVATE OR INDEPENDENT UNITS OF ORGANIZATION
A3.1: USE PRIVATE FOR-PROFIT ORGANIZATION
A3.2: USE NON-PROFIT INDEPENDENT ORGANIZATION

No less disputed than uniformity and scale is the what-type question of what type of agency is best for getting any particular job done. Here we concentrate mainly on 'agency type' doctrines for public services rather than on their parallels in private business.

A1: Use Classic Public Bureaucracy

A1 holds that it is best to provide public services by public bureaucracies which are 'classic' in the sense that they are directly controlled by elected politicians and are part of a 'core' public service. In general, A1 is unfashionable today, but a century ago it was a new orthodoxy, and supported by advocacy just as strong as that which underlies today's orthodoxy of corporatization and privatization. Schaffer (1973, 4) gives a sense of the universality of the claims for A1 in Victorian Britain:

> ...it was...held to be the best, and even the only, form of organization for central government. The nineteenth-century invention was ... the belief that Ministerial responsibility demanded departmental organization of this and only this type, and that Ministerial responsibility and departmental organization should be applied throughout central government.

Part of the case for A1 rests on lambda- and sigma-type justifications commonly advanced for doctrines U1 and B1 – the putative advantages of using standardized components in administrative design in terms of the flexibility it offers in rearranging the parts, and the potential coordination possibilities and promotion pool advantages of large scale organization. Overshadowing these, however, the standard case for A1 rests on theta-type claims about the 'democratic' character of this form of organization.

Such claims go back to the nineteenth-century attack on boards and collegial forms of organization – the Prussian conversion to single-headed forms of organization after Prussia's defeat by Napoleon in 1807, and the English utilitarians' dislike of 'boards' as means of evading Parliamentary oversight of administrative action (see Bentham 1931, 451; Mill 1910, 331). This orthodoxy survived well into the present century, for example in the view of the 1918 British Haldane Report on the Machinery of Government (Cd 9230 1918, 11) which expressed strong, if futile, disapproval of the trends which it saw away from classic public bureaucracies:

> Attempts have been made...to distribute the burden of responsibility by other means [than classic public bureaucracies].... We feel that...there should be no omission, in the case of any particular service, of those safeguards [i.e. direct accountability to Parliament through a Ministerial head] which Ministerial responsibility alone provides.

Even later, as we will see in Part III, the 1937 Brownlow Committee Report in the USA (President's Committee on Administrative Management, 1937) argued for A1 as making for clear political accountability and lines of command; and similar claims have played a part in reactions against the growth of non-departmental bodies in Britain in the 1940s and 1970s (see Hood in Hood and Schuppert 1988).

A2: Use Independent Public Bureaucracy

A2, the doctrine that public services should be provided by some form of public organization which is *not* a classic public bureaucracy, has probably never been argued with the same degree of general applicability as A1. But A2 has come into increasing favour in many countries since the 1920s and 1930s (see Sharkansky 1979; Hood and Schuppert 1988).

Whereas A1 rests mainly on justifications similar to those normally used for doctrines U1 and B1, A2 tends to be based on justifications similar to those used for U2 and B2, though it has some special variants too.

One is the sigma-type claim that A2 is a formula for effectiveness, for at least two reasons. One is the potential ability to gain the service of people who would not be attracted to, or perhaps capable of, a full-time career as elected politician or state bureaucrat under the normal rules of the game. Such people can be attracted by independent public bodies, the argument goes, by the greater freedom of independent bodies to offer terms and conditions outside normal public service rules. The other reason is the idea that A2 can avoid the characteristic drawbacks attributed to classic public bureaucracies – administrative paralysis, entanglement in red tape, long decision and clearance queues, hypercaution in the face of possible political embarrassment and political interference, truncated memory and steep learning curves through lack of continuity in direction.

Such claims have a long history. Independent regulatory commissions were extremely important in the growth of US federal government after the formation of the ICC in 1887, and variants of the same idea were used to justify A2 in the USA in the New Deal period, notably the famous Tennessee

Valley Authority (Selznick 1949). There were influential nineteenth-century enthusiasts in Britain for non-classic forms of public organization; even Bentham thought that independent boards could be useful for very open or very routine work. And much the same justification was given for the development of the 'parastate' sector in Italy and Spain as a reaction to the constipation and incompetence of the mainline bureaucracies.

Perhaps the two leading twentieth-century exponents of the case for A2 were Francesco Nitti and Herbert Morrison. Nitti, an economics professor who came from the underdeveloped south of Italy, argued that A2 was preferable to A1 for many tasks because independent bodies could more easily be insulated from political pressures to adopt inefficient hiring and management practices. (see Cassese 1988). Nitti developed this idea when he was Minister of Agriculture, Industry and Commerce in Italy in 1911 (Nitti 1974, Vol. 2, 520–67).

Herbert Morrison (1933), a leading British Labour politician, espoused A2 in the 1930s, for much the same reasons as Nitti and to counter claims from other parts of the socialist movement that trading enterprises set up by the state or taken over from private owners should be controlled by workers' cooperatives (syndicalists), by all-purpose elected local authorities (municipal socialists), or should follow the early Leninist model of post office organization (centralized, pluralized, ministerially controlled). In order to counter such claims, Morrison argued that state trading enterprises should be set up as independent public bodies, not directly controlled either by their workers or by central or local government.

Other justifications for A2 mix theta-type with sigma-type claims related to collegiality and independence. Vesting authority in a board rather than a single minister or politician is normally held to have at least three advantages. First, it allows the blending of experience with new blood (for example, through retirement by rotation, as in doctrine D3) in a way that ministerial direction cannot do. Second, it allows direct representation of interest groups in the direction of the enterprise, to gain the benefits claimed for doctrine Z1 in the use of stakeholders.

Third, board government makes it possible to create built-in checks and balances, ensuring that the arguments of one interest group will normally be countered by arguments from a rival group; even Bentham saw mutual checking as a potential merit of independent boards.[1] Not only the composition of each individual board, but also a structure of overlapping or rival boards can be used as a device for setting ambition to check ambition (following Madison's famous precept in *Federalist 51*).

In addition to the case for A2 related to board government are theta-type claims linking A2 to trusteeship. The claim is that A2 can provide impartiality by distancing an organization from day-to-day electoral politics and mainstream public bureaucracy. This claim often has winning force in fields such as decisions over pay and top salaries, the investigation of allegations of political corruption (as with the New South Wales Independent Commission Against Corruption, set up in 1988 on the model of a Hong Kong Commission) and the regulation of business (as with the American style of independent regulatory bodies, developing from the Interstate Commerce Commission of 1887).

The claim is also often applied to 'adversary bureaucracies' designed to challenge decisions or proposals by mainstream public bureaucracies in a range of areas from financial audit to equal opportunity in employment, or even in financial areas where it is held that electoral pressures will lead to imprudent decisions unless there is some independent check (as with the German Bundesbank, with its constitutionally guaranteed independence from government). The economist J. M. Keynes was a general advocate of what he termed 'public sector trusts' on the basis of this argument (see Keynes 1952), and A2 has often proved to be an appealing doctrine when mainstream politics or bureaucracies are distrusted.

A3: Prefer Private or Independent Units of Organization

A3 holds that private or independent units of organization should be preferred to public bureaucracies to provide services wherever that is possible – and, typically, claims that it is possible more often than advocates of A1 or A2 allow. Even where the nature of the 'problem' is such that some kind of 'public' intervention is required, advocates of A3 argue that this need not mean direct service delivery either by classic or by non-classic public bureaucracies.

'Public' provision can take place through private or independent forms of organization by one or more familiar measures, notably (a) compelling consumption or performance, for instance in obligations to insure (doctrine F1, considered below) (b) vouchers enabling consumers to choose among a variety of suppliers, for instance in food stamps or schools (c) subsidies to private or independent producers, for instance in rescue services. Advocates of A3 argue that most public services, including many kinds of law enforcement, can readily be provided in this way. Beyond that, A3 divides into two main doctrines.

A3.1: Use Private for-profit Organization

This variant of A3 puts the emphasis on private profit-making institutions as preferred suppliers of services. A3.1 came strongly back into vogue in the 'privatizing' 1980s, but it was by no means invented then. It was, for instance, held both by the eighteenth-century German cameralist Johann von Justi and by the English utilitarians of the eighteenth and nineteenth centuries, despite their very different economic orientations. Bentham, for example, in his famous 'poor plan', advocated that a joint-stock company should organize poor relief on a profit-making basis. The joint-stock form was chosen so that stock in the company might be sold to the frugal working class. Such a measure was calculated to divide the 'independent poor' from the 'dependent poor' (by making the former stand to profit from the least generous possible treatment of the latter) and thus lessening the chances of revolution (see Bahmueller 1981, 104–5 and 125–6).

A3.1 is typically justified by sigma-type claims about the efficiency consequences of transferable property entitlements. These ideas go back to Aristotle and Aquinas. The claim is that self-interest and transferable property entitlements produce pressure for maximum efficiency in management of resources; therefore exclusive and transferable property rights should be adopted wherever it is technically possible to do so (Wagner 1973, Ch. 7).[2] Specifically, it is held that transferable titles to ownership in production units:

a) avoid the diffusion of gains or losses arising from more or less productive efficiency among the population (or taxpayers) as a whole, and therefore create stronger incentives to search for innovative methods of operation designed to cut costs;

b) mean that investment choices are more likely to be taken from a longer time-perspective than if titles to ownership were not transferable. Where titles of ownership are transferable, managers and workers can be rewarded by stock holdings and therefore have a direct personal interest in the long-term profitability of investment projects. Where such titles are not transferable, managers and workers can only lose or gain from investment choices during their term in office, and hence (it is argued) will tend to opt for projects which enhance their prestige or the attractiveness of their work conditions in the short run, to the possible detriment of long-term prospects.

A3.2: Use Non-profit Independent Organization

A3.2 holds that independent non-profit institutions are the best vehicle for providing public services. It draws on a communitarian or co-operative ideal for dealing with problems of collective action. Its best known form is the 'subsidiarity principle', which is rooted in Roman Catholic doctrines of the state. It has its origins in the Papal Encyclicals *De Rerum Novarum* (1892) and especially *Quadragesimo Anno* (1931), which represented an attempt by the Roman Catholic Church to protect its interests in welfare provision and education in the context of the expansion of the welfare state from the late nineteenth century (see Isensee 1968, 18–21; Wegener 1978; Hood and Schuppert 1988).

The 'classic levels' of the subsidiarity principle are (running from low to high): the individual, the family, private associations, parish and local state bodies, state and federal levels of government and supranational organizations (Kunst 1975, 2592). The doctrine holds

a) that public services should be provided at the lowest level of organization which is compatible with efficiency and effective provision. Lowest-level provision is the negative part of the subsidiarity doctrine, since it restricts state activity.
b) that the state is obliged to assist lower level organizations to provide public services, especially through financial support. The declaration of an entitlement to assistance is the positive side of the subsidiarity doctrine (Eichhorn 1985, 892–3).

A3.2 is not, of course, a doctrine exclusive to the Catholic state tradition. Today, it is commonly advanced by other ethnic and religious groups (such as muslims in Western countries) to reject a uniform 'statist' style of service provision. And the argument that charitable or volunteer organizations, supported by public finance if necessary, can out-perform public bureaucracies in many fields, has become increasingly commonplace in the complex societies that have developed during the long peace since World War II.

In its secular form, the case for A3.2 has two main elements. One is the sigma-type claim that subsidiarity leads to lower costs and greater reliability arising from volunteer service (as discussed under R1 above). The other is the theta-type claim that A3.2 produces organization which is less intrusive and 'closer to the people' than other types of agency, particularly for sensitive areas such as child abuse or animal cruelty. In a generally wealthy, sophisticated, telephone-based society, it is held that many forms of social provision can be carried out more effectively by support of a group devoted to maintaining the appropriate network and 'putting the money where the talent is' rather than by the inevitable expense and industrial relations conflict which goes with a 'dedicated' public bureaucracy. A3.2 has recently been a winning doctrine in areas such as education, crime surveillance, counselling services for crime victims (rape, housebreaking, etc.), services for religious or ethnic minorities (translation, intermediation), 'meals on wheels' and a growing set of 'self-help' services.

V DOCTRINES OF CONSUMER–PRODUCER ORGANIZATION

F1: COMPEL CONSUMPTION
F2: ALLOW CONSUMER CHOICE
F2.1: ALLOW CHOICE TO OPT OUT
F2.2: ALLOW CHOICE OF SUPPLIER

F1: Compel Consumption

The doctrine that everyone should be obliged to consume a particular service has some affinities with the doctrine G5 that everyone should be obliged to help provide the service. Indeed, there are some activities (such as compulsion to vote in elections, as in Australia, Singapore, Austria), where it is debatable whether 'consumption' or 'provision' is the more accurate term. Obligation to consume does not necessarily imply obligation to pay for the service at the point of delivery, nor does it have any particular implications for whether the service should be provided by public or private organization: those are separate issues.

F1 is often applied to public services, for example in mandatory education, garbage collection, pilotage and insurance. But it is applied in many other contexts too, for instance where use of common cleaning or maintenance services is prescribed as a contractual condition of tenancy in a building.

F1 is normally justified by the lambda-type claim that compulsory consumption can prevent 'free-riding' from damaging a collective asset. The argument usually consists of some variant of Albert Hirschman's (1970) well-known thesis that 'exit' of customers from a service can lead to a deterioration rather than an improvement in service quality.

Hirschman argues, in contrast to the orthodoxy of mainstream economics, that the effects which economists normally expect from competition (i.e. lower costs, higher standards of service) cannot always be realized. In some circumstances, 'exit' means opportunities for 'cream-skimming', sometimes through offering a higher grade of service at a higher price, such as priority paid mail or private couriers. With such alternatives, the more articulate and resourceful clients will vote with their feet. In our example, they will not press for a general improvement of mail delivery. If these customers exit from the postal service, the overall result might well be a further deterioration of the service. Hence arguments for locking key clients (particularly the articulate middle class) into particular services such as public schools or public transport.

F2: Allow Consumer Choice

Contrary to F1, F2 advocates choice, usually on the basis of orthodox liberal ideas which hold individuals to be the best judge of their own interests, and see welfare as being diminished wherever choices are imposed from outside. F2 comes in two main variants.

F2.1: Allow Choice to Opt Out

F2.1 is the purest form of the 'free to choose' doctrine. It holds that consumers should be free to opt out of receiving a particular service altogether if they wish to. Examples of its application include the removal of compulsion on citizens to take out health insurance by the Fraser government in Australia in 1976 and 1978 (Gray 1984, 5–6), the removal of compulsion on parents to make their children attend school on the part of several American state governments over the past decade, the removal of compulsion for university students to belong to student unions by the UK government in 1988.

F2.2: Allow Choice of Supplier

F2.2 is a half-way house doctrine between F1 and F2.1, in that it prescribes freedom to choose among two or more suppliers but not to opt out of the item to be consumed altogether. F2.2 may be expressed through voucher-type provision for some kinds of compulsory-consumption services such as education, but it can be used with individualized payment too. An example is to prescribe (as in countries such as Australia, the UK and Singapore) that vehicles be subjected to tests of roadworthiness, but to allow vehicle owners a choice of testers. The same often applies to obligations to insure. This is a half-way house in that it seeks to prevent the potential for damaging collective assets through free-riding while still aiming for the welfare gains based on the view of individuals as the best judge of their interests in choosing a supplier.

VI DOCTRINES OF INTERNAL COMPOSITION

Aggregation Doctrines

C1: PUT UNLIKES TOGETHER
C2: PUT LIKE WITH LIKE.
C2.1: PUT LIKE WITH LIKE BY PURPOSE
C2.2: PUT LIKE WITH LIKE BY PROCESS
C2.3: PUT LIKE WITH LIKE BY CLIENTELE
C2.4: PUT LIKE WITH LIKE BY AREA

C1: Put Unlikes Together

C1 is the doctrine that the way to put the building blocks together within an area of responsibility is deliberately to put *unlike* pieces together, or to keep apart functions because they are similar. Schaffer (1973, 62) shows that C1 sometimes wins the day in administrative design. An example is the traditional fragmentation of responsibility for justice among UK ministers, in conscious contrast to the standard model of a single Ministry of Justice followed by countries in the Napoleonic administrative tradition. Another example (now superseded) is the traditional division of responsibility for control of staff and financial resources in government between Treasury departments and Public Service Boards in Australia.

C1 is usually based on two justifications. One is a theta-type 'checks and balances' case for administrative pluralism (like those used for doctrines V2.1 and V2.2) to avoid excessive concentration of power over sensitive functions. The other is the lambda-type argument that juxtaposition of unlike items can be a formula for creative, 'synergistic' activity or covering all the angles. This is a claim often advanced to justify the composition of multidisciplinary 'task force' units. It can be argued that a combination of unlikes can be a positive antidote to 'groupthink' – that is, excessive homogeneity in outlook or assumptions which may lead to dangerously faulty judgements (see Janis 1972).

C2: Put Like With Like

More familiar than C1, C2 holds that the best way to design organization is to put 'like with like' in some way when dividing up responsibilities. C2 is a doctrine which can be justified on the sigma-type grounds that it brings benefits to one or more of three groups: the *top directorate* (because of the flexibility and substitutability that such a structure may afford to managers); the *workers* (because of the possibilities of interaction with others having common concerns or 'speaking the same language' in professional or disciplinary terms); or the *clients* (because of the greater convenience of dealing with a coherent unit).

The assumption that homogeneity is the proper basis for organizational design underlies many arguments about composition. For instance, when academics battle over the boundary lines of departments and faculties, it is often on the basis of what are held to be intellectual family groups or commonalities of research programmes, on the (typically suppressed) premise that C2 rather than C1 should be the design principle for the overall structure.

Beyond that, the 'like with like' doctrine splits up into advocacy of different bases on which 'like with like' can be determined. This is one of the hoariest areas of administrative argument. Aristotle identified two contrasting doctrines within C1 when he asked (Aristotle 1984, 2063):

...should offices be divided according to the subjects with which they deal, or according to the persons with whom they deal: I mean to say should one person see to good order in general, or one look after the boys, another after the women, and so on?

The debate between organization by subject and by client has since raged.

Since the work of the 'scientific management' school of the early twentieth century, it is now conventional to identify four different doctrines within C1. The ambiguity and contradiction among these four doctrines is often stressed in textbooks on administrative science, although from our perspective this feature is simply a microcosm of the much larger set of contradictory doctrines in administrative argument.

C2.1: Put like with like by purpose   C2.1 holds that organization is best divided up according to programmatic goals. This assumption often underlies management techniques such as management by objectives and programme budgeting, which take organizational units as essentially goal-oriented.

Typically, C2.1 rests on three major justifications. One is a theta-type claim which holds that organization according to defined purposes is the best way of ensuring accountability, in that the relevant goals provide some 'bottom line' against which performance can be judged. A second is the sigma-type claim that organization according to purpose is likely to minimize the roadblocks to goal achievement that may arise from organization based on some other principle. A third is based almost on the diametrically opposite principle, in that it holds that organization according to major goals brings the resolution of goal conflict directly to the top, where (it may be held) such conflict properly ought to be resolved.

The third principle was the basis of an interesting proposal by the New Zealand Treasury in the mid-1980s for the division of ministerial responsibilities according to the basic values to be pursued, for example with a minister for wealth maximization, a minister for environmental purity, a minister for cultural values, a minister for equality of opportunity, and so on. The idea (stillborn, of course) was to ensure that Cabinet discussion focused explicitly on trade-offs between these basic goals.

C2.2: Put like with like by process   Contrary to C2.1, C2.2 holds that is often best to group around specialist equipment or skills, which can then be put to a variety of purposes. This doctrine is often used to justify institutions such as the typing pool, the computer centre, the PR unit, the transport pool, the central purchasing agency, even the 'administration block'.

C2.2 usually rests on sigma-type claims about appropriate use of resources, typically in the realization of scale economies. This claim conventionally consists of one or more of three basic assertions. First, it can be argued that C2.2 makes possible the effective supervision of specialists in a way that cannot be achieved where organization is on some other basis, in which case the scattered specialists must be overseen by people who are 'lay' to that particular specialism.

Second, it can be argued that C2.2 provides a more challenging and stimulating working environment for scarce and expensive specialists and avoids the 'de-skilling' that may occur where specialists are not interacting on a daily basis with those who share their expertise. Third, it can be argued that C2.2 makes it easier to smooth out variations in demand for particular processes, and spreads out the cost of particular specialties in staff and equipment, so that the organization as a whole can enjoy better-quality or lower-cost process skills than would apply if the processes were divided among units constituted in some other way.[3]

C2.3: Put like with like by clientele   C2.3 holds that it is likenesses among types of clients or customers around which units of administration should properly be built. Although C2.3 is often hard to distinguish from C2.1, in that clients and purposes often go together, it was distinguished by Aristotle (as we saw above) and certainly there is no logical identity between clients and purposes. For example, feminists might debate whether the removal of gender-based discrimination in teaching was better achieved by setting up anti-discrimination units in an integrated system, or segregating students into single-sex schools (as advocated by Sarah, Scott and Dale 1989): the segregationist argument is a case for C2.3, the integrationist one is a case for C2.1.

As in that example, C2.3 is often defended as a political device to 'flag' the importance of particular groups and fit in with their demands. Beyond that, C2.3 in some ways is the administrative analogy of 'holistic medicine', the view that medical treatment is most effective when it is based on close experience of the particular patient rather than separately dispensed expertise for particular parts of the body (heart, lungs, bladder, etc.). Such a form of organization is held to enable an organization to get to a deeper level of understanding than can be achieved by organization according to analytic units.

Such is the traditional case for the division of foreign affairs ministries by country expertise, or for central finance departments according to expertise in the particular departments being monitored.[4] Only that way, it is held, can an organization get 'deep down', know its enemies and friends intimately, know where the bodies are buried, build up a close network of contacts.

C2.4: Put like with like by area   C2.4 holds that the best way to divide up organizations is by territorial area, with all-purpose units in each area.

Like C2.3, C2.4 can be justified in terms of its symbolic value and its possibilities for conveying political 'clout' to areas which matter. A different justification for C2.4 is the lambda-type claim that that an all-purpose field structure is less likely to be totally disabled by communications failures than an organization using some other form of division of responsibilities, and in that sense may be capable of greater robustness. This argument is likely to be a winning one in circumstances where organizations operating over a large area face a hostile environment, which may explain why it has traditionally been favoured for organizations such as churches, armies and colonial governments.

Length of Hierarchy Doctrines

Y1: USE LONG HIERARCHIES
Y2: USE SHORT HIERARCHIES

Y1: Use Long Hierarchies

Currently unfashionable, the doctrine that hierarchies should consist of an elaborate gradation of ranks, with many rungs on the ladder, was once widely advocated. A prime example of the latter is the Table of Ranks introduced by Peter the Great into the civil and military service of Russia and extended by his grandson's wife Catherine II in the late eighteenth century (MacLean 1978). Bentham (1962, 194) considered this to be

> ...an invention in politics, which matches the most ingenious discovery in art that the present century has witnessed.

The main justification for Y1 is the sigma-type claim that it extends the motivational advantages generally claimed for H2 (discussed later) by spacing the rungs of the ladder in such a way that there is always another rung of the ladder to be reached and so that at every point in a person's career, however distinguished, there is always an incentive to try to reach that next rung. Advocates of Y1 claim that short or widely-spaced hierarchies cannot provide such continuous incentive to advance. This was, for instance, a common criticism of academic hierarchies in the UK and Australia in the 1970s, where it was held that the insertion of more rungs on the ladder would increase pressures to perform according to the dictates of top academic managers.

Y2: Use Short Hierarchies

Y2 is the 'flat hierarchy' doctrine that the number of rungs in the ladder of authority should be kept limited. Organizations, the doctrine goes, work best when there are not too many steps between the top and the bottom. Advocacy of 'flat' hierarchies came into high fashion in the 1970s and 1980s in both business and public administration.

Conventionally, Y2 rests on two standard justifications. One is the sigma-type claim that Y2 makes for easy information flow within an organization. Long hierarchies, the argument goes, result in excessive distortion of information as it travels up and down the line, as a result of self-serving distortion, simple distortion by 'noise' and the need to simplify or spell out messages as they cross from one level to another (see Hood 1986, 107–8). Many theories of bureaucratic pathology have been built on cumulative distortion of information as it travels up and down the line.

The other, closely related, justification for Y2 is a hybrid sigma/theta claim that it limits the scope for buck-passing up the line of command and for unnecessary duplication of work between levels of rank – features which advocates of Y2 believe to be endemic in long chains of authority. Y2, it is held, will be more likely to lead to 'buck stops here' attitudes, and to avoid make-work practices such as overpedantic correction of draft documents produced by subordinates.

VII   CONCLUSION

Our 27 specimens of what-type doctrines are merely a selection of some of the commonest varieties. They do not exhaust the field. Moreover, the boundary line between what-type doctrines and doctrines relating to administrative whos and hows is bound to be a ragged one. This is not surprising, given that questions of organizational form are usually related to the kind of people to be involved and the way in which business is to be done. Indeed, it could be that all administrative 'whats' are ultimately reducible to 'whos' and 'hows', as the hidden agenda of every debate on organizational form.

NOTES

1   See Bentham 1931, 450–1; also Schaffer 1973, 9–10.
2   This is related to the argument for venality of office (doctrine G2 above), as advanced by Montesquieu and Bentham.
3   The assumptions underlying that proposition are (i) that transaction costs among such units would be greater than zero and (ii) that organizational slack would be no greater under C2.2 than any other basis of division.
4   The 'porthole principle' – see Shapiro 1978.

5   How-type Doctrines

Yuan Hui inquired how to govern a state. 'Use the Hsia calendar. Ride in a Yin carriage. Wear a Chou hat...'. (Pocock 1971, 47)

I   INTRODUCTION

As we said earlier, it is often thought that the 'who-type' questions matter most in administration. But there is, of course, a counterpoint. Equally familiar to the stress on individuals is the view that a bad *system* can defeat even the most vigorous and talented individuals – and thus that administrative 'whats' and 'hows' can be just as important as the 'whos'.

Beyond that, it can even be argued that administrative systems should be designed in such a way that their working ought not to depend on persons of exceptional talent or integrity. This is the idea advanced by Jeremy Bentham (Hume 1981, 134) and other 'rule-minded' thinkers who hold that in a properly designed system the units ought to be replaceable and interchangeable, and should work by rule and rote.

Accordingly, we must include some specimens of what we can loosely term 'how-type' administrative doctrines – that is, doctrines having to do with what *procedures* or *methods* should be used rather than organizational building blocks or the type of people which are to be preferred.

How-type doctrines in this sense include precepts relating to (1) how *authority* should be distributed; (2) how *leadership* should be exercised; (3) how *information* should be managed; (4) how *cases* should be handled; and (5) how *control processes* should operate.

101

II DOCTRINES OF AUTHORITY

Doctrines of *authority* come at the intersection of the 'what' and 'how' spheres – the area labelled 'c' in Figure 2.1 earlier. They relate to the proper distribution of entitlements to make decisions or issue commands.

Shape of Hierarchy Doctrines

H1: EQUALIZE AUTHORITY
H1.1: EQUALIZE AUTHORITY BY INDIVIDUAL CONSCIENCE
H1.2: EQUALIZE AUTHORITY BY VOTING ENTITLEMENTS
H2: USE DIFFERENTIATED RANKS
H2.1: USE DIFFERENTIATED RANKS, WITH SINGLE-PERSON RESPONSIBILITY
H2.1A: MIX INDIVIDUAL AUTHORITY WITH STRONG STAFF SUPPORT
H2.1B: USE INDIVIDUAL AUTHORITY WITH A 'LEAN' CENTRE
H2.2: USE DIFFERENTIATED RANKS, WITH MULTIPLE SUPERIORS
H2.2A: USE COLLEGIAL OR BOARD AUTHORITY
H2.2B: USE 'FUNCTIONAL' SUPERVISORS

H1: Equalize Authority

H1 doctrines, usually based on theta-type claims, hold that entitlements to command or decide should be equalized in some way. But 'equality' can take several forms.

H1.1: Equalize authority by individual conscience H1.1, the strongest variant of H1, is a doctrine of organized anarchism which holds that no individual should be absolutely subject to the authority of another, or of any collectivity or hierarchy. It is the administrative equivalent of those religious doctrines which stress the paramountcy of each individual's conscience (the extreme case perhaps being that of the Quakers, who will not even have a 'minister', let alone a priest). On this view, the model for organization should be that of judges on a bench, fellows in a college, members of a legislature, with no final obligation for any one member to take direct orders from another. (LeGuin (1974) offers an interesting science-fiction account of H1.1.)

Conventionally, there are two justifications for H1.1, both of a 'theta' type. One is the claim that H1.1 is an effective antidote to corruption in high places. This claim underlies the argument for giving each individual the legal entitlement to bring cases to court as an alternative to a centralized (hence corruptible) state prosecution system. It underlies the argument for giving police officers formal equality on the basis of an oath of office which obligates them to enforce the law without fear or favour, rather than subjecting them to orders from above as to which laws are to be enforced and which are to be set aside. Applying H1.1 in such cases is held to increase the chances that citizens or police officers will pursue and prosecute erring politicians and high officials (cf. Marshall 1984, 142).

A second justification for H1.1 is that it is a bulwark against morally objectionable actions by a hierarchy or collectivity, even where no technical corruption or illegality arises. Such tendencies can only be kept in check if each individual is free to reject orders, to 'blow the whistle' on colleagues and superiors, to act according to the dictates of conscience or of some broader *jus gentium*.

H1.1 was used in the Nuremburg Trials after 1945 to counter the defence of former Third Reich officials who were accused of war crimes and who argued that they had 'only followed orders'. The same happened in the trial of Adolf Eichmann in Jerusalem in 1961. Eichmann, a former lieutenant-colonel in the Nazi SS, had been responsible for carrying out the 'final solution' of killing Jews. Eichmann kept telling the court that he had simply done his duty, obeyed the orders of his bureaucratic superiors and strictly obeyed the law of Nazi Germany (Arendt 1964). He argued that 'ein Befehl ist ein Befehl' (Jackson 1984). The court used H1.1 to reject this defence. We can expect the issue to recur, particularly with regime changes in Eastern Europe and perhaps South Africa.

Some would extend H1.1 well beyond such apocalyptic circumstances. For instance, some of the American 'New Public Administrationists' of the late 1960s and early 1970s applied H1.1 to matters of everyday administration, such as the determination of social security eligibility. They argued that those who did the 'actual work' in public administration, particularly 'street level' employees serving socially disadvantaged clients, should set their own goals if the directions coming from above did not satisfy their sense of social justice (cf. Marini 1971). The same general idea has been advanced by environmental and consumerist campaigners who hold that each member of an organization should be entitled and even encouraged to 'blow the whistle' on unethical or possibly illegal behaviour on the part of colleagues or superordinates (see Nader et al. 1972).

H1.2: Equalize authority by voting power   H1.2, a weaker version of H1, holds that all affected persons should be equally entitled to vote or participate in any decision-making, but should be bound to the collective decision once it has been taken.

There are many detailed ways in which H1.2 can be put into effect. The differences relate to the ways in which 'those affected' are defined, and to the nature of the decision rule. At one extreme is a rule of unanimity, which prevents collective action unless everyone agrees. In practice, such a rule is virtually the same as H1.1. At the other extreme is a plurality rule, allowing collective action if there are more votes for than against of those who choose to be present at a meeting. Or, as commonly happens, collective decision may not involve formal head-counting at all, but simply a convention of consultation before action and decision according to an informal 'sense of the meeting'.

H1.2 is applied in many contexts, from collective self-management by workers (see Dahl 1984) to residents' committees of apartment blocks or other communal living arrangements. The former idea goes back to medieval guilds, but has more recent origins in nineteenth-century mutualist and syndicalist thinking, and particularly the ideas of Pierre-Joseph Proudhon and the French 'Proudhonists' of the First International (for an account, see Vincent 1984). From these ideas the syndicalists advanced the doctrine of self-governing workplaces, rather than central state authority or 'bourgeois individualism', as the proper basis of a free society. H1.2 was the central theme of the 'workers control' movement after the February 1917 Revolution in Russia, until it was suppressed by Lenin after the October revolution.

Conventionally, the case for H1.2 is the theta-type claim that democratic administration requires decisions to rest on a broad basis of consent among those who have to do the work (or of 'those affected' in some other sense).

In addition, H1.2 is often justified on the basis of the sigma-type claim that it is a more effective and less wasteful method of organization than H1.1 or control from above. The reason for greater effectiveness and less waste, according to this argument, is that H1.2: improves the quality of the information base on which decisions are taken; improves the quality of working life for those who actually carry out 'doing' activities; and removes waste and demoralization arising from decisions made by some outside 'managerial' authority which are likely to be ignorant and self-serving.

This claim comes in many varieties. Quality circles and other forms of collegial work have been developed in business organizations from Finland to Japan. Peters and Waterman (1982, 240), in their famous book on 'America's best-run companies', see peer group control rather than direct controls from the top as one of the factors associated with corporate 'excellence'. Cathy Ferguson's (1984, 27 and 206–7) feminist attack on bureaucratic hierarchy is built on this double argument. But it has a specifically feminist element in its claim that viable models of non-hierarchical organization can be drawn from the experience and practice of women's groups in handling collective decisions.

Shan Martin (1983) uses the sigma-type claim for H1.2 to attack the recent 'new public management' trend of importing stereotypes of private sector authority into public bureaucracies, with a proliferation of 'managers' at every level. She claims (ibid., 131) that this trend – a version of H2 – is propagated mainly by the people who benefit most from its acceptance –

managers, management educators, trainers and consultants (a conclusion which comes as no great surprise to those who see administrative argument from a rhetorical perspective). She argues that the trend will tend to reduce performance rather than to lift it, because

> ...hundreds of persons labeled and paid as managers ... not only perform largely unneeded functions but ... also *interfere with the effective performance of others.* (ibid., 166–7; our emphasis).

Observers as different as Charles Lindblom and Michel Foucault have argued that hierarchy masks power more than it aids performance. Those of this persuasion are fond of citing examples of employee participation schemes which have been ended because they were too successful – in showing the managers to be unnecessary (cf. Ferguson 1984, 70).

H2: Use Differentiated Ranks

Contrary to H1, it is often taken for granted that unequal division of authority is essential for efficient administration; and this view is not confined to the conservative side of politics.

H2 is typically justified by four sigma-type claims. One says that the distribution of political skills and gifts for leadership is inherently unequal in any real-life society. Theoretically, it might be possible to achieve equality in such capacities, but only by measures so draconian as to be unacceptable on human-dignity grounds (such as drug treatment or frontal lobotomies to reduce virtually everyone to the status of a human vegetable). Devices which fail to recognize and make use of inherent inequality in human leadership skills, such as automatic rotation of office or equalization of powers, will lead to serious inefficiency and comparative disadvantage for the organization concerned (Williamson 1975, 53).

The second common justification for H2 is that it provides a means of *motivation* which is not available under H1. The motivating force comes from the fact that it is usually thought to be preferable to wield authority than to be subjected to it – to 'hand it out' rather than to 'take it' from others. So H2 gives an effective stimulus to persons on each rank to devote effort to the struggle to reach the next rung of the ladder of authority. This vital incentive for hard and effective work, the argument goes, cannot be provided under any pure form of H1. It is closely linked to justifications for Y1, as considered earlier.

A third argument for H2 says that dividing organizations into ranks of differing authority brings respect from outside to those in the higher ranks, which would not be available if all members in the organization have equal authority. This claim also parallels the justification for Y1, considered earlier.

The fourth justification for H2 says that it is the only way to avoid the characteristic weaknesses of any system of self-direction or group decision-making. Those weaknesses are usually held to include: decision deadlocks; the squandering of resources in endless debate and committee 'politicking'; shirking of unpleasant work; free-riding; inconsistent activity by one part of an organization undoing what another part does; lack of decision resolution through the working of voting paradoxes (Black 1958); the tendency for participative democracy in practice to result in much more power for some than others - a result which one author has dubbed 'zealocracy', the rule of activists (Tivey 1978, 129).

It is common for H2 to emerge as a winning doctrine in organizations originally founded in idealistic dedication to H1. Robert Michels (1949) saw such a progression as an inevitable 'iron law of oligarchy' applying to such organizations. An example is the move of Circus Oz, the Australian circus group, from H1.2 to H2. Originally the troupe decided its acts on the basis of a collective view emerging from meetings of all the company. The result was an endless series of 10-hour meetings, leading to the perhaps inevitable decision to save time and energy by adopting an hierarchical authority structure. Something similar seems to have happened in Portugal after the 1974 revolution.

H2.1: Use differentiated ranks, with single-person responsibility   H2.1, the commonest form of H2, holds that the best way to get things done effectively is to rest authority with one individual at each level, and so '...every administrative activity should be set up with a single responsible head' (Report of the President's Committee on Administrative Management 1937, 46).

H2.1 is easily the most powerful, most enduring and best-known of all administrative doctrines. In the sixteenth century, Niccolo Machiavelli saw H2.1 as the epitome of good government, drawing his inspiration from Romulus and Moses. And for a long time, H2.1 was virtually synonymous with administrative 'science', as Dunsire (1973a) shows. It has a long history in military administration, and was carried over into civil administration in Europe under Napoleon Bonaparte and his Prussian imitators.

Apart from the general justification for H2, H2.1 usually rests on two specific claims. One is the sigma-type claim that, compared with group or collegial direction, H2.1 saves decision time and avoids ambiguity or deadlocks. This claim was made by Max Weber, in the tradition of the Prussian adoption of the Napoleonic style of monocratic administration after 1807 (Gerth and Mills 1948, 214), and has been repeated by later writers in the same tradition, notably Charles Perrow (1972).

The other typical justification for H2.1 is the theta-type claim that only by placing authority in the hands of a named person is it possible to assign clear blame when things go wrong. It is a condition and incentive for personal responsibility. This claim was made by Jeremy Bentham and John Stuart Mill and by more modern writers such as Victor Thompson (1976), and it relates to typical justifications for doctrine A1, as considered above – particularly the idea that (representative) 'democracy' requires that bureaucracy be directed by identifiable public officials elected by the people.

H2.1A: MIX INDIVIDUAL AUTHORITY WITH STRONG STAFF SUPPORT H2.1A, the famous doctrine of 'staff and line', asserts that, in order for individual authority to be effective in large organizations, the single person in charge needs to be assisted by a staff of helpers who do not themselves have the authority to issue commands but whose role is to process information for the chief. Broadly, the justification for H2.1A is that it combines the advantages of H2.1 in terms of clarity of purpose and direction with the advantages which H2.2 offers in terms of the information base available for high-quality decisions.

H2.1A has military origins, and 'staff work' has a long history in that context. In modern Europe, the idea is associated with the development of the famous Prussian General Staff. The *Generalstab* came into existence after 1655, mainly, it seems, as a means of unifying the diverse units within the Prussian army; but apparently it was not until the late eighteenth century that coherent general staff doctrines developed within the military general staff (Craig 1955, 6 and 31).

In 1801 Colonel von Massenbach argued that the purpose of a general staff should be: to develop operational studies in specialist areas; to prepare plans for war which took account of all possible contingencies; to become familiar with problems of terrain by the holding of regular staff exercises; and to collect and store intelligence about foreign conditions and forces. He further argued that the military staff should be divided into brigades specializing in particular operational areas, that its members should alternate between service with the staff and service with line units, and that its head should have direct access to the king to express his opinion on military matters (ibid., 31).

In the twentieth century analogies to the military general staff doctrine have gained ground in business administration and public service. The early 'scientific managers' argued for the development of 'staff' units to augment the analytical functions of the chief executive of a business corporation, and the same doctrine was applied to public administration. The 1937 Brownlow Committee on Administrative Management, which we examine in Part III as a case study of administrative argument, offered a famous modern exposition of this doctrine. By the 1960s, the doctrine that chief executives need to be surrounded by a formidable battery of special advisers, personal assistants and analysts, had become a cliché of administrative argument.

H2.1B: USE INDIVIDUAL AUTHORITY WITH DELEGATED POWERS Contrary to H2.1A, H2.1B is the doctrine of delegation and a 'lean centre'. It holds that single-person authority works best when power is delegated directly to line managers rather than maintained through an extensive general staff. H2.1B was advanced against von Massenbach's doctrine in 1801 by critics from rival units within the Prussian army, who naturally saw Massenbach's assertion of H2.1A as no more than a bid for extra turf for his own agency, the *Generalquartier-meisterstab*. This conflict was but a rehearsal for many subsequent battles between staff and line.

H2.1B is conventionally justified on the sigma-type grounds that delegated power: keeps lines of command and responsibility clear-cut; avoids the muddle and confusion caused by the inevitable plotting and power-struggles which will occur within any general staff; and maintains the power to act in the hands of those who are assumed to be in the best position to know the conditions on the ground. Such claims for H2.1B were widely accepted in corporate management circles in the 1970s and 1980s, when 'lean centres' became all the rage (Peters and Waterman 1982; see also the discussion under M2.2). Such claims for H2.1B have been accepted in other contexts too, for instance by the Roman Catholic Church, where Vatican II substituted 'freedom to manage' by bishops instead of the previous centralized structure, with all decisions concentrated on the Papal office.

The other standard justification for H2.1B is the theta-type claim that it avoids the anti-democratic potential of H2.1A (which is said to result in rule by unelected general staff 'advisers', usurping power which elected officials should wield directly). For instance, German liberals traditionally regarded the Prussian General Staff with great suspicion, because of its very deliberate use as a bulwark against the claims of the Prussian legislature from the 1870s. Similarly, H2.1B briefly came into favour against H2.1A in the USA after the downfall of the Nixon Presidency in 1974, when the general staff of the 'Imperial Presidency' became politically discredited. Hence Jimmy Carter's shortlived election promise in 1976 not to have a formal chief of staff in the White House.

H2.2: Use differentiated ranks, with multiple superiors

H2.2A: USE COLLEGIAL OR BOARD AUTHORITY   H2.2A says that (contrary to H1) effective administration requires that there be a directorate set over those who do the actual work, but holds that (contrary to H2.1) such direction is better vested in a group than in a single individual. Such direction may be effected by face-to-face committee meetings (cabinets, boards of directors, etc.) or by administrative procedures which give validity to a decision only when two or more persons have signified their agreement to it.

The tradition of collegial administration goes back to the German cameralists and their imitators (as with the twelve-person colleges introduced into Russian administration by Peter the Great). There is also a radical tradition, classically embodied in the administrative practice of the 1871 Paris Commune, the 'workers' government' which was set up in Paris during and after the Prussian part occupation of Paris in 1870. Many of its members saw the Commune as a collective 'administrative commission' (Rihs 1973, 149). More recently an extreme version of collegiality has been portrayed in the

Cold War espionage bureacracies of novelists like John le Carré and Len Deighton.

Traces of both traditions survive today in the Soviet bureaucratic system, and Japanese bureaucratic procedures also reflect H2.2A (possibly as a result of German administrative influence in nineteenth-century Japan). The Japanese system of *Ringi* involves the drafting of a document by a low-ranking official and its circulation up the hierarchy, eventually reaching the very top, involving the rule that a decision is only made when all the relevant officials have attached their seals. The corresponding Soviet procedure of *vizirovanie* involves the formal circulation of a draft decision among bureau chiefs in advance of that decision being considered by the *collegium* (top level board) of a Soviet Ministry (for both of these cases, see Fortescue 1988). How far this procedure differs in practice from informal processes of 'clearance' operated in most bureaucracies is debatable; but all such collegial decision procedures attract heavy criticism from advocates of H2.1, arguing that H2.2A dissipates authority and wastes time and resources (ibid.).

Conventionally, H2.2A is justified by theta- or lambda-type claims. The theta-type claim is that H2.2A offers a check to corruption, on the principle of multiple-key locks; and that, by institutionalizing 'multiple advocacy' (George 1972), it allows a number of different and opposing viewpoints to be represented, which will check one another to produce moderate and balanced decisions (such claims parallel the case for A2 considered earlier). The lambda-type claim is that H2.2A can provide *robustness and continuity* in direction in the face of resignation, retirement, infirmity and death.

H2.2B: USE 'FUNCTIONAL' SUPERVISORS H2.2B is Frederick Winslow Taylor's (1911) famous principle of 'functional foremanship'. Like all variants of H2, H2.2B holds that administrative effectiveness demands that human work be checked and directed from a centre of authority. But it holds that work should be supervised by a number of *separate* directors, not by the collective wisdom (if that is what it is) of a group. Directors should act independently of one another, each director having authority to oversee that part of the work in which the director is expert, but not the whole.

Perhaps the most familiar application of H2.2B is higher education, where students are typically directed by a series of specialist teachers, each responsible for one field of the overall work, but none responsible for all of it. (For example, the typical undergraduate student works for three lecturers and three tutors, each of whom may have distinct pedagogic goals and values as well as different subject expertise.)

Taylor's doctrine of functional foremanship never became 'mainstream' in either public or private administration in the way that his ideas about reward did. But H2.2B was reinvented by management theorists in the 1970s under the slogan of 'matrix organization' (cf. Mintzberg 1979, 168–75), which became fashionable in some large organizations. The link between such an organizational design and performance in an objective sense is (of course) disputed; but the adoption of H2.2B at least involves some private benefits for the management training industry in that such a structure requires many more managers to run it than one-boss forms of authority.

The justification for H2.2B is that it combines the advantages of H2.1 and H2.2A. That is, it is held to ensure that direction is better informed than can be achieved under any version of H2.1, but that it avoids the 'mish-mash' or 'lowest common denominator' quality often associated with group decisions under H2.2A. Advocates of H2.2B may concede that the application of the doctrine may lead to some degree of overlap, underlap and contradiction in direction. This is indeed the typical problem encountered by students working for different specialist teachers who compete with one another to get the student's attention. It is the standard objection to H2.2B by advocates of H2.1. But they argue that single-boss organizations also tend in practice to put incompatible demands on their members, and hence suffer from the same disease without securing the advantages of specialist expertise.

III   DOCTRINES OF LEADERSHIP

L1: GIVE LEADERS THE BEST
L1.1: GIVE LEADERS THE BEST CONDITIONS
L1.2: GIVE LEADERS PRIVILEGED WORK AWAY FROM THE FRONT LINE
L2: GIVE LEADERS NORMAL WORK AND CONDITIONS
L3: GIVE LEADERS THE WORST
L3.1: GIVE LEADERS THE WORST CLIENT CONDITIONS
L3.2: GIVE LEADERS THE WORST, FRONT-LINE, WORK

Leadership doctrines are precepts about how persons in positions of authority should lead. Should such persons be isolated from the squalor of the 'front line' or 'coal face', cultivating a sense of majesty and distance, dealing with high matters which the mean intelligences of their underlings can only guess at? Or should they be found at the 'business end' of organization, drawing authority precisely because they are in the front line?

L1: Give Leaders the Best

The L1 family of doctrines holds that leadership should be associated with privilege in terms of comforts, subject-matter and conditions of work. The normal justification is the sigma-type claim that such practices lead to efficient division of labour and motivation, in providing effective incentives for people down the line to want to move into leadership positions, and to enhance the quality of decision-making. (There is a rough analogy here to

John Rawls' (1971) 'difference principle': special conditions for leaders are just if they benefit the worse-off, by producing better decisions or other behavioural effects.)

L1.1: Give Leaders the Best Conditions

L1.1 holds that those at the top of the leadership tree should enjoy the most comfortable conditions. Thicker carpets, larger offices, more powerful automobiles, longer and more sumptuous lunches: these are the prerogatives and the badges of institutional leadership.

Common justifications for L1 span the sigma-theta-lambda divide. One is the case put by the pigs in George Orwell's *Animal Farm*. Leaders should be cossetted so that they are in peak condition to make the difficult choices and perform the demanding intellectual tasks or special acts of courage that leadership demands. One of the earliest arguments on these lines is put by Sarpedon to Glaucus in the *Iliad* (Homer 1950, 229). Kings are 'given the best seats at the banquet, the first cut off the joint, and never-empty cups...they live on the fat of the land they rule, they drink the mellow vintage wine ...'. But these lunches are not free. In return, kings are expected to fight in the front line of battle and make extreme efforts when circumstances demand it.

A second justification goes that respect for leaders will be increased by their ability to command the good things of life. Hence the seductive claim that if the directorate of organization *A* is expensively tailored and coiffed and equipped with lavish executive toys, organization *B* will be somehow diminished if its leaders have more ordinary accoutrements. Similarly, those of higher rank will only draw respect from those below them if they are seen to be valued more highly by the organization.

A third, and related, claim is that there must be visible payoffs for the exercise of leadership if it is to appeal to any but the most power-hungry individuals. Insofar as leadership involves making unpleasant choices, performing under pressure, attempting to deal with hostile or recalcitrant people, there has to be something substantial 'in it' to encourage psychologically normal people to aspire to such positions.

L1.2: Give Leaders Privileged Work away from the Front Line

L1.2 is that variant of L1 which holds that leaders should be special in terms of the kind of *work* they do rather than of the general comforts and conditions in which they work. L1.2 holds that leaders should engage themselves in high-level 'policy' work, separated from the tedious routine work going on below them.

L1.2 is normally defended by sigma-type claims about efficient division of labour. In protecting leaders from mundane matters which would reduce their concentration on broad strategic issues and other higher matters, L1.2 is held to apply resources to their most appropriate uses.

L1.2's ancestry goes back at least as far as Plato's *Republic*, where the philosopher-monarchs left the daily direction of the realm to auxiliaries and guardians. And L1.2 became familiar in British government administration following the 1854 Northcote–Trevelyan Report. Using ideas which were apparently borrowed from Sir Henry Taylor (Dunsire 1973a, 18), the Report made a controversial case for the separation of 'intellectual' and 'mechanical' work in government bureaucracy. Intellectual work, naturally, described what the administrative elite did, while the mass of underlings were restricted to mechanical work. The doctrine has been resuscitated in many forms since, as a way of keeping separate the 'doing' and 'deciding' aspects of administration. Oddly enough, some avowedly socialist organizations make a similar distinction between a leadership (intellectual) committee and a management (mechanical) committee.

But the distinction is deeply contested. Northcote–Trevelyan's idea went against all the evidence as to how administration was actually conducted in the nineteenth century. Many nineteenth-century administrators held that there was no firm distinction between intellectual and mechanical work, and that trying to make such a distinction would lead to severe pathologies. There is a striking parallel with today's anti-managerialist dissidents who rail against the cult of the MBA as deeply destructive of organizational morality and effectiveness (cf. Mintzberg 1990).

L2: Give Leaders Normal Work and Conditions

L2 holds that effective leadership can only be exercised by someone who is continually engaged in the normal work of the organization, not raised above it to full-time work on special duties. Sometimes L2 is based on the sigma-type claim that leadership can only be effectively exercised from someone engaged in normal work – an idea which is often applied to sport team leadership. Perhaps a more common justification for L2 is theta-type concerns with keeping leaders representative and continually 'in touch' with their constituencies. Such concerns underlie the traditional case for labour union leaders who actually work on the shop floor, or for academic leaders who actually teach and do research (both unfashionable practices today).

L3: Give Leaders the Worst

At the opposite extreme from L1 is the doctrine that leaders should work in abnormal conditions – but the conditions should be abnormally severe, not abnormally privileged.

L3.1: Give Leaders the Worst Client Conditions

L3.1 says that leaders should not simply work in normal conditions, but that they should be made to experience the conditions of the most disadvantaged persons to whom their work relates. It is usually justified by theta-type claims about the conditions for vigorous and responsive leadership. The Cultural Revolution of Mao's China, once much admired by some Western scholars, was ostensibly a large-scale application of this doctrine (but there is no evidence that its distant admirers were ever moved to imitate it).

At its weakest, L3.1 implies that the leader should periodically set out to experience what it is like to be a client or customer, in the tradition of monarchs adopting an incognito to experience the life of their subjects (the modern equivalent is the executive who tests the organization's defences or client-friendliness by anonymous phone calls or visits to the public counter; see Townsend 1970).

A stronger variant is the view that leaders should have much more than casual and occasional experience of the conditions faced by the most disadvantaged people for whom they are responsible – for example, that social welfare ministers should themselves try to live on the public dole, that transport chiefs should use peak-hour public transport to get to work, that housing bosses should sleep on the streets along with the homeless, or that those responsible for policies towards the Third World in the rich countries should be made to go hungry (see Thompson 1976, 120). Only in this way, the doctrine goes, will leaders have both the information and the urgent motivation necessary to change the conditions of those at the bottom of the heap.

L3.2: Give Leaders the Worst, Front-line, Work

L3.2, the mirror-image of L1.2, holds that leaders should work in the most demanding conditions at the front line of their organizations. Like L3.1, L3.2 has weak and strong variants. The weak variant is that those in positions of authority should occasionally experience conditions at the 'coal face' of their domains. This is the doctrine that the police chief should periodically go on the beat in person, or that the agency head should work from time to time at the public counter where the public and the officials meet. For instance, the head of the Australian Tax Bureau (Trevor Boucher) spent a week on the inquiries desk in 1990. The claim is that such activity will improve the quality of the leader's decisions away from the front line, and improve the leader's standing with the troops (perhaps with the 'enemy' too).

The stronger variant of the doctrine asserts that leaders should work at the front line as a matter of course. A (rare) application of L2 in social welfare is the case of the Smith Family, a private welfare agency in New South Wales in Australia, which used its most senior staff as the first point of contact for the public (see Wilenski 1977, 272). And there are many points along the continuum between the weak and strong variants of this doctrine. For instance, Budget Rent-a-Car Australia used to require its executives to work one day per month on the counter to keep them alive to the priority of customer service.

This version of L3 thus advocates a reversal of what some would see as the 'normal' relationship between high official rank and closeness to the front line. It has no time for the principal who does not teach, the general who does not fight, the sport captain who does not play. Nor are legislatures exempt from the extreme variant of L3, which logically implies that those who make the laws should themselves see to the enforcement and implementation of the laws which they have made. (Another doctrine which is not likely to appeal to today's politicians, though it was applied by the 1871 Paris Commune). Counter staff in difficult line agencies like social security often say that the quickest way to make an exception is to bring a supervisor face to face with a client. The implication is that if managers were more accustomed to the human drama of the interviewing cubicle, their decisions would be more humane or at least more informed. The same might even be true for legislators.

IV   DOCTRINES OF TASK SPECIALIZATION

J1: SPECIALIZE WORK
J1.1: SPECIALIZE WORK AS FAR AS THE MARKET WILL ALLOW
J1.2: SEPARATE 'POLICY' AND 'EXECUTION' SPECIALISMS
J2: CONSOLIDATE WORK

J1: Specialize Work

The idea that specialization of tasks leads to more informed decision-making or to higher productivity, or both, has a long pedigree. By 1820 Georg Hegel had advocated that government needed to mirror the division of labour in society if it was to be effective. Similarly, for Adam Smith and Jeremy Bentham, it was almost axiomatic that division of labour was the foundation of good administration, both private and public; and their ideas continually reappear in new guises and contexts.

J1.1: Specialize Work as Far as the Market Will Allow

J1.1 is one of the familiar, mainline staples of administrative argument. It holds that labour and equipment should be divided into specialized fields as long as it is possible to keep the specialist labour or equipment fully occupied (which in turn depends on the size and stability of the market or clientele).

The orthodox justification for J1.1 is the claim that specialization: creates the best possible knowledge base for administrative action, by avoiding a situation in which everyone has to be 'jack of all trades and master of none'; limits 'learning curve' problems (that is, inefficiencies associated with shifting from one kind of work to another, unfamiliar one); and may result in cheaper and faster operations through rationalization.

J1.1 is commonly linked to B1 (the 'big is beautiful' doctrine) and is commonly justified by the pin-factory argument discussed earlier under B1. Dunsire (1973a, 189–93) has applied the idea to public-service products, using examples such as teaching specialization in schools or the specialisms associated with modern road-mending technology. J1.1 is often used as an argument against rationalizations involving hybrid work (for example, combining teaching and management), which can be condemned as 'de-skilling' on the conventional justification used for J1.1.[1]

J1.2: Separate 'Policy' and 'Execution' Specialisms

Closely related to L1.2, J1.2 is a variant of J1.1 which is one of the most venerable doctrines of Public Administration. It holds that good administration requires specialization along the lines of 'policy' and 'execution'. Policy specialists should concentrate on clarifying values, goal-setting, overall control frameworks. Executive specialists should concentrate on 'getting things done' or keeping the machinery running. This is the famous 'policy-administration dichotomy' doctrine, introduced into US Public Administration by Woodrow Wilson (1887) and used to justify the development of a professional civil service.

The conventional case for J1.2 is that it combines the sigma-type advantages of administrative or managerial expertise with the theta-type advantages of popular election and finely-tuned political antennae at the top.

J1.2 is often condemned by academics as an untenable model of how administrative processes do or ever could work (cf. Appleby 1949). But, though pronounced dead by the 'doctors', the doctrine obstinately refuses to lie down. It continually reappears in new guises. A recent example is the New Public Management movement of the 1980s, which is built in part on the idea that operational management can be clearly separated from goal-setting by 'corporatization' of the public service. For instance, J1.2 was the keynote of the influential 1988 UK Efficiency Unit Report, *The Next Steps* (1988, 10, para. 23), which argues (with hope triumphing over experience):

Ministers and civil servants must...stand back from operational details...leaving managers free to manage. (ibid., 11, para. 27).

J2: Consolidate Work

J2 holds that it is best to combine rather than to specialize separate types of work, so that each worker can perform a variety of different tasks. Karl Marx thought that J2 should apply to work in the communist utopia, in order to avoid the stultification of narrow task specialization. J2 was also espoused by the French student radicals of the 1960s, in their opposition to all division of labour and knowledge (Dunsire 1973a, 187).

But, like so many administrative doctrines, J2 is not the exclusive property of any single political tendency. It was advocated with equal vehemence by Sir Edwin Chadwick, who was an enthusiastic admirer of industrial capitalism and a strong opponent of labour unions. Chadwick (1854, 194) attacked narrow specialization in government bureaucracy, ridiculing the idea of '...assigning to every function a functionary, to every book a book-keeper..., to each set of returns a clerk...'. He argued:

> By such divisions of labour, the public is... served much in the same way as a Hindoo household, where one servant brings up the meat, another the vegetables, one has the charge of the pipe, another the business of cooling the water, and so on with each service; more than a dozen serving men being required to do work which with us is better done by one servant on the principle of consolidation.

J2 is conventionally justified on two sigma-type grounds. One is an idea which is often applied to factory or routine office work. It claims that extreme specialization makes work so uninteresting or so dangerous to health that the potential benefits of specialization are outweighed by the costs of ill-health or the negative effects of boredom on workers' motivation and morale. Hence the rise of the idea of 'job enrichment' and multi-skilling, as applied in corporations such as IBM in the 1960s and 1970s.

The other conventional justification for J2 is that specialization can be wasteful because it makes it impossible to adjust inequalities in workload and thus may result in practice in underutilization of resources. This is a criticism commonly made of academics with tenure. Worse, rigid specialization may actually hamper the smooth passage of work if particular tasks are claimed as the exclusive preserve of an entrenched group, which can then use its monopoly of such tasks to obstruct the work of others in the pursuit of feuding or power-play.[2] A variant is the idea that J2 leads to less compartmentalized and better-quality decisions – for example that combination of 'policy' and 'administrative' work leads to better administration (through politically responsive handling of casework) and better policy (through grounding in experience of administrative work).

V INFORMATION-MANAGEMENT DOCTRINES

I1: PREFER SECRECY
I2: INFORM ONLY THOSE WHO 'NEED TO KNOW'
I3: PREFER GENERAL OPENNESS

Information-management doctrines are precepts about who should be entitled to what information, on what terms, and when. Here we identify only the three commonest specimens. Like most administrative doctrines, the three are often advanced with passionate intensity in relation to particular cases, but rarely with complete consistency. For instance, lawyers, academics and journalists tend to be vigorous advocates of general openness of information when it applies to government, but are typically much less enthusiastic about its application to sensitive areas of their own affairs.

I1: Prefer Secrecy

I1 holds that good administration demands extensive confidentiality and secrecy. Information should be available only to those with the appropriate rank and security clearance, or with a particular password, PIN number or biometric profile. Normal and seldom questioned in private industry, I1 is currently unfashionable in public administration, under pressure of 'consumerism', liberal academia and bureaucratic reformism. But I1 was taken for granted as the correct way to do public business by the eighteenth-century Prussian cameralists (see Parry 1963, 186) and was also seen as a key to bureaucratic efficiency by Max Weber. Nor are such views by any means dead today.

Some of the justifications conventionally used to defend I1 come from the sigma family. One of these is the claim that effective judgements of performance or competence can only be made when a veil of secrecy encourages frankness and candour in the expression of opinions. Another is the intellectual property argument for restricting availability of information, as conventionally applied to commercial secrets, and to academic research before publication. A third is the 'professional confidence' claim that effective service to clients demands guarantees that privacy will be respected, in order to win trust and avoid shame or embarrassment.

A further common justification for I1 which belongs more to the theta/lambda family is the security case for confidentiality. A conventional application is the claim that information about wrongdoing can only be obtained by investigatory agencies if the provenance of such information is kept strictly secret, for otherwise the life and property of informants is liable to be imperilled. The same idea was applied to the debate over anonymity of blood donors which occurred in the UK in 1989. Against a demand that the identity of blood donors be revealed so that victims of AIDS-infected blood received in transfusions could sue donors for damages, it was argued that such a move would destroy the integrity of the voluntary blood donation system. Exactly similar issues arise with sperm donation.

I2: Inform Only Those Who 'Need to Know'

I2 holds that information should be available only to those who meet some criterion of merit or have some standing in a legal sense – for instance, '*bona fide* researchers' but not 'muck-raking journalists', people with material interests at stake but not casual inquirers, public officials but not private citizens, senior managers but not junior staff. A common application of I2 is the idea that individuals ought to be allowed to see certain files relating to themselves, for example to check on the accuracy of information in their credit rating files, but should not have access to the files of other clients.

Else Oyen (1982) shows that I2 is commonly espoused in the professions. The real argument, of course, turns on *who* is defined as 'needing to know'. For example, physicians often allow particular information that they hold about their patients to be given to other physicians, but not to psychologists or social workers – sometimes not even to the patients themselves. Equally, psychologists often allow their particular information about their clients to be passed on to physicians but not to social workers.

More subtle is the application of the 'need to know' principle in the field of espionage bureaucracy as depicted by novelists like Len Deighton and John le Carré. Here the argument tends to go that field agents should be given only limited information, partly so that they have fewer secrets to reveal if captured by the other side, but also to ensure that they 'stir things up', doing risky things that they would not undertake if possessed of all the information in the hands of C(ontrol).

I3: Prefer General Openness

I3 holds that secrecy is generally repugnant and that information ought wherever possible to be available to anyone who wants it. Conventionally, there are four main justifications for I3, all belonging to the theta family.

One is the radical claim that effective democracy requires all citizens to have access to all information used by the administration in its decision-making. Hence Mably's sweeping assertion that 'Rien ne doit être secret chez un peuple libre' (quoted in Legendre 1968, 239).

A second theta-type claim for I3 is the idea that general openness will serve to prevent intentional or unintentional abuses of office. Jeremy Bentham (1931, 411), argued for publication of public accounts and fees of office as a means of checking tendencies to malfeasance by public officials. To check such tendencies: '... the worst principles have their use as well as the best; envy, hatred, malice...'.

Bentham also argued for publication of annual reports to Parliament as a form of accountability for public boards and for publication of the reasons and facts on which administrative acts are founded, to prevent abuse of authority. A recent application of Bentham's idea is the suggestion that UK juries ought to give reasons for their findings, in order to check miscarriages of justice.

A third, sigma-cum-theta claim is that I3 can prevent abuses by clients or citizens at large, not just those in office. This idea is sometimes applied to fields such as tax administration, where publication of details filed for tax purposes may encourage honesty by giving others an opportunity to check on false statements (Bentham's 'envy, hatred, malice' again, this time directed against other citizens rather than public officials).

A final justification is the idea that I3 can help to make society better informed about its collective problems. This argument is developed by Else Oyen (1982). She claims that the application of I1 and I2 to information about particular clients prevents the aggregation of information, and so protects the professions and bureaucracies from challenge either by pooling of information among their clients or by independent social science research. As she puts it (ibid., 8):

> The clients are cut off from the opportunity to teach each other the rules of the game and ways to handle this client role. They are prevented from furnishing the public with information about themselves and from organizing pressure groups against the system.

I3 is rarely advanced without any qualifications. Though 'freedom of information' became legally enshrined in several democracies in the 1970s, the 'freedom' was invariably hedged by reference to security and intellectual property restrictions, and in some cases with significant user charges and a user-hostile request system which made 'freedom of information' something of a paranym.

VI   DOCTRINES FOR HANDLING CASES

Rule-boundedness and Discretion

K1: DECIDE BY RULE AND ROTE
K2: DECIDE BY DISCRETION
K2.1: USE DISCRETION TO ADOPT AN 'ACTIVE' STANCE
K2.2: USE DISCRETION WITH A 'PASSIVE' STANCE

K1: Decide by Rule and Rote

K1 holds that administrative casework should be handled like a computer program. Decisions should be completely governed by rules specifying every contingency, without any need for the application of human judgement. Some computer-based 'expert systems' today perhaps come close to turning the computer-program metaphor into fact (Snellen and van de Donk 1989).

K1 is linked with traditional aspirations to a Rechtstaat and 'a government of laws and not of men' (cf. Hood 1986, 21). It became the reigning doctrine in some fields of business regulation in the USA in the 1970s, under the pressure of consumerist lobbying (Bardach and Kagan 1982). It has a following in welfare policy, on the ground that the dignity of welfare claimants ought to be established by a system of rules which makes them independent of the prejudices and petty tyranny of 'street level bureaucrats' (cf. Howard 1978).

The justification for K1 is almost invariably a theta-type claim based on a low view of the ability of human decision-makers to make fair decisions free of bias or considerations of personal gain (cf. Allott 1980, 256). The assumption is that only a 'no-discretion' system can prevent laxity, corruption and lack of zeal among office-holders. K2 is held to protect citizens from administrative tyranny, the process of 'rigid rules and lax enforcement', as Tocqueville (1949, 75) put it in his famous description of *ancien régime* France.

K2: Decide by Discretion

K2 holds that good administration requires that decision-makers be able to use their own judgement or common sense within a broad ambit, and are not constrained to operate like a slot-machine. For example, environmentalists may urge K2 in opposition to corporate justifications of polluting activity in terms of the common defence that 'If it's legal, it's OK', urging instead that discretion be used to pursue higher standards. In the context of social security, Richard Titmuss (1971) advanced K2 against the doctrine that welfare entitlements should be fixed by rule and rote; and the same idea often comes up in education and social work.

General justifications for K2 tend to rest on sigma-type claims about the advantages of flexibility relative to a 'Procrustean bed' approach to casework which reduces everything to an undesirable uniformity, and on lambda-type claims about capacity to respond to the unexpected. The claim is that it is impossible and undesirable to reduce all administration to a computer program, because it is never possible to foresee all possible contingencies.

K2.1: Use discretion to adopt an 'active' stance   K2.1 is a variant of K2 which holds that decisions should be made or cases handled by taking an 'active' stance relative to clients or customers. Activity in this sense can be *literal* – the 'street theatre' approach to administration, involving a deliberate seeking of custom and generation of 'happenings'. Or it can be *metaphorical*, meaning demonstrated commitment to a particular cause, the wearing of hearts on sleeves rather than the cultivation of neutrality and 'distance'. In this form, K2.1 holds that administrators should *not* be like disinterested judges, impartial to who wins and who loses. Rather, the system should be actively geared to achieving a preferred outcome, with the dice clearly loaded in favour of the desired policy goal. Doctrines of 'proactivity' and a 'roadshow' (rather than wait-by-the-telephone) approach to management often have appeal to those who are dissatisfied by current outcomes or by 'new brooms' who wish to have demonstrable effect.

Proactivity is often held to be virtuous because it is equated with being in control, cutting through the inertia or institutional biases or informational handicaps which hamper a wait-to-be-asked approach to administration. This doctrine is popular in social work, where the disadvantaged are often held to be unable to master the system sufficiently to acquire the support and services to which they are entitled according to the legislation. More than once a welfare programme aimed at the deprived has been captured by the educated middle class as a result of its ability to study legislation, fill out forms, and marshall political support. Proactivity is commonly argued as the correct strategy for regulatory agencies, for instance in the field of equal opportunity or trading standards, where 'passivity' can be argued to lead to ineffectiveness. The same goes for art and culture administration, where a 'roadshow' approach has become fashionable. And K2.1 is also frequently advanced in debate about the conduct of industry policy, for example in the common argument that poor Anglo-American economic performance lies in a 'hands-off' approach of government to economic planning, in contrast to the wonders allegedly worked by 'proactive' planning agencies such as the French Planning Commission or the Japanese MITI.

K2.2: Use discretion with a 'passive' stance   K2.2, less fashionable and less media-approved than K2.1, holds that discretion should be applied passively and neutrally. It should be used 'without sympathy or enthusiasm' (Thompson 1976), and strictly in response to demands initiated by customers or citizens. Passivity may mean waiting for cases to present themselves (as in a law court) rather than in seeking them out, responding only when a question is correctly phrased and accurate, or by decision on a basis of studied neutrality or impartiality rather than of demonstrated 'commitment'.

K2.2 is often linked with achieving fair and indiscriminate judgement, with avoidance of undue intrusion into private affairs. At first sight, K2.2 may look conservative, but in fact, like most administrative doctrines, it is by no means the property of any particular partisan stripe. A stereotype pro-market right-winger might favour K2.1 as the correct operating principle for the police and security forces (favouring an 'active' approach to law and order and the quelling of political dissent) but see K2.2 as the correct operating principle for industry policy agencies (favouring a non-discriminatory policy by government on the ground that 'business knows best'). On the other hand, a stereotype socialist libertarian might apply the doctrines in reverse – K2.2 for the police and security forces, but K2.1 for industry policy agencies.

Decision Doctrines

W1: TREAT LIKE CASES ALIKE
W2: TREAT UNLIKE CASES ALIKE

W1: Treat Like Cases Alike

W1 is a doctrine of *variable* treatment. In order that like cases can be treated alike, it holds that response should be tailored to each individual case, either by rule or by discretion. Debate may well rage as to what 'likeness' should mean and what the indicators of 'likeness' should be.

The case for W1 is normally made in terms of sigma-type and theta-type claims. The theta-type claim is that W1 is the only way to achieve *fairness*, by linking treatment to varying need or to desert. The sigma-type claim is that W1 is a key to *efficiency* or avoiding waste (for example in giving food stamps only to the poor rather than to everybody), or that it is a recipe for *effectiveness*. Rather than giving all patients identical treatment, results will only be obtained if treatment is varied according to the disease or complaint.

W2: Treat Like Cases Unlike

Contrary to W1, W2 is a doctrine of uniform treatment. It says that all cases should be treated the same, irrespective of their particular characteristics. This is typically justified on theta-type grounds of fairness. Examples include the idea that teachers or doctors should spend the same amount of time with each pupil or patient, regardless of need, or that education or health authorities should spend the same sum of money per pupil or per patient. For instance, some feminists argue that teachers should equalize time spent with each student, to prevent undue attention being paid to boys.

There are some interesting treatment doctrines in the border territory between W1 and W2. For example, the use of a lottery system (often used in allocation, for instance in conscription) treats each case alike in terms of *chances*, but achieves unequal treatment in terms of *outcomes*. And in long-linked systems, such as health or education, we typically see one doctrine applied at one level and the other at another level. An example is the application of W2 in the idea of funding hospitals through standard payments (from governments or insurers) based on 'disease-related groups' (DRG). Here the aim is to avoid costly over-servicing of patients by hospitals by a process of fixing separate categories of disease and establishing a median cost for each disease, such that a hospital gets a standard fee for each treatment within a DRG (say $150), irrespective of what the doctors actually do. Whether such a regime merely exchanges simple over-servicing for over-diagnosis and undertreatment is not the issue here. The point is simply that such a regime is a compound of doctrines W1 and W2 – W1 at the funding level, W2 at the treatment level.

VII   DOCTRINES OF CONTROL OVER OPERATIONS

X1: CONTROL BY INPUT
X2: CONTROL BY PROCESS
X2.1: CONTROL BY OPEN ADVERSARIAL PROCESSES
X2.2: CONTROL THROUGH STANDARDS OF PROFESSIONAL PRACTICE
X2.3: CONTROL THROUGH 'BUSINESS METHODS'
X3: CONTROL BY OUTPUT
X3.1: CONTROL BY OUTPUT MEASURES
X3.2: CONTROL BY OUTCOME MEASURES

X1: Control by Input

X1 holds that control should focus on inputs, such as the amount of money spent or staff hired. Despite obeisances to other doctrines of control, many administrative control systems in practice follow X1.

X1 is sometimes justified in pragmatic, sigma-type terms. Inputs are often far easier and cheaper to measure than throughputs or output. For instance, it is simpler to keep a check on the number of hours a person works than on the quality of work they do. Similarly, provided that waste, greed and opportunism can be kept within reasonable bounds, materials used may be a rough-and-ready indicator of 'need'.

X1 is also sometimes justified in 'principled', theta-type terms, in circumstances where 'non-interference' is particularly prized, say in cultural affairs, international aid, scientific work. Here the typical claim is that respect for national sovereignty, artistic or academic freedom, requires that outside control be based primarily on the funding stage or the hiring stage of operations – controlling who gets what funds or what quality of staff is appointed, rather than focusing control on how the operation works or what concrete results it produces.

X2: Control by Procedure

X2 holds that control should be applied to the procedures according to which business is done. X2 has traditionally been important in public administration. The normal justification is the theta-type claim that the conduct of government business needs to meet procedural standards more rigorous than those typically prevailing in private business – for instance in procedures for access, for coordination of decisions to achieve consistency, for avoidance of conspicuous waste, for careful recording of decisions, for avoidance of arbitrary proceedings which may give scope for abuse of office.

X2.1: Control by Open Adversarial Processes

This variant of X2 holds that effective control means oversight conducted according to the sort of procedure traditionally associated with a criminal or civil court trial. X2.1 holds that close attention must be paid to rules of evidence and procedure. It means that the 'parties' in every case should have the opportunity to be represented by professionals. It means that considerations of cost and time taken over decision-making should be secondary to the aim of (eventually) arriving at a correct judgement. It means that evidence should be heard impartially from all sides affected in the case, and (as in the traditional model of 'a fair trial') that proceedings should be held in public.

X2.1 is mainly applied to public management. It is beloved by lawyers, for whom it conveniently combines self-interest with professions of high (theta-type) principle; and it has been unstoppable in areas such as statutory land-use planning processes.

A variant of X2.1 is sometimes advocated on sigma or lambda-type grounds. This is the claim that where significant policy choices (for example, on public safety) need to be made in complex fields where final proof is infeasible, they should be based on carefully staged adversarial processes involving the best available expertise (Lindblom 1965; Majone 1986 and 1989). The procedures need to be devised to test the best available evidence from the most persuasive sources. Such an idea lies behind Robert Dahl's (1985) argument for 'guardianship' in nuclear weapons control, and Giandomenico Majone's case for 'science courts' in high-technology policy. Majone (1986, 449) uses the example of deciding whether the effects of low-level radiation from X-rays, radioimmunoassay, etc., are harmful to human health. He claims that, since it would require an experiment with 8 billion mice to determine at the 95 per cent confidence level whether a level of X-ray radiation of 150 millirems would increase the spontaneous mutation in mice by half a percent, there is no practical alternative to deciding the issue by the best *prima facie* evidence available, and by carefully structured methods of hearing out the arguments.

X2.2: Control through Standards of Professional Practice

X2.2 holds that the best method of control is to model operations on the caring professions, with the decision-makers applying discretion within a climate of professional ethics.

Central to X2.2 is the assumption that decision-makers do, or can at least be made to, follow some equivalent of the Hippocratic oath. That means that they can be bound to serve the interests of their clients rather than their own interest.

On this assumption, X2.2 holds that control works through professional ethics and peer-group pressure. Decisions should be made by applying professional judgement to each particular case, using the best available knowledge, and should be based on personal examination and counselling, not on adversarial hearings involving agents or professional advocates for each 'side'. Accuracy and good practice should be checked through a structure of peer review. Like X2.1, X2.2 implies subordination of cost considerations to other desiderata in order to serve the 'needs' of a clientele.

X2.3: Control through 'Business Methods'

X2.3 is particular to public management and it overlaps with some of the other 'how-type' doctrines considered here. But it deserves a place of its own, in view of its recurring popularity. It holds that the correct procedures for controlling public business are those which are used in private business. As long ago as the 1850s, Sir Edwin Chadwick (1854, 177) argued that 'the best private practice' should be the model for public business, and the same idea emerged more strongly in the United States in the 1890s, in the emphasis on professional private business-style management which underlay the 'city-manager' and 'commission plan' models of urban government.[3] Subsequently, it was augmented by Taylorist ideas of 'scientific management' and extended to federal government level in the 1930s, as we will see in Part III.

X2.3 has a continuing attraction. Businessmen seconded to British government departments during World War I later advocated the introduction of private business methods to cure the ills of bureaucracy (Thomas 1978, 199). Since the 1970s, business-type methods have been an emphatic part of the administrative recipe of the 'New Public Management', which we will discuss in Part IV.

The typical justification for X2.3 is the sigma-type claim that bureaucratic 'rigidity' can be removed by a business-style no-red-tape approach and that the inefficiency and corruption of 'politics' can be dissipated by nonpartisan 'management' experts who concentrate on getting the job done rather than in 'playing politics'. Normally, the suppressed premises in the argument are the assumptions that the management methods associated with successful private corporations (a) represent a causal link between organization design and performance and (b) are readily portable to apply to public management.

X3: Control through Outputs

X3 holds that the focus of control should be the *results* which are achieved, not the procedures through which the results are achieved. The idea that control should be aimed at the achievement of policy goals within a cost ceiling is Jerry Mashaw's doctrine of 'bureaucratic justice' (Mashaw 1983, 172). X3 conventionally comes in two forms.

X3.1: Control through Outputs

X3.1 holds that control should be exercised by constructing 'output indicators' for operations and relating them to inputs. If we follow X3.1, we will be keenly interested in indicators such as number of traffic tickets issued per traffic police officer-hour, length of red tape used or tonnage of forms stamped per bureaucrat-hour, metres of chalk on blackboards per teacher-hour.

X3.1 is widely applied in both public and private management. It is normally justified in sigma or theta-type terms as a key to efficiency and accountability. By focusing on items which are readily controllable by the actions of workers and bosses, it holds them accountable for what they can change and raises pressures to 'get the job done' at maximum efficiency. X3.1 figures heavily in the ideas of the 'New Public Management', which is discussed in Part IV.

X3.2: Focus on Results in Terms of Outcomes

X3.2 holds that control should focus on the *final*, not the intermediate, output. If we follow X3.2 we will be interested in controlling sewerage authorities by indicators of the changing incidence of water-borne communicable diseases, not by the number of pipes laid or homes connected; in judging police performance by the changing incidence of crime in society, not by the caseload handled; in controlling health care workers by the number of patients remaining in good health, not by the number of sick people being treated in hospital, as in the currently fashionable concept of 'health maintenance organizations'.[4]

The case for X3.2 is that an effective control system needs to focus on results without setting up a system which causes statistics to be produced for the record in a way which encourages 'working stupid' and diverts resources from substantive goals. X3.2 is more often advocated than applied.

VIII CONCLUSION

The 99 administrative doctrines in our collection are not intended to be an exhaustive listing of the doctrinal 'bunch of keys' available for administrative argument. If we had driven our research army further, rigorously following the method of classification *per genus et differentiam* (or Bentham's variant of archetypication and phraseoplerosis), we could greatly expand the number. But the 99 do include many of the commonest doctrines which are found in administrative argument. The sameness can be hard to recognize, because the doctrines are frequently re-invented and re-named. As we noted in Chapter 2, continuous relabelling is a characteristic feature of administrative doctrines, which can obscure lines of parentage. It is true that some of our 99 doctrines are comparatively modern, but many of them can be traced back to classic sources in mainstream political theory, as we have seen.

To label and classify administrative doctrines in this manner is not to trivialize them, but to make them easier to identify, analyse and discuss. To the extent that administrative debate is an 'issue-machine' processing a more or less fixed stock of available arguments, to which fundamentally new variants are very seldom added, a labelling approach enables us to discuss and identify received ideas with greater economy than is possible when each doctrine must be described in full whenever it is introduced.

Laying out the 'keys' in this way enables us to analyse and juxtapose the doctrines advanced by different classic authors or reports, the received doctrines of different national traditions, or (as Braybrooke used his method) to portray the arguments which are led in recurring cycles of administrative argument, by presenting them as a compound of the 99 doctrines which we have described here. Standardizing terminology is the best way to pick up structurally similar administrative arguments which appear in very different administrative or political contexts. This can help us to pinpoint commonalities which often get covered up if we follow specialist accounts, for example of the administrative politics of different times or places or of particular policy domains.

Few of these doctrines are specific to any particular time or place. Still less are they limited to any particular partisan or ideological outlook. In spite of the efforts of a generation of administrative theorists in the Simonian tradition, all of them remain contested, in that their applicability and results are open to question. Most of them are still justified in practice by forceful use of a few predictable clichés, some of which we have identified in the discussion above, and *not* by a 'natural science' mode of demonstration. What remains puzzling is why some of these doctrinal keys open the lock of acceptance so readily in some times and places, and why the door remains firmly shut to them in other circumstances.

In the next Part, we move from looking at the available range of keys to the analysis of the acceptance factor, or how a particular doctrinal key comes to fit a particular rhetorical lock.

NOTES

1   Proponents of such ideas, naturally, tend to talk in terms of 'multi-skilling'.
2   A phenomenon which is so common in most real-life organizations that colourful examples are never lacking to support the argument.
3   See Karl 1963, 93; Downs and Larkey 1987.
4   Like so many administrative doctrines, the HMO idea is not as new as it seems. Bentham (1962, 239, fn) reports an attempt to set up a similar system for the charitable *Hôtel Dieu* establishment in Paris in the eighteenth century, when M. de Chamousset and Co. offered to manage the establishment on the basis of a fee only for those who were cured, with no charge for any patient who died.

PART III
THE ACCEPTANCE FACTOR

Introduction

There is no need of *Cameralwissenschaft und Polizei*; Austria has been prosperous a long time without anything of that sort. If people are only pious and say their prayers, God will bless the country without such stuff. (The views of the Rector of the University of Vienna on cameralistics, as expressed to von Justi, who was appointed as the first professor of economic sciences in 1750; see Small 1909, 288–9.)

In Part I, we conceived administrative doctrines as a bunch of keys available to open a rhetorical lock of acceptance. Instead of Simon's preferred recipe for the study of administration, which involves use of the methods of natural science to explore the relationship between administrative design and performance, we suggested that an alternative programme was to catalogue the keys in the bunch and to investigate the conditions for opening the lock.

In Part II, we identified and discussed 99 different doctrines of administration as a means of illustrating how the first kind of investigation could be conducted. In this Part, we start to explore the second area – the acceptance factor. In Chapter 6, we will look at three 'classics' of administrative argument, using 'classic' to denote phenomena which have acquired a significance beyond their own particular time and location. Why were these classics persuasive? In Chapter 7, we will explore further the idea of metaphor as the key to persuasiveness in administrative argument.

6 Three Cases of Administrative Argument

...he who persuades must show that those things to which he exhorts are just, lawful, expedient, honourable, pleasant and easy of accomplishment. Failing that, when he is exhorting to that which is difficult, he must show that it is practicable and that its execution is necessary. (Aristotle [Rhetoric to Alexander] 1984, 2272)

I INTRODUCTION

In this chapter we look at three well-known specimens of administrative argument. They are:

1   the British Northcote–Trevelyan Report of 1854, (*Report on the Organisation of the Permanent Civil Service*, C 1713, 1854), which heralded the later development of the classified civil service, recruited and promoted on merit;
2   the US Brownlow Report (President's Committee on Administrative Management, 1937), which heralded the later development of the 'Imperial Presidency' through the thoroughgoing application of the German General Staff principle to the US President's office;
3   the Wilenski Review of New South Wales Government Administration of 1977 (interim report) and 1982 (further report), which developed an agenda for a wide range of developments in modern Australian public administration, including affirmative action for women and minorities, freedom of information, new methods of budgeting and resource planning.

Our three cases are thus taken from different countries, different levels of government and different points in time. They both precede and follow Simon's call for a positivist science of administrative design and performance. If it was correct to suggest, as we did in Part I, that administrative argument has common features produced by its essentially rhetorical nature, those common features ought to show up in spite of the differences of time, level and place in these three cases. The three cases can also serve as subjects for exploring the six conditions for explaining the 'acceptance factor' which we noted in Part I.

II   THE BACKGROUND TO THE THREE CASES

Our examination of the three cases aims to explore what they tell us about the acceptance factor in administrative argument. We are not trying to replicate the work of those scholars who have given definitive historical accounts of the cases. And we concentrate mainly on the written documents. But each of the cases has its own special political context and has a particular history; and we need briefly to sketch out the background to the three reports in order to make the story intelligible.

The Northcote–Trevelyan Report

The orthodox interpretation of the Northcote–Trevelyan Report is that it reflects the 'crisis of patronage' which developed in the UK civil service with the extension of the franchise beginning in the 1830s and the shift away from aristocratic government.[1] As the middle class became enfranchised, the patronage system became difficult to manage politically, with more voters to be squared with government jobs than there were jobs readily available. Moreover, with growing pressure to extend the franchise still further, patronage was passing out of the hands of the traditional ruling class (Mueller 1984).

Patronage also created a perverse incentive structure which made the bureaucracy hard to manage. Junior clerks were recruited on the basis of patronage and promoted by seniority. This meant that people in such positions had no incentive (other than the dictates of conscience) to work hard or effectively. They could not better themselves by doing any more than the minimum required.

Further, the patronage system (and the incentive structure built into it) often served to bring people of only mediocre ability and application in the lower ranks of the bureaucracy. Notable families used the public service as sinecures for second and successive sons. The idleness and incompetence that such recruitment produced was described in some of the novels of Charles Dickens and Anthony Trollope. So it was often necessary to bring people in from outside when someone of real drive and ability was needed for higher-level responsibility. This system produced some bureaucratic leaders of exceptional youth and talent, such as Sir Charles Trevelyan himself. But at the same time it further strengthened the lack of incentive for the lower ranks to work hard and completed the vicious circle of indolence and mediocrity.

The Northcote–Trevelyan Report offers an answer to this 'problem'. The Report offers a set of doctrines, based on theta-type justifications, involving recruitment by competitive examination, promotion on merit, a separation of 'intellectual' and 'mechanical' work and a central classified pay scheme common to all departments. Chapman and Greenaway (1980, 50–1) see such ideas as part of a long-term internal logic of administrative evolution (a slow but steady move towards 'tests of fitness'), linking with a set of changes taking place in the world outside the bureaucracy (growing size of firms, developments in the educational system) and with the broader middle-class political push towards meritocracy reflected in the Liberal ascendancy of the time.

The Report ran into a political storm after it appeared and Lord Aberdeen's government fell in 1855 before any action had been taken on it. But despite its short-term failure, the Northcote–Trevelyan Report acquired international significance in administrative argument, became a landmark document in the development of European bureaucracy, and succeeded in 'setting the agenda' for UK public management for 70 years in a manner reminiscent of 'the new public management' of today.

Indeed, it retains strong symbolic power even to the present day. Our third case, the Wilenski review of NSW government administration, laid claim to its mantle, arguing that its own proposals were simply a logical extension of Northcote-Trevelyan principles (Review of NSW Government Administration 1982, covering letter to Minister). On the other hand, the 1968 Fulton Committee Report on the UK Civil Service (Cmnd 3638 1968, 9) used the Northcote–Trevelyan Report in its opening paragraph to symbolize everything that it claimed to be outdated about the UK civil service in the 1960s. In both cases it served as a touchstone.

The Brownlow Report

The Brownlow Report is part of the politics of the New Deal and the Roosevelt Administration. It is a landmark statement of 'managerialism' in public administration and is closely associated with the alliance between Progressivism and the scientific management movement (see Merkle 1980). It reflected the attempt by a President supported by an exceptionally strong and durable winning electoral coalition to use his office for the pursuit of interventionist social policies designed to benefit and maintain that coalition.

However, the realization of this programme was hampered by the limits of the President's formal authority – not only in the constitutional engineering of separation of powers between the Presidency, Congress and the judiciary, but also within the bureaucracy of which the President was nominal head. The classic Roman/Napoleonic structure of five departments into which the US federal government had been divided in 1789 had grown to over 100 separate units, many of them more effectively controlled by Congress than by the President. More than a dozen of them were independent regulatory commissions which had grown up since 1887 and which reflected ideas about economic management that tended to conflict with the thrust of the New Deal programme. Some of them were quasi-independent boards, which spread executive responsibility around a set of pressure groups.

The Brownlow Committee offers a solution to this 'problem'. The Committee's solution is couched in terms of a more centralized top-down reporting structure based on a private business management analogy, with a large general staff apparatus around the chief executive. Like the Northcote–Trevelyan Report, the Brownlow Report ran into political trouble immediately after it was issued. The legislation designed to implement its proposals was dubbed a 'dictatorship bill' and defeated in Congress. But like the Northcote–Trevelyan Report, the Brownlow Report had an 'agenda-setting' effect in the longer term and has acquired unquestionably 'classic' status.

The Wilenski Review of NSW Government Administration

Our third case is too recent to be generally recognized as a 'classic', coming thirty years after Simon's manifesto for a new administrative science. But it certainly has some of the marks of a 'classic', in that, like the Northcote–Trevelyan and Brownlow reports, it pointed the direction of administrative change in the Australian state of New South Wales (NSW) for over a decade prior to the advent of the 'new public management' in the late 1980s.

Politically, the Review reflects the attempt of a political party long out of office in NSW to regain control over the state's bureaucracy after winning government in 1976. After more than a decade of rule by the conservative coalition of the Liberal and Country (now National) parties, the new Labour Government, headed by Neville Wran, sought to put its stamp on the government structure, in part by putting its own people into key positions in the bureaucracy.[2]

A crucial part of the background was the experience of the 1972–5 Labour government led by Gough Whitlam at the Commonwealth (federal) level of Australian government. The election of the Wran government in NSW came closely after the high drama of Whitlam's fall in 1975. The Wran government set out to overcome inertia resistance from the bureaucracy, since, in Labour Party folklore, bureaucratic inertia was to blame for many of the mistakes of the Whitlam government. One of the Wran government's chosen instruments for realizing its bureaucratic agenda was a 'whizz-kid' from the Whitlam government, who had seen the Whitlam government's mistakes at first hand, had the appropriate party political connections in NSW, and knew what could be done. This was Professor Peter Wilenski, who had been Prime Minister Gough Whitlam's Principal Private Secretary from 1972 to 1974. He went on to other high offices in the Whitlam government before it fell.

Like Northcote–Trevelyan and Brownlow, Wilenski offered a doctrinal 'solution' to the 'problem' of a public bureaucracy which was out of tune politically. His solution was couched in terms of an extension of political control over the bureaucracy, more 'flexible management and attitudes', an extension of merit hiring and promotion to give more opportunities to women and members of minority racial/ethnic groups, and improved public access to services. The Wilenski Report differs from the two earlier ones in that it spreads itself over a broader range of issues, with more of a 'scatter-gun' approach to reform. It also differs in that in this case the key turned in the acceptance lock much more quickly. The Wilenski Report was not blocked immediately after its production in the same way as happened to the other cases. But by no means all of its proposals were put into effect at once. For example, its proposal for the introduction of Freedom of Information legislation was left aside for over a decade in NSW.

General

At first sight, the styles of the three cases appear very different. The Northcote–Trevelyan Report is a slim document. Unlike most official reports, it is evidently designed to be *read*. It consists of only 23 pages[3] of magisterial precepts, devoid of any real supporting evidence in the sense of a battery of statistics and supplementary reports. It has the assertive brevity of an expensive consultant's report today. The credibility of its proposals rests in large part on the weight and standing of its proponents, and those who support its ideas. By contrast, the Brownlow Report runs to 53 pages for the report itself, plus over 300 pages of appendices.[4] Instead of the terse, plain-man's style of the Northcote–Trevelyan Report, it appeals to the march of history and the laws of administrative science to back up its assertions. The Wilenski Report, by comparison with both Brownlow and Northcote-Trevelyan, is a massive tome. Its two documents together run to 538 pages exclusive of appendices. It is a blockbuster – evidently designed *not* to be read. Unlike the other two, it is closely packed with figures and tables, cartoons, copious references to overseas developments, even some citations of academic work. All of this, including the learned apparatus of footnotes, gives it an academic aura, an important part of its claim to authority.

However, in spite of their differences in time, place, style and level of government, these documents all have some things in common. They are all attempts to select a sub-set of administrative doctrines from the larger set of available doctrines, and to back these up with justifications, in such a way that the 'acceptance key' will turn in the lock. Moreover, as we will see, all of these documents justify the doctrines which they advance by the use of enthymeme[5] and argument-by-example, rather than by the kind of 'hard-data' demonstration which Herbert Simon believed should take the place of administrative 'proverbs'. To show this, we need to look a little more closely at the way in which these three documents are argued, the sorts of doctrines about 'who', 'what' and 'how' that they advance, and how they are justified.

III   THE 1854 NORTHCOTE–TREVELYAN REPORT

Most of the doctrines advanced by Northcote and Trevelyan belong to the 'who-type' family discussed in Chapter 3, and the justifications offered belong largely to the sigma family. Six main doctrines are advocated:

1   Q1, the doctrine of recruiting the best and brightest that society has to offer.
2   E2, the doctrine that it is best to recruit people at an early age without experience of any other walks of life.
3   P2, the career service doctrine, linked with L1.2, the doctrine that the bureaucratic elite should do only 'intellectual' work, and should be placed in a separate class for recruitment and promotion from those who do 'mechanical' work.
4   P2.2, the doctrine that promotion (and other important items too, such as retirement pensions and pay increments) should be awarded on the basis of merit rather than of seniority or political patronage.
5   A variant of N3, the doctrine that the skills required of administrators are general literary and analytic skills (plus some specialist skills for particular departments) as testable in open competitive examinations.
6   U1, the doctrine of a uniform structure of public service, involving uniform base pay rates and a bureaucracy-wide system of job classification.

Justifications for this array of doctrines are sigma-type claims about greater effectiveness, limitation of waste by the ability to adjust workloads, to motivate junior staff and to get the best value for money in hiring and promotion.

Simon would not be surprised to find that the Report's style is 'proverbial'. It does not offer a 'hard data' demonstration of the theta-type claims advanced for the six doctrines. Instead, it relies on maxims and examples to show that what it advocates is (in Aristotle's language), just, expedient, practicable and necessary. Contradictory maxims and examples are ignored, and the six doctrines are presented as truths: self-evident to those with proper experience of the matters under discussion. The Report opens with one of the most-quoted passages in public administration (C 1713, 1854, 3):

> ...it may safely be asserted that...the Government...could not be carried on without the aid of an efficient body of permanent officers, occupying a position duly subordinate to that of the Ministers, who are directly responsible to the Crown and to Parliament, yet possessing sufficient independence, character, ability and experience to be able to advise, assist, and, to some extent, influence those who are from time to time set over them....

No evidence, of course, is given for this allegedly 'safe' assertion. There is no mention of the rival doctrines that might be advanced (for instance, G3, Q2, T2). Nor is there any indication that the 'safe' assertion might be countered by the view that a permanent administrative staff promotes elitism and lack of bureaucratic responsiveness to changing electoral preferences, as declared with fully equal vigour by President Andrew Jackson some 25 years earlier, in defence of G6. (His argument, too, was unencumbered by evidence.)

The next doctrine to be advanced is Q1 (ibid., 7)

> It is *of course* essential to the public service that men of the highest ability should be selected for the highest posts. (our emphasis)

The 'of course' implies that the assertion is self-evident, but this claim too, fundamental as it is to the argument of the Report, is not demonstrated or further substantiated. Not even considered is the contrary doctrine Q2, the view that the appropriate place for people of the highest ability is in the private sector. Ignoring Q2 allows the conclusion to be drawn that urgent corrective action is needed to change the disproportionate presence in the bureaucracy of persons of mediocre ability, indolence and poor health, instead of the alternative conclusion that a public service staffed by second-rate people is exactly what is needed for a vigorous capitalist economy.

The Report's persuasive strategy is to establish at the outset the assertion that a permanent staff is needed and that the best and brightest are needed for that permanent staff, so that the central 'problem' for action quickly becomes (ibid., 8):

> What is the best method of providing it [the civil service] with a supply of good men, and of making the most of them after they have been admitted?

The 'answer' comes in general terms on the next page:

> The general principle...which we advocate is, that the public service should be
> carried on by the admission into its lower ranks of a carefully selected body of
> young men, who should be employed from the first upon work suited to their
> capacities and their education, and should be made constantly to feel that their
> promotions and future prospects depend entirely on the industry and ability with
> which they discharge their duties....

Even with the problem carefully defined in this way, this 'answer' again rests
on persuasive assertion rather than on exhaustive demonstration. Indeed,
every component of the Report's 'answer' to its carefully contrived question
could be opposed by an equally plausible but contrary 'answer' – for example,
E1 against E2, Q2 against Q1, U2 against U1, T2 against T1.

How does the Report deal with the counter-doctrines and justifications
which could be matched with the doctrines which it asserts? One of its
methods, already noted, is a blatant one-sidedness, ignoring the contrary
doctrines. For instance, the Report concentrates on the 'evils of patronage'
(ibid., 12), and does not discuss the possible *benefits* of patronage in creating
a politically responsive or representative bureaucracy or in putting some
people of exceptional ability into high office at an early age.

Elsewhere, the Report deals with possible objections by partly admitting
contrary arguments. For instance, it is admitted that it may sometimes be
desirable to make some 'lateral entry' appointments (ibid., 7), that specialist
qualifications may sometimes be more appropriate than general ones (ibid.,
12), even though general ability is described (ibid., 14) as 'a matter of more
moment than...being possessed of any special acquirements'.

The Report's third approach to contrary doctrines is to anticipate them in
an attempt to deflect their force. For instance, the stock objection to merit
promotion (doctrine P2.2), that it would lead to favouritism and corruption in
practice, is anticipated by a scheme to make superordinates give their reasons
in writing for selecting a particular candidate, and to make supervisors give
to departmental heads a list of several possible candidates for a post, with a
report on each, rather than a single one. [6]

Perhaps the most striking overall feature of the Northcote–Trevelyan
Report is its apparent simplicity. It may be relevant to note in this context that
Aristotle (1984, 2224) considered simplicity to be part of the power of
enthymeme in rhetorical argument. Sir Stafford Northcote and Sir Charles
Trevelyan were far from 'uneducated' men. But they here adopted a style of
argument, involving short chains of deductive reasoning, which Aristotle
(ibid.) considered to be characteristic of the power of the rhetoric of uneducated men:

> It is this simplicity that makes the uneducated more effective than the educated
> when addressing popular audiences.... Educated men lay down broad general
> principles; uneducated men argue from common knowledge and draw obvious
> conclusions.

The Northcote–Trevelyan Report is a classic case of argument from 'common knowledge' in order to draw (apparently) obvious conclusions.

IV   THE BROWNLOW COMMITTEE REPORT 1937 (PRESIDENT'S COMMITTEE ON ADMINISTRATIVE MANAGEMENT)

Our second specimen, the Brownlow Report of 1937, is an American classic of administrative argument which is just as famous as the Northcote–Trevelyan Report. The Report has been much written about, notably in Barry Karl's (1963) account of the development of its ideas and of the three men who wrote it, Louis Brownlow, Charles Merriam and Luther Gulick.

The Brownlow Report is concerned with the 'problem' of how to structure the cockpit of modern administrative government. It has something to say about 'who-type' and 'how-type' doctrines, but much of its argument is concentrated on the area of 'what-type' doctrines. The justifications used are a mixture of sigma-type, theta-type and lambda-type claims, relating to effectiveness, value for money, democratic oversight and the capacity to respond to a crisis. Nine important doctrines are advanced:

1   H2, the doctrine that 'administrative' work (which is not defined) is best conducted by single-headed hierarchy rather than collegial organization.
2   V1, the doctrine that executive authority ought not to be divided.
3   H2.1A, the doctrine that hierarchical management should be assisted by a general staff.
4   A1, the doctrine that most forms of administration should be conducted within classic public bureaucracies. 'We have no hesitation...in recommending that every activity and agency be brought within a department...' (President's Committee on Administrative Management, 1937, 36).
5   A variant of G6, the doctrine that recruitment to all 'policy-determining' positions (including staff positions) should be by political patronage. This is said to be 'of the essence of democratic government' (ibid., 39).
6   G7, the doctrine that all positions other than 'policy-determining' ones should be filled on the basis of objective merit.
7   C2.1, the doctrine that the boundaries of government departments and agencies should follow the lines of major purpose.
8   B1, the doctrine that administrative departments should be large, so that there need not be many of them.
9   R2.1B, the doctrine that reward for administrators should be at least as high as rewards obtainable for comparable work in the private sector (ibid., 13).

Many of these doctrines are recognizable as standard 'managerial' lines of argument about the organization of government, and the Report itself is often cited as an exemplar of the high tide of American 'scientific management' theory.[7] One of its authors (Luther Gulick) was a highly successful management consultant and prominent late exponent of the 'scientific management' school.[8] The 'Notes on the Theory of Organization' prepared by Gulick for the Brownlow Commission are of central importance in academia, including the famous idea of POSDCORB as encompassing the essence of management. Another (Charles Merriam) was a vigorous academic advocate of the view that the practical problems of government could be solved by the application of 'science' (see Karl 1963, 61–70). Louis Brownlow himself was a former journalist and one of the pioneer American 'city managers'. Hence the Report reflects the application of city management rhetoric to the federal level of government.

The Brownlow Report was written nearly eighty years after the Northcote-Trevelyan Report, by people who tended to wear their pretensions to administrative 'science' on their sleeves. But at bottom the structure of the Brownlow Report's argument is not very different from that of the Northcote–Trevelyan Report. The similarity lies in the advancement of doctrines which can be met and matched with counter-doctrines of at least *prima facie* plausibility, and in the assertion, but not actual demonstration, of the superiority of the measures being advocated.

For example, V1, the doctrine that executive authority should not be divided, could be countered by V2, the doctrine that Madisonian checks and balances, the pitting of ambition against ambition, is the best, and indeed ultimately the only, way of preventing abuse of public office. A1, the doctrine that most forms of administration should be conducted within classic public bureaucracies could be countered by A3, the 'subsidiarity' doctrine (that community or private organizations ought to provide public services, with subsidies if necessary) or by the currently fashionable doctrine (A2) that hived-off agencies are more efficient than classic public bureaucracies. H2.1, the doctrine of the superiority of single-headed hierarchy for 'administrative' work[9] could be opposed by doctrines H2.2B ('functional foremanship') or H2.2A (collegiate self-management). H2.1A, the doctrine of a general staff to augment the power of the chief executive could be opposed by doctrine H2.1B, also fashionable today, that chief executive establishments should be 'lean', with control achieved through competition and delegation of authority. And if appointment by political connections to the topmost 'policy-determining' administrative positions is claimed to be 'of the essence of democratic government', why should the application of the doctrine stop there?

The Brownlow Report, in fact, no more demonstrates the validity of the measures it advocates than does the Northcote–Trevelyan Report. It claims but does not demonstrate, that large savings will result from the application of its recommendations,[10] just as it claims, but does not demonstrate, that the costs of higher salaries in the bureaucracy will be outweighed by savings arising from lower turnover and the retention of more able staff. (That high executive salaries are associated with productivity is a thesis usually accepted without evidence in the world of private business, too (see Broom and Cushing 1977).)

Rather than making its point by an exhaustive analysis of all the available cases, the Report seeks to make its argument persuasive by associating the doctrines which it favours with sources of authority. Broadly, six kinds of 'authority' are invoked.

The first is 'history' and its 'lessons'. The Report claims (*President's Committee on Administrative Management* 1937, 12) that the lessons of history prove the superiority of strong hierarchical authority and of the dangers of a spoils system of appointment to public office. The 'evidence' for the first proposition comes from selecting the pre-1787 history of the American states under the Articles of Confederation and ignoring counter-examples, such as the Swiss model. The 'evidence' for the second proposition comes from selecting the case of President Garfield's assassination by a disappointed office-seeker and ignoring cases where exceptional talent has been recruited to public office through the route of party spoils.

The second kind of authority is 'science' rather than 'history', with the claim that the measures being advocated represent universal principles of human organization (ibid., 3):

> ...the foundations of effective management in public affairs, no less than in private, are well known. They have emerged universally whenever men have worked together for some common purpose... Stated in simple terms, these canons of efficiency require the establishment of a responsive and effective chief executive as the center of energy, direction and administrative management; the systematic organization of all activities in the hands of qualified personnel under the direction of the chief executive; and to aid him in this, the establishment of appropriate managerial and staff agencies ... Taken together, these principles... may be considered as the first requirement of good management....

According to this passage, universal human experience shows that an able chief executive is essential to any organization.

A third kind of authority is found in successful practice elsewhere. The claim is that the 'problem' has been satisfactorily solved elsewhere – usually in state or city governments. Hence the conclusion is drawn that the measures adopted in other very different contexts are also applicable to the special institution of the Presidency. In what is now a very familiar cliché of administrative argument, an ideal private business organization is held up as a model for government to follow (ibid., 33–4):

> Any large industrial or commercial enterprise with plants, stores or services scattered over a Continent would, for the sake of good management, organize the business on the basis of the separate services, plants or areas. Each one of these

divisions would then have a manager who would direct the whole enterprise, working through 8 to 10 executive assistants in accordance with the policies determined by the stockholders and the board of directors. This is in general what we propose for the Government of the United States....

In this case alleged conclusions from other entirely different forms of organization (and types and levels of government) are taken to support arguments about national government.

A fourth powerful symbol of authority which is held to justify the Report's doctrines is the US Constitution itself. Thus it is claimed that the Constitution 'clearly intended' to design the American Presidency according to the precepts of 'scientific management' (ibid., 3), but that current practice falls short of this design. Likewise the development of independent regulatory commissions is held to constitute 'a headless fourth branch of government', at variance with the constitutional principle that there should only be three branches (ibid., 39).

A fifth and related justification for the Brownlow Committee's recommendations is that they are 'democratic'. The Report anticipates the (all too plausible) objection that the measures it proposes will mainly be to the benefit of technocrats, consultants and bureaucrats, through higher salaries and more opportunities. Hence it is at great pains to assert that the aim of its proposals is to strengthen 'democracy', not to realize a hidden agenda to aggrandize the President and his 'administrative managers'. This claim is frequently repeated throughout the Report. To take one example (ibid., 4):

> There is but one grand purpose, namely to make democracy work today in our National government; that is, to make our Government an up-to-date, efficient and effective instrument for carrying out the will of the nation. It is for this purpose that the Government needs thoroughly modern tools of management.

Rather than developing a model of 'democratic administration' along the lines advocated by Vincent Ostrom (1974), in the formula $B2 + G3 + M2 + O1 + U2 + V2$,[11] 'democracy' is claimed to require $V1$, quick and effective oversight from a single controlling centre (President's Committee on Administrative Management 1937, 1). $V1$ is held to be desirable partly because, in standard 'managerialist' fashion, the value of democracy is held to lie in 'results' rather than in process (ibid.):

> We are too practical a people to be satisfied...with mere plans, talk and pledges. By democracy, we mean getting things done that we, the American people, want done in the general interest. Without results we know that democracy means nothing.,...

Indeed, the Report goes so far as to say that the 'best and soundest practices of government' which its recommendations embody, could only be opposed on the basis of 'treasonable design' (ibid., 2–3). Contrary views are thus associated with lack of patriotism rather than with honest doubt or disagreement.

The final source of authority claimed by the Report is its frequently repeated claim that its recommendations represent the leading edge of 'modernity' contrasted with the old-fashioned and haphazard structure which the then existing state of affairs is portrayed to be (ibid., 37). This too has since become one of the most familiar clichés of administrative argument:

> The Executive Branch of the government of the United States has thus grown up without plan or design like the barns, shacks, silos, tool sheds and garages of an old farm....

Planning, we are to conclude, is better than spontaneity.

Much of the persuasive claims of the Brownlow Committee Report thus rest on marshalling the heavy artillery of science and historical inevitability. It is a classic of administrative argument by example and by enthymemes built on pithy and quotable maxims. Easily the best known of these maxims is the four-word sentence (penned by Louis Brownlow) 'The President needs help' (ibid., 5). Why does the President 'need help'? The answer supplied in the following pages of the Report is the growing complexity and magnitude of the work of the President's Office.

Aristotle in fact (1984, 2222) believed that the use of maxims was a risky strategy, suitable only for the elderly or rhetoricians experienced in their subject matter. It is a mark of how effectively the Brownlow Committee assumed an aura of scientific expertise that it carried this mix off so successfully.

V   THE WILENSKI REVIEW (REVIEW OF NSW GOVERNMENT ADMINISTRATION) *DIRECTIONS FOR CHANGE* 1977 AND *UNFINISHED AGENDA* 1982

Our third specimen of administrative argument is a comparatively modern document, which differs from the other two cases in five respects.

First, it is directed to the administrative system of a state government in a federal system, rather than the national level of government to which the two reports considered above were directed. Second, unlike either Brownlow or Northcote–Trevelyan, the report comes in two parts, produced five years apart – an 'interim' report produced shortly after the review was set up in 1977 which consists of a broad survey of the field and a tentative canvassing of alternative ideas, and a 'further' (final) report appearing at the end of the review's life in 1982.

Third, it ranges over a broader span of doctrinal territory than the other two cases. Whereas the Northcote–Trevelyan Report is mainly concerned with who-type issues and the Brownlow Report is heavily (though not exclusively) concerned with what-type issues, the Wilenski Review is concerned with who-, what- and how-type issues in almost equal measure. But the justifications come largely from the theta-type family, in contrast to the thrust of the other two cases.

It differs markedly from the other two specimens in style. Its style is in a sense post-positivist compared to the optimism and rationalism of the Brownlow Report and the 'plain man's commonsense' style of the Northcote–Trevelyan Report. Though the Wilenski Report is written in full awareness of Simon's attack on administrative 'proverbs', it is not a statement of faith in science and rationalism in the same way that the Brownlow Report is. Instead, it goes out of its way to achieve 'street-wise' credentials. The text makes explicit and continuous reference to the devious processes of bureaucratic politics which govern implementation of administrative reforms. It was written in the light of two other 'reforming' reports which shared some of its ideas – the UK Fulton Committee Report on the Civil Service of 1968 (Cmnd. 3638 1968) and the Report of the Royal Commission on Australian Government Administration (1976). It very self-consciously tried to avoid the fate of those two reports: the aim was to pre-empt tokenism, resistance, partial and selective implementation (see Wilenski 1986, 172–83).

It also differs significantly in other matters of style. The text is much longer than our other two specimens, as we have already noted. Though it is elegantly written, it draws heavily on the terminology and format of modern social science. For instance, the Interim Report is densely packed with tables and figures, using 'number-magic' as part of its persuasive force in a way that neither Brownlow nor Northcote–Trevelyan did. An element of this is the use of opinion polling and attitude surveying – commissioned by the Review – as a source of 'scientific authority' for its findings.

A further persuasive device is the use of cartoons (drawn by the popular Australian satirist Peter Cook), interleaved with the text, usually to exaggerate and stereotype the positions it is trying to change. For example, in order to discredit what it portrays as an ethos of excessive administrative secrecy, a cartoon in the *Further Report* (Review of NSW Government Administration 1982, 50) shows a male public servant sharing a double bed with a filing cabinet, a shotgun at the ready in order to fend off intruders. The cartoons appear on every few pages of the Report. They are another 'language' in which the Report speaks, turning opposing ideas into grotesque stereotypes and disparaging them in ways which could not be done in the more measured style of the text.

Twelve of the most important doctrines which figure in the Wilenski review are:

1   Q1, the doctrine of recruiting the best and brightest in society at large. The Review (1977, 87) considers but explicitly rejects Q2, the 'mediocrity doctrine'.

2   P1, the doctrine of promotion on merit.

3   H2.1A, the general staff doctrine.

4   E1, the doctrine that recruitment to the public bureaucracy of those who have worked in other occupations is beneficial to the public service.

5   U1, the doctrine that the public bureaucracy ought to be as far as possible unified for the purposes of promotion and transfer.

6   A variant of R2.1A, the doctrine that the public service ought to be a model employer, treating its employees better than short-term market considerations alone would require. In this case, the argument goes that the public service ought to develop the skills of its employees to the maximum extent.

7   H2.2A, the doctrine that single-headed hierarchy ought to be modified by collegiate practices, in the form of team projects, task forces and worker participation in management.[12]

8   S2.1, the doctrine of representative bureaucracy, used here to justify affirmative action.

9   U1, the doctrine of unitary management applied to the public service, to advocate a centralized budgeting process and close oversight of all units from the overseeing centre.

10   A variant of X2.2, the view that administration should be driven, as in the ideal of the 'caring' professions, by a concern with the best interests of the customer or client.

11   A3, the subsidiarity doctrine (applied here to information services).

12   I3, the freedom of information doctrine.

Some of the doctrinal bunch of keys selected by the Wilenski review are identical to those selected by the Northcote–Trevelyan and Brownlow Reports. Some are opposites, for instance, in the preference for E1 rather than E2. Some are simply different – such as the idea of one-stop information shopping, or of putting the most senior, rather than the most junior staff at the 'front line' of the bureaucracy in direct contact with the public.

Despite its self-conscious modernity, the Wilenski review seeks to persuade by means that are essentially the same as those employed in the Northcote–Trevelyan and Brownlow Reports. By this we mean that it justifies its preferred doctrines by example and enthymeme, not by irrefragable evidence. In spite of its battery of statistics and social science jargon, the review does not use 'test' and 'control' group methods to prove its assertion that elaborate priority-setting staff work results in better government. It does not use 'test' and 'control' or systematic 'before' and 'after' comparisons to prove its assertion that freedom of information laws lead to greater equity and fewer errors. It does not use such methods to prove that affirmative action measures bring about changes that would not have occurred anyway, or that such measures do more than advantage the most privileged members of the 'disadvantaged' group at the expense of the most disadvantaged members of the 'privileged' group.[13] Nor does it even recommend that such methods be used in the future to determine these questions.

Though the Wilenski review differs from the Northcote–Trevelyan and Brownlow Reports in its copious use of statistics and in its consideration (in many, though not all, cases) of objections to the doctrines it is canvassing, it is just as vulnerable to Simon's charge of 'proverbiality' as the other two cases. The tone is generally didactic, with little interest in trial and error and experimentation. The message is that the review knows what 'Reform' is, who its enemies are and how it should be carried out.

In the absence of evidence, it justifies its doctrines in three main ways. First, like the Brownlow Report, it presents NSW of the late 1970s as chronically out-of-date in relation to what is claimed to be 'best practice' elsewhere. The idea of 'imitating best overseas practice' (if short skirts are worn in Miami, then they must also be worn in Leningrad) involves the suppressed premise that is the hallmark of argument by enthymeme. The Wilenski review also follows the Brownlow Report in its implicit philosophy of 'Newism', the familiar rhetorical figure of 'if it's new it's better'.[14] But it does not follow the stock argument of recent managerial approaches to public administration that private business practice is the model to be emulated. The reason, of course, is that such an argument would not always support the courses of action for which Wilenski is arguing.

Second, it draws authority from an aura of scholarship. Unlike the Brownlow Report, it does not try to ground its proposals in allegedly 'universal' principles of organization. But it does show itself to be versed in the academic study of administration, particularly where reference to academic studies is convenient for supporting the argument.[15]

Perhaps more important is its extensive reference to what is presented as the most up-to-date public management practice elsewhere, carefully selecting the cases to fit the argument. The concept of 'leading democracies' is a loaded and selective idea. The 'models' for NSW to follow are taken from faraway places whose practices are not sufficiently known in NSW for local critics to fasten on to the obvious snags - general staff priority-setting machinery from the UK and Canada (ibid., 14ff), budgeting formats from Ontario, management accounting and decision analysis techniques from North America, worker participation schemes from the Federal Republic of Germany, affirmative action schemes from the USA, Canada and Sweden.

Third, like the Brownlow committee, the Wilenski review uses a particular definition of 'democracy' to justify its proposals. Unlike the Brownlow committee, it adds 'equity' as another way of justifying its proposals. Neither of these terms is very closely defined, which enables the report to shift from one meaning to another to suit the argument. For example, the word 'equity' is sometimes used to mean treating like cases alike (as in the case against gender discrimination), but sometimes it is used to mean giving preferential or special treatment to the least advantaged in order to achieve greater equality of outcomes. 'Democracy' is never used to mean direct democracy, but it is sometimes used to mean participatory democracy, and at other times to mean orthodox representative democracy (ibid., 3):

> The *first* theme of this Report is that the decision-making processes of NSW Government should be so ordered that it is the elected politicians who make the most important decisions.

This is a conclusion which is bound to flatter any elected politician, though the message has two constituencies: the elected politicians and the electors who vote them into office.

The Wilenski review is an exceptionally skilful and self-conscious piece of modern administrative argument. Its strategy for persuasion is not the 'obvious conclusions drawn from common knowledge' of the Northcote–Trevelyan Report, nor the claims to universal science of the Brownlow Report, but the appearance of utter command of its subject-matter and the claims to modernity, justice and democracy. It does not in general use maxims like the Brownlow Report nor oracular utterances like the Northcote–Trevelyan Report, and its text (though not its cartoons) is more balanced than either of the other two. At bottom, however, its argument is also based on example and enthymeme – probabilities, examples and signs (Aristotle 1984, 2236). The fact that this is not immediately noticeable is a tribute to the skill with which the argument is presented.

VI CONCLUSION: EXPLORING THE ACCEPTANCE FACTOR

The analysis of the available doctrinal 'bunch of keys' illustrated in Part II can help us to make sense of administrative arguments such as the three specimens considered here. We can make sense of them in several ways. To the extent that the basic set of keys available is limited, each specimen can be analysed as a special configuration out of a standard stock. Table 6.1 summarizes how we can represent and compare the doctrinal components of the three documents examined here, as vectors of the 99 doctrines sketched out in Part II. This helps us to compare what otherwise seem to be qualitatively unique statements. Such a treatment can help to demystify the process of administrative argument, by making it easy to identify the doctrines which have *not* been chosen in any particular piece of administrative argument. 'Knowing the above facts, we know their contraries...' (Aristotle 1984, 2178).

Table 6.1   The three cases: doctrinal composition

	Northcote-Trevelyan 1854	Brownlow 1937	Wilenski 1977 and 1982
Who-type doctrines	E2		E1
	Q1	Q1 [4]	Q1
	G7	G6/G7	G6/G7
	N3		
	P2		P2
	P2.2B		P2.2A
	P2.1		
	T1		
	R2.2C [1]		
	R2.1 [2]	R2.1C	R2.1A
	D1		
			S2.1
What-type doctrines	U1	U1	U1
		B1	
		A1	A1 [5]
		C2.1	
		V1	
How-type doctrines		H2.1	H2.1
		H2.1A	H2.2A
	J1		J2
			I3

Notes
1 for superannuation and increments
2 for base pay
3 for 'policy' positions
4 for non-'policy' positions
5 for information

The other element to be explored here is how and why the key fits the lock. Why did the Northcote–Trevelyan and Brownlow Reports (eventually) become accepted as classic agenda-setting arguments? Why did the Wilenski review become accepted as setting out a new agenda for NSW administration? In Part I, we set out six items which have been identified as related to the 'acceptance factor'. Can these items help us to understand the acceptance factor? The six items, it will be recalled, were.

1   the achievement of *symmetry* between 'problem' and 'solution';

2   the use of *metaphor* to achieve persuasive power;
3   the use of *ambiguity* to appeal to multiple groups of hearers;
4   a concentration on *public benefits* rather than private advantage in the adoption of proposals;
5   a *selection of arguments* and evidence to fit the desired conclusions, ignoring contrary arguments or evidence;
6   the *suspension of possible sources of disbelief* in the rhetorician's argument.

We will be looking more closely at these six elements when we compare two philosophies of public management in Chapter 8. Here we must content ourselves with briefly noting how the six elements relate to the three specimens considered here.

First, symmetry. As was shown earlier, each of the specimens fits into a broader political and social context. The Wilenski review is a mirror of a range of 'progressive' causes in Australian administrative politics in the mid 1970s. The Brownlow Report fits the political logic of the New Deal programme and the trend towards the 'imperial presidency'. The Northcote–Trevelyan Report fits with the threat to aristocratic government posed by the nineteenth-century extension of the franchise.

Second, metaphor. The Brownlow Report contains some powerful metaphors – government as corporate management, public management as engineering, the parental (or 'Big Daddy') theme involved in its preoccupation with single-headed hierarchy. The Northcote–Trevelyan Report's dichotomy of 'intellectual' and 'mechanical' work also has a metaphorical ring, with its obvious analogy to the head and the hands or the brain and the body (Douglas 1987). The Wilenski review, however, lacks a major metaphorical theme of this kind; to the extent that it employs metaphor, the metaphors are small and multiple, or bound up in the use of citations or statistics (cf. Edmondson 1984; McCloskey 1985).

Third, ambiguity. All of these specimens can be 'read' in different ways. The Wilenski review's slogan of 'democratic administration' can be read as a call for strengthening 'top-down' control over the bureaucracy by Ministers or as a formula for participatory democracy aimed at the new pressure groups of the 1970s. The Brownlow Report's ideas about 'administrative management' can be read by the 'Roosevelt coalition' as a political recipe for cutting away the shackles restraining the New Deal programme, or by the traditional middle-class constituency for Progressivism and 'scientific management' as an extension of 'apolitical' city-managerialism to the federal level. The Northcote–Trevelyan Report can be read by the rising middle class and university reformers as thoroughly 'republican' – the advent of a Napoleonic-style *carrière ouverte aux talents*. At the same time, it can be read by the traditional aristocratic governing class as a means of *preventing* the lower orders from filling the ranks of the civil service by making a university education a necessary condition for appointment to the higher civil service – at a time when admission to English universities was in practice limited to the masculine offspring of the gentry. Hence the proposal can also be read as thoroughly *un*-Napoleonic – a conservative counter-stroke against pressures for a representative bureaucracy, aiming to maintain the social composition of the service, by picking the best and brightest of the aristocracy (cf. Mueller 1984).

Fourth, private advantage and public good. The three cases fit the general expectation that people who recommend administrative changes typically make recommendations that will *tend to benefit people like themselves*. In the case of the Northcote-Trevelyan Report, the replacement of patronage by recruitment and promotion on merit may or may not have public benefits; but such a move is likely to increase the power of senior career public servants – such as Sir Charles Trevelyan[16] – relative to elected politicians. The move makes the senior civil servants the sole purveyors of promotion within the bureaucracy, and makes it easier for them to dominate their subordinates by recruiting only youthful and inexperienced people as junior staff. In the case of the Brownlow Report, attaching a general staff to the Presidency may or may not result in the better expression of the people's will, as the Report claims. But what it is bound to do is to increase opportunities for, and the power of, management and policy specialists – such as Brownlow, Merriam and Gulick. In the case of the Wilenski review, an increase of staff appointments, lateral entry and the increase of Ministerial power vis-à-vis career administrative chiefs may or may not deliver the public benefits that Wilenski claims. But it will certainly help ministers in an incoming government to tighten their grip on the bureaucracy, by planting partisan advisers and aides in high places in the bureaucracy. It brings benefits to in-and-outers as a class. Many high-flying careers in Australian government have been built on such a structure.

Fifth, selection of argument and evidence. As we showed in the discussion above, each report is highly selective in its treatment of argument and evidence. As we saw, the Northcote–Trevelyan Report ignores the potential advantages of political patronage as a vehicle for 'democratic administration'. It ignores the case for channelling the best and brightest into the private sector, and it plays down the scope for favouritism, corruption and political partisanship in a merit promotion scheme. It stresses the success of the earlier, analogous reform of the Indian Civil Service (Mueller 1984, 195–8) and plays down the egoism of those with a university education. Similarly, the Brownlow Report presents a one-sided interpretation of 'democratic administration', ignoring the counter-doctrine that democratic administration means decentralized, competitive administrative structures rather than an imperial centre. It plays down or ignores the risk which actually materialized in the Watergate case over thirty years after it put forward its proposals – namely that the unelected general staff would in practice make the key executive decisions, bypassing the constitutional organs of government. Again, the Wilenski review, in its constant reference to the administrative practices of leading overseas countries, carefully leaves out those 'advanced' administrative systems – such as Japan, Switzerland or California – which do not present the

Table 6.2   The three cases: keys to persuasion

	Northcote-Trevelyan 1854	Brownlow 1937	Wilenski 1977 and 1982
Private Advantage	Greater power to senior civil servants over promotion vis-à-vis elected politicians and more power over subordinates (raw, inexperienced)	More scope for experts in policy and administration	More scope for partisan advisers in government. Easier for ministers to put own people into high positions
Major Doctrines Ignored		A2/A3 B2 C2.2-C2.4	
	E1		E2
		H1/H2.2	
			I1/I2
	J2		J2
	P2.2A		
	Q2	Q2	Q2
		R1	
		R2.2	R2.2
	S2.1/S2.2	S2.2	
	U2.2	U2	U2
		V2	
Method of Suspending Disbelief	'Obvious conclusions drawn from common knowledge	Scientific validity 'modernity'	Scholarship extensive knowledge of leading cases 'modernity'

convenient models of 'modernity' for NSW to emulate. It ignores private business practice where that would not help its argument, for instance in affirmative action.

Finally, suspension of disbelief. All three cases aim to suspend disbelief in the practicality of the proposals by pointing to cases which it is claimed are analogous and which are held to work satisfactorily. In its references to the time of trial awaiting the American people and the perils of unpreparedness or poor administrative equipment, the Brownlow Report uses the traditional (and in this case prescient) device of pressing deadlines for action, in order to foreclose attempts to look more closely at the proposals and the argument. The Wilenski review, as noted above, attempts to suspend disbelief by its aura of scholarship (its bulky text, extensive footnotes, battery of figures and tables, attitude surveys) and by its appearance of detailed knowledge of the 'leading' countries for the various issue-areas that it discusses. But the Northcote–Trevelyan Report uses an exactly contrary style, presenting its ideas as plain common sense by practical men of affairs, with the central 'problem' and the resulting 'answer' apparently falling 'naturally' into place – once the argument has fast-forwarded through the contestable areas of permanence and excellence.[17]

Conclusion

Table 6.2 sums up the last subsection. The difference in style of the three cases discussed here is striking. It is impossible to imagine Northcote and Trevelyan using cartoons or opinion polls to back up their case, or Wilenski putting in purple passages about the practical political genius of the Australian people. But, when we look more closely, this set of cases seems to support the claim made in Part I that, while the superficial style of administrative argument may vary over time and from one political context to another, there may be some underlying similarities in basic form.

The six elements which we identified in Part I as possible clues to the 'acceptance factor' seem to give us some purchase on understanding the three cases. However, our discussion here was necessarily brief, and more than these three cases would be needed before we could say whether these items are common to *all* successful administrative doctrines. Accordingly, we shall return to these elements in rather more detail in Chapter 8, when we ascend to the 'philosophy' level of administrative argument and compare the earliest and latest European philosophy of public management. Before doing so, however, we take a closer look at one of the six elements – the role of metaphor and fiction in administrative ideas.

NOTES

1   See Finer 1952a; Parris 1969; Chapman and Greenaway 1980.
2   For the background, see Chaples, Nelson and Turner 1985; Painter 1987, 94-115.
3   Not including a letter of support from Benjamin Jowett, a prestigious Oxford academic and translator of Plato's *Republic*.
4   These were the 'nonsupporting documents', as Charles Merriam, one of the Committee's three members, is said to have jokingly called them (Karl 1963, 222).
5   An enthymeme is an argument with missing premises, a standard rhetorical figure.
6   The possibility that the departmental head might also be biased and corrupt is never, of course, considered.
7   See, for instance, Dunsire 1973a, 94–5; Merkle 1980, 265.
8   Though Ostrom (1974, 39–40) shows that he came close to rejecting its central hierarchical ideas.
9   Whatever 'administrative' means here: it is not defined.
10 President's Committee on Administrative Management 1937, 51.
11 That is, polycentric, competitive, decentralized administration, with direct participation by the relevant communities of interest.
12 This idea is advanced in the *Interim Report* but not pursued in the *Further Report*.
13 The commonest objection to such schemes; it is not considered in the Wilenski Report.
14 See Eaton 1986, 71.
15 For example in relation to the dysfunctions of traditional hierarchical bureaucracy, or to the redesign of bureaucracy from the viewpoint of equitable access.
16 It has to be noted that Sir Stafford Northcote was not a career civil servant at the time of the Report. According to Parris (169, 146) he quit the civil service in 1850 on the death of his father and entered the House of Commons shortly after the Report's publication in 1854, later becoming Chancellor of the Exchequer.
17 At the same time, when defending the Report in a letter to a newspaper, Trevelyan blithely used Greek phrases without transliterating or translating them (Mueller 1984, 203).

7 Fiction and Metaphor in Administrative Argument

It is from metaphor that we can best get hold of something fresh. (Aristotle 1984, 2250)

...very different (is) the Fiction of the logician from the fiction of poets, priests and lawyers... By the priest and the lawyer, in whatsoever shape Fiction has been employed, it has had for its object or effect, or both, to deceive, and, by deception, to govern, and, by governing, to promote the interest...of the party addressing, at the expense of the party addressed...Fiction, in the logical sense, has been the coin of necessity - in that of poets, of amusement - in that of the priest and the lawyer, of mischievous immorality in the shape of mischievous ambition....(Bentham, quoted by Ogden 1932, 17–18)

I INTRODUCTION

In the last chapter, we started to look at the factors which seem to play a part in opening the lock of acceptance for administrative doctrines. In this one, we look at a little more depth at one of the six elements raised there, and return to a question posed at the outset. Why do some administrative arguments open the acceptance lock more readily than others? More particularly, the question is, Why has the *auctoritas suadendi* in administrative argument belonged to groups such as 'econocrats' (Self 1975) and 'managerial consultocrats' rather than to other groups or specialities?

Our hypothesis is that part of the answer to these questions lies in the use of metaphor and fiction to achieve persuasiveness. This hypothesis would explain the persuasiveness of economics in administrative argument by its

157

fictions rather than its truths.   The paradox is that the relative lack of persuasion in 'mainstream' Public Administration may be a product of its determined search for unvarnished verisimilitude or 'concrete factual realism' (henceforth 'CFR'). If there is anything in this hypothesis, it has implications for administrative science that deserve attention.

II METAPHOR AND FICTION IN LAW, ECONOMICS, MANAGEMENT THEORY AND OTHER 'DISCIPLINES'

The distinguished anthropologist Mary Douglas (1987) has offered an analysis of the roots of institutional thought. By 'institutional thought', she means ideas which are sufficiently pervasive and persuasive to be held in common by collectivities and to form the basis of enduring social rules, customs, organizations and habits. The force of Douglas's argument is that, to be instituted, thought needs to be metaphorical. Institutional knowledge must be grounded in reason and nature in some way, particularly through analogy with universal phenomena. Obvious examples are the metaphors of parent and child, the unity of the body, the sun and the planets – all of which are recurring themes in religious and political thought. Only metaphorical knowledge can become institutional knowledge.

Douglas's idea suggests that winning arguments in administrative what-to-do debates will tend to be those which are grounded in metaphor and fiction. Administrative arguments that follow Bentham's precept, aiming at 'CFR', will lose. Reality is complex and diffuse, seldom yielding a single clear meaning. Metaphor, on the other hand, simplifies, while fiction persuades. Against such powerful forces CFR is at a double disadvantage.

Law, as the traditional source of persuasive argument, is obviously a key case. Extravagantly counterfactual assumptions, far-fetched almost to the point of absurdity, are one of the best-known hallmarks of legal argument. Who, for instance, could really believe that the scattered stockholders of a large American corporation are necessarily all citizens of the state which incorporates it (Gray 1921, 34)? Or even that everybody can or does know the law? Why is legal argument so full of such extraordinary flights of fancy, when the same technical effect could usually be served without resort to fiction (for instance, simply by holding arguments based on legal ignorance as inadmissible)?

Douglas's answer would be that the use of fiction adds more persuasion than could be achieved if the relevant argument or rule was presented without fictional elaboration. On that point, both those who see legal fictions as pernicious and those who see them as constructive and convenient, seem to agree. Indeed, the bolder the fiction, the more it seems to be capable of capturing attention and developing its own intellectual momentum. Moreover, just as fire sometimes needs to be fought with fire, fictions are often best fought with other fictions. An example is the medieval fiction of corporate bodies as persons, which is said to have been originally developed by church interests to counter the fiction of the state as the sole or supreme person in society (ibid., 54).

Economics is also distinctive in its propensity to reason through explicit fictions, notably in the fiction of the economic person as opportunistic and self-seeking to the exclusion of all else. This is generally recognized as the greatest – or most notorious – fiction in all of social science. It has been carefully developed and reformulated over two centuries. It has been incubated in clinical isolation from the empirical observations of social psychology and group behaviour (cf. Fuller 1967, 106, fn 23; Douglas 1987). Though one empirical study after another has shown the assumption of the rational economic individual to be false, the fiction continues to dominate economics and intrude into other social sciences. Of course, there are many other examples of fictions in social science. But economics is distinguished from other less prestigious social sciences, in that it involves not just one 'big lie', like the original contract in jurisprudence and political theory, but also a host of other smaller ones.

As with the case of law, metaphor and fiction seem to lend persuasion to economic arguments in several ways. To the extent that they are fresh and bold, they can capture attention. An example is the application of the metaphor of the market to areas of social life which are not ordinarily thought of as a market. Such an application carries with it the accompanying baggage of standard fictions about given technology, perfect and symmetrical information, an even distribution of market power, and so on. These conditions may not be appropriate to the case at hand, but if the metaphor is striking enough, who will think to ask if it is appropriate? Cases in point are behaviour and decision-making within public bureaucracies, the sexual division of labour and changing family structures, charitable donations, adoption, crime.

But economists get more out of their fictions than novelty value. To the extent that the fictions are complex and arcane, they command respect and awe. McCloskey (1985) sees the rise of the 'econocracy' over the past fifty years as a product of the successful use of mathematical metaphor to portray economics as an arcane 'hard science', establishing for economists a claim to a special expertise beyond the realm of the laity's understanding. McCloskey likens the algebraic and geometrical symbols of economics to the classical quotations which an earlier generation of scholars used in order to present their arguments. The symbols, like the quotations, are the product of the most recondite learning, rather than of common knowledge and observation.

The work of the 'strategists' in international relations theory – particularly that group which addressed the new issues of nuclear weapons strategy after 1945 – could also be said to fit this pattern. On the fiction of the Clausewitz paradigm of international relations, i.e. states as persons, the strategists built the metaphor of those 'persons' as players of simple games with evocative titles, notably Prisoner's Dilemma and Chicken (cf. Rapoport and Chammah 1965; Brams 1975, 1–50).

Other influential metaphors from the strategists include the 'domino theory' that helped to form the doctrines leading to US commitment of troops in the second Indo-China war between 1965 and 1973 or the related 'nut-cracker theory' which had some influence up to 1965. To recall, the domino theory treated the complex political systems of the South East Asian countries as a set of dominoes which would all fall to communism if one did, while the nutcracker thesis held that South East Asia was a nut being cracked by two arms of a communist nutcracker, the arms being the People's Republic of China and the Soekarno regime in Indonesia (Fromkin and Chace 1985, 742).

Organization theory and corporate management literature is also rich in metaphor and fiction, though it is rarely as elaborate and fine-grained as in law, economics or strategic studies. We can note, for instance, that the word 'management' is itself metaphorical in origin. It was originally drawn from the Italian word for the skilful control of a horse by its rider (still reflected, for example, in the term '*manège*' for riding-school). The same is true for the word 'organization', which originally meant a biological entity and was only later extended metaphorically to the social sphere (Morgan 1980, 610). Much of the modern literature on organization, from 'pop management' to more scholarly works, is saturated with metaphor. Examples include titles with reference to corporations as having 'minds' (Heirs and Pehrson 1982) or 'brains' (Beer 1972), or the ability to 'dance' (Kanter 1989).

III   TRADITIONAL PUBLIC ADMINISTRATION AS A SEARCH FOR 'CFR' (CONCRETE FACTUAL REALISM)

Here, then, we have an instructive contrast. On the one hand, the mainstream of academic Public Administration over recent decades has been marked by a search for CFR - and has not been persuasive. On the other hand, economics, strategists and management theorists have shunned CFR and have exercised a palpable influence over policy-makers. Our argument is that the CFR and the lack of influence are causally related. The path to influence may lead through metaphor, the better to understand confused and confusing reality.

Why did Public Administration develop these aspirations to CFR? There are several possible explanations One of them could be the influence of Jeremy Bentham, the intellectual progenitor of utilitarianism. Bentham considered fictions in general to be 'impossible, yet indispensable'. Why? Because he thought they were rooted in language. Language if only used literally, according to his philosophy, could do no more than describe the physical arrangement of bodies in space. Interpreted in this way, Bentham was an earlier anticipation of twentieth-century physicists who have called for an O-language, a language in which only observational statements could be made (Carnap 1966, 252–4). In fact, Bentham realized that fictional thinking was useful and inevitable (see Ogden 1932, 15). But he repeatedly condemned fictions in the law and government in the most outspoken terms. He began his intellectual career at an early age by a strong attack on the fiction of an original social contract as the basis for constitutional law. 'Fiction of use to justice?' he sneered, 'Exactly as swindling is to trade' ('Legal Fictions': see Ogden 1932, Appendix A, 141). One of Bentham's many extravagant tirades against lawyers' fictions appears in the epigraph to this chapter. Bentham saw – or at least feigned to see – fictions such as the original contract as reflecting deliberate mendacity, a means for gaining power and wealth which could not be obtained by more direct means. There are, as we will see shortly, rival and much less negative views about the value of fiction in the law.

The question is, of course, how much influence Bentham has had on the development of mainstream Public Administration, and this is hard to assess. To the extent that Bentham has been a factor in promoting the cult of CFR, it would have been through an indirect process of diffusion. Few students or teachers of public administration have devoted themselves to a study of Bentham's voluminous works. All the same, any one educated in the social sciences comes across many references, some explicit, many implicit, to Bentham.

A second explanation, not necessarily incompatible with the first, could lie in the historical development of mainstream Public Administration. Much of its original *raison d'être*, as it developed towards the end of the last century, was to replace fiction by CFR. Its ambition was precisely to go beyond the legal fictions which traditionally covered (in more than one sense) the working of public organizations, to look at what actually lay behind these notions.

The sort of fictions that mainstream Public Administration scholars have examined over the last few decades were often what we will later discuss under the heading of *tatemae* – accounts of practice or institutional working which seemed threadbare, out-of-date and deceptive. The thrust and the challenge was to get at and discuss the true, living 'practice' which underlay the formal and implausible account of structures and procedures – to *de*fictionalize, to *de*mystify the way that the administrative system worked and how it was built.

Many of the fictions subjected to this scrutiny, as we will see in section IV below, were fictions of authority which had grown out of what once was literally the case. They were not originally and self-consciously conceived as fictions. In this way they differ from many of the fictions in science and law which were deliberately created as fictions. Hence it is tempting to think that the fictions of administration could easily be dismissed as no more than outmoded and mistaken descriptions of actual practice. Those fictions were not assessed as assumptions adopted in full knowledge of their falsehood, whose value is to be debated in terms of their *convenience* rather than their *veracity*.

A third explanation – which may complement the two already mentioned – is that mainstream Public Administration may have been peculiarly insulated against 'academic drift' and metaphorical flights of fancy, by the nature of its students and teachers. Much of its 'bread and butter' student clientele has consisted of people with some experience of bureaucracy, who are likely to be impatient with 'simplistic' perspectives based on fictional models. Many of its traditional (and distinguished) teachers have likewise been drawn from the ranks of public bureaucrats, whose background has often led them to aspire to describe things 'as they really are'. Focus on relevance does not encourage imagination.

These characteristics, shared with other fields of study which are caught between 'academic' and 'professional practice' perspectives, like business administration, mean that fictional thrusts will tend to be repulsed as inappropriate attempts to enliven an essentially dull subject (see Spann 1966, 4–5 and 15). Such ideas are likely to be seen as out of line with the self-image of a practical, nuts-and-bolts subject concerned mainly with practitioners' career development and concrete applications (see McCurdy and Cleary 1984, 52).

However, these features have applied to mainstream Public Administration since its earliest beginnings. Johann von Justi complained of these tendencies as stultifying the subject in the middle of the eighteenth century (see Small 1909, 297). Yet the long-standing 'professional' orientation has not prevented some important fictions – such as that of the policy–administration dichotomy – from being adopted in the past, nor has a similar orientation restrained the growth of fictions in the law. Just as in business administration the demand of the clientele for relevance has not entirely impeded flights of the imagination in that domain.

A final explanation is that the desire for CFR may derive from the overwhelming masculine domination of both the supply and demand for Public Administration, to say nothing of Business Administration. This conclusion follows from Ricca Edmondson's (1984, 5 and 15) claim that a rejection of 'personalism' and components of discourse which are not exclusively intellectual is associated with traditionally masculine personality traits such as suppression of emotion and imagination in preference to rules, logic, and consistency. It is certainly true that masculine and feminine responses to situations can differ (Jackson 1989). If that is true, an academic field so dominated by male writers as Public Administration is likely to exhibit those traits to a high degree.

However, it must be said that a similar masculine domination has not manacled other intellectual fields to CFR. Moreover, this explanation is also open to the objection which can be levelled at the one considered above, namely that this characteristic is a permanent feature of academic Public

Administration, but it has not prevented fictions from being devised and employed in the past.

It may be judicious to conclude that each of the four factors have contributed something to the nature of Public Administration today. Pressed to determine which of the four has had the most affect, we would suggest the second of the four outlined above, the drive to make Public Administration a science. Often those most determined to be scientific are those who least understand how science works, including the use of metaphors (Jackson 1972). Innocence breeds enthusiasm. The other three factors, the influence of Bentham, the drive to be practical, and the masculine orientation have contributed to but not initiated developments.

IV TYPES OF METAPHOR AND FICTION IN ADMINISTRATIVE ARGUMENT

Whatever the explicit agenda of mainstream Public Administration, fictions continually appear in administrative argument and ideas. In this section we will take a look at some of the types, discussing them under the headings of (i) *tatemae*, (ii) devices for innovation, (iii) devices for dealing with rule contradiction and overinclusiveness, and (iv) devices for explanation.

Tatemae

Tatemae is a long-established term for what is said to be a Japanese phenomenon of adopting explanations or descriptions of phenomena which no-one actually believes for a moment, but which are convenient to adopt for public utterance (see Lebra and Lebra 1986, xii; Dale 1986, 105). In Japanese cultural analysis, it is conventional to distinguish between *tatemae*, overt but fictional principles, and *honne*, real intent or privately held feelings.

A common form of *tatemae* in administrative doctrine is the pretence that particular practices or institutions do not exist at all. For over half a century British governments formally denied that there was any such thing as the espionage and political police agencies MI5 and MI6. A Japanese parallel is the denial that government agencies exert directive influence over financial markets.

Closely related types of *tatemae* are fictions of agency and independence. The 'class action' in US legal practice in practice involves lawyers acting as independent entrepreneurs of law enforcement; but it is built on the fiction that the attorney is acting on the clients' instructions (Posner 1977, 462). Organizations which are in fact fostered by or dependent on government, are often fictionally 'private'. A classic example is the Irish Hospitals Sweepstakes, a lottery originally promoted by an Irish Cabinet Minister, but constituted as a 'private' concern in order to avoid government embarrassment about operating an illegal lottery within the UK. Other examples include strategic firms, national civil aviation 'flag-carriers', national 'armourers', economic 'power-house' concerns (see Peters 1988, 77). To judge from these examples, *tatemae* are hardly limited to Japan.

A third common type of administrative *tatemae*, also related, is the fiction of command – the pretence that the reins of power are held by someone other than the person who is actually in charge. A well known example is the case of the Tokugawa regime in Japan. Central to that regime, before the Meiji restoration of 1867, was the fiction that the Emperor was the real ruler and the *shogun* only an aide. It was this fiction that was reversed at the end of World War II when it was decided not to hold the Emperor responsible for either the initiation of the war or its conduct. In 1990 Belgium pretended to have no king for one day in order to allow the passage of controversial legislation.

A final common type of *tatemae* in administration relates to matters of motivation, purpose, procedure or justification. One variant of this last type of *tatemae* is the common practice of giving false reasons for a particular course. False reasons are given because they are easier to defend than the true reasons, within the constraints of legal or political prudence. A second variant is the pretence that the purpose or activity of a particular institution is quite different from what everyone knows it to be. Examples are the Ministries of Truth, Love, Peace and Plenty in George Orwell's *1984*. Life has imitated art all too well in the case of the so-called State Research Bureau, the notorious secret police of the Idi Amin regime in Uganda from 1975 to 1979. A third is the case of fictions of procedure – for example, the fiction that company personnel read and understand every paper that crosses their desks (however impossible this may be in practice), the fiction that the insurance policyholder has read the small print before taking out the policy, the fiction that the electorate is well-informed about the policies of candidates or parties offering themselves for election.

Tatemae in this sense are universal in administrative argument. In so far as they frequently operate as a thin veneer over what may be unpleasant, widely known but for some reason unmentionable truths, they fit fairly closely to Bentham's equation of fictions with lies which serve particular interests.

Why are they so common? Is it just an attempt to fool the gullible? Bagehot (1963), in a famous analysis, saw the function of the 'dignified' fictions of the British constitution (monarchical government, Parliamentary government) in these terms. According to him, the uneducated or unsophisticated might believe or cling to *tatemae* such as royal government, while the reality was essentially republican. Today's equivalent might be the belief in the rule of the people through democracy.

But the problem with explaining the prevalence of *tatemae* in these terms is that, particularly in a society much more educated than that of Bagehot's day, many of these fictions so manifestly *fail* to persuade those who question them. Who – apart from very young children, the uninterested, or the exceptionally gullible – seriously believes that the British have no political police; that the Japanese stock market response to the 1987 crash was not coordinated by the authorities; that high permanent officials are mere drudges of their minister; or that all decisions are made by reference to the wishes of the people? An alternative and perhaps more plausible explanation for the prevalence of such fictions might rest in the way that they provide solid legal (or quasi-legal) cover for a given action or decision when admission of the truth would leave the decision-maker far more vulnerable to attack.

If the Bagehot 'fool the gullible' approach is the true explanation of administrative *tatemae*, then we might expect such fictions slowly to disappear with increasing sophistication in the society at large, although some allowance would have to be made for the fact that many people are uninterested in political administration. By contrast, if the 'covering rear' explanation has more force, we might expect such fictions actually to grow in incidence, particularly in a context of growing legal and political challenge to administrative decisions, allied with measures such as freedom of information legislation and generalized anti-discrimination legislation. The truth is that new *tatemae* are generated while old ones lose credibility and are discarded. Things change but remain the same.

Devices for innovation

Fictions often enter into administrative argument as a means of innovation. Here they are being used, in Aristotle's language, as 'a way of getting hold of something fresh', by putting a new situation or case in the clothes of something more familiar and straightforward. For the moment we will concentrate on practical innovation, leaving the discussion of intellectual innovation to a later sub-section.

The classic account of fictions as devices for innovation in the law was given by the eighteenth century German jurist von Savigny. Von Savigny (1967, 32-3) argued that fiction was central to the development of the Roman law from the third century AD, from a scheme of 'the grossest simplicity' to one of great sophistication and power. Later jurists have elaborated Savigny's argument. For instance, Esser (1969, 5) claims that whole areas of legal development would scarcely have been conceivable without the creation of fictions. Lon Fuller (1967), in his brilliant survey of legal fictions, is more ambivalent. At one point (ibid., 68), he claims that fictions are part of the pathology of the law, but later he follows the general lines of von Savigny's argument, to the effect that fictions are almost invariably an aspect of legal innovation:

Developing fields of the law, fields where new social and business practices are necessitating a reconstruction of legal doctrines, nearly always present 'artificial constructions' and in many cases, outright fictions. The doctrine of vicarious liability for tort began with such notions as that the master should be 'deemed negligent' for hiring a careless servant.

Fictions of this type are equally common in administrative argument. They serve to persuade that a new kind of case can be fitted into traditional categories (as with the treatment of aircraft as if they were ships). The fictions of command discussed earlier often consist of a pretence that ways of exercising authority which have been practically superseded are still literally in existence. Such fictions reconcile current reality with traditional practice and thus provide a convenient cover for institutional development. A case in point is the enlargement of the General Staff in Prussia in the late eighteenth century after the death of the brilliant soldier-king Frederick the Great, in order to deal with the new reality, that Frederick's successors had neither talent nor inclination for military command. The change was covered by the fiction that the Chief of Staff was only an 'aide' and that the real command was still exercised by the king (Tullock 1965, 146). This is a common pattern with the emergence of bureaucracies and Parliamentary government displacing an older and simpler pattern of royal command.

A similar example is the fiction built in to the Westminster model of representative government, which pretends that a government minister performs in person all the functions of a department – the fiction that *qui facit per alium facit per se*. Like the Prussian fiction of royal command of the military after 1786, this may once have been a literal description of the way that government departments were run, for instance in the days when the British Foreign Secretary Lord Palmerston, in the early part of his career, personally read and answered every letter that came into the Foreign Office (Parris 1969, 24 and 109–19). Later, even in Palmerston's career, the idea became manifestly false as a description of reality, but remained convenient as a means of assigning responsibility for the actions of rapidly growing bureaucracy.

Although it is rarely discussed in these terms, the American concept of the policy–administration dichotomy, as expounded by Woodrow Wilson (1887), could also be interpreted as an innovative fiction of the same general type. That is, the distinction may have once been a literal description of reality in the days when the functions of government were so simple that elected representatives could perform all but the most obviously mechanical tasks of government themselves. With the age of 'big government', the doctrine could no longer be a literal description of how business was or could be done, but it provided a pretext for institutional innovation in reconciling the reality of bureaucratic government with the theory of representative democracy. If there is no difference between policy and administration, then all administration is policy. So, participatory democracy is the only possible form of democracy, since a limited number of representatives obviously cannot monitor every action of a large bureaucracy. But participatory democracy on the scale required is itself impossible because, as Oscar Wilde said, there are not enough evenings in the week (Mulgen 1988, 25). CFR in such matters can take us to the abyss. Fiction helps to square the circle and allow practical development to take place.

Means of Coping with Rule Contradiction and Overinclusiveness

A common practical use of fictions in law and administration is as a convenient way of escaping from the consequences of incompatible or 'overinclusive' rules (Posner 1977). Overinclusiveness means the framing of rules in such a way that they prohibit more kinds of behaviour than the framer really intended to stop. In any situation where there are well-organized and resourceful interests in getting round a rule (as in the case of tax law), overinclusive framing of rules is a tempting way of forestalling the loophole problem. The problem then arises of cases being caught in the trap which the framers or administrators of the rule had no real intention to prohibit – for example, the ambulance which enters a public park in order to rescue a badly injured child, ignoring the overinclusive 'no vehicles' rule posted at the park gate (Hart 1961, 123–6; Gottlieb 1968, 45, 108, 113; Twining and Miers 1976, 118–19, 122, 240–2).

Reinterpreting facts to fit bureaucratic rules is common enough. But fictions are not the only way to cope with situations for which the rules were not designed. For instance, the problem can be handled by selective enforcement of the rules, turning a blind eye to the inconvenient cases. Or it can be handled by refinement of the rules, covering all the contingencies by ever more precise specification. Both of these methods, however, have their limits. The first can only be applied in those areas where the state or some other single actor has a monopoly of law enforcement. The second is hard to apply with retrospective effect, so that it can deal only with future cases, not current ones.

However, resort to fiction is not restricted in either of these ways. It offers an instant exit from rule incompatibilities, by the simple means of changing the facts to fit the rules rather than the rules to fit the facts. During the American Indian wars, a group of Indian scouts employed by the US army went home after a conflict without being mustered out of service. According to army rules, this action was desertion, and the wheels of officialdom would have started to turn against the 'deserters' had not the field commander changed the facts. The deserters, he said, were on home leave (Dunlay 1982, 156).

The same goes for one of the most famous fictions of the English law, namely the pretence by the Court of King's Bench, in the *Mostyn v. Fabrigas* case of 1775, that the Mediterranean island of Minorca was part of the city of London – indeed, that it was located in the parish of St Mary Le Bow, in the ward of Cheap (*English Reports* Vol. XCVIII, KB Division XXVII, 1 Cowper 161–81). By changing the facts, the court got round an overinclusive rule which made the Governor of Minorca (then General Sir John Mostyn) absolute in the district of St. Phillips, where the event in question actually took place. By pretending that the Mediterranean island was in the centre of London, the court made it possible for Anthony Fabrigas, a native Minorcan, to bring an action against the Governor for assault and false imprisonment.

Fictions and Metaphors as Devices for Explanation and Interpretation

There is a fine line between the use of fiction and metaphor for justification and for interpretation or explanation. For example, the German cameralist metaphor of the state as a large farm or family estate (Small 1909, 321) clearly functions in both ways.

The same perhaps applies to the common contemporary fiction of taking corporate actors as if they were individuals, just as traditional international relations theory took states as persons. But (*pace* Bentham) such a fiction does not necessarily imply deliberate attempts to deceive or reify. Such an approach may simply be convenient for brevity and prediction. For instance, as Mashaw (1983, 69) puts it:

> It is habitual at commonsense level to view organizations, if not as having goals of their own, at least as behaving as if they did.

A more striking example of an explanatory or interpretative fiction in administrative argument is the device used by Bernard Schaffer (1973, 252) to explain the development of the British civil service in the nineteenth and early twentieth centuries. That is the fiction of the 'public service bargain'. In this fictional bargain, concluded between elected politicians and senior bureaucrats in the nineteenth century, the latter exchanged overt partisanship, some political rights and a public political profile in return for 'permanent careers, honours and a six-hour working day'. Like the larger social contract which this 'bargain' resembles, it was never concluded. Schaffer's fiction simply reflects the view that the development of the system can be conveniently understood exactly *as if* such a bargain had actually taken place.

Beyond fictions of this type lie a range of metaphors which have been influential in administrative argument and in the development of new academic perspectives on administration. Morgan (1980) relates the adoption of new kinds of metaphor to intellectual innovation in organization theory.

Smith (1981) argues that the development of new metaphors is critical to advancement of techniques of evaluation – that is the assessment of the effectiveness of social programmes, measures and organizations. The dominant metaphor of evaluation in the 1970s was that of the controlled laboratory experiment (with quantitative observation of a range of cases divided into a control group and an experimental group). Smith argues, in a post-Modernist vein, that this metaphor has reached the limit of its usefulness as a spur to development in evaluation and he argues for experimentation with alternative ones, such as the making of a piece of investigative journalism, the assembly of evidence by a lawyer, the assessment of a movie by a film critic, even the production of a picture by a watercolour painter (ibid., 46).

The two explanatory metaphors which have dominated the study of administration have been the images of the metaphor of the machine and of the organism. The metaphor of bureaucracy as a 'machine' has a very long history. It figured prominently in the writings of the eighteenth-century German cameralists (Parry 1963, 182), to whom it was convenient in presenting Public Administration as a technical science appropriate for fulfilling the goals of enlightened absolutism. The cameralists' machine metaphor carried into Max Weber's famous account of bureaucracy, with his attribution of machine-like efficiency to bureaucracies, his conception of individual workers as 'cogs' in the machine and of judges as mechanical vending machines (Gerth and Mills 1948, 228). Frederick Winslow Taylor (1911) and other pioneers of 'scientific management' took the machine metaphor even further in their approach to organizational design (see Kassem and Hofstede 1976, 4).

The explanatory power of machine metaphors lies in their consistency with some of the well-known properties of bureaucracies. They fit with the commonly observed tendency of bureaucracies to operate with stability under standard operating conditions, regardless of their consequences. The machine view is consistent with the apparent absence of any imagination or insight in the way that bureaucracies conduct business day by day, while at the same time fitting with their capacity to be 'reprogrammed' for very different purposes, within some limits.

Treating organizations as machines sets in train a broader mind-set. Machines need to be *designed*, and so administration or management can be thought of as a design science. Design means the capacity to apply knowledge about the properties of materials in order to realize particular values in a given context (cf. Bobrow and Dryzek 1987). Machines need to be controlled, repaired and maintained, and so the administrative specialists can see themselves as engineers or mechanics, as Frederick Winslow Taylor and his followers did. If bureaucracies are machines, they can be evaluated by the sort of criteria which are normally applied to machines – reliability, safety, power output, energy consumption, service life, availability of spare parts, ease of repair.

The machine metaphor remains fertile as a source of interpretation and explanation of administration and bureaucracy. Over recent decades it has turned away from the Weberian steam-age imagery of cranks, cogs and wheels to the more modern imagery of information-processing machines. David Braybrooke's (1974) image of an 'issue-machine', which we discussed in Part I, is one example of this. Another is Andrew Dunsire's image of public bureaucracies as a kind of computer system, at least in relation to language hierarchies, and of their control as an hierarchy of servomechanisms – engineered 'collibratory' devices which use a pent-up energy source to intervene in an opposed balance of forces (Dunsire 1978 and 1989).

The logical conclusion of the new machine metaphor is to interpret and explain organization through explicit and applied computer-engineering notions such as access time, compatibility, read only memory, multi-tasking, processing capacity. Information processing machine metaphors also have the interesting property that they cut across the traditional dichotomy of machine versus organism, since the science of information processing systems, cybernetics, sees living organisms as 'machines' for processing information (see Deutsch 1963; Hage 1974; Turkle 1984).

The other traditional interpretative and explanatory metaphor in administration is that of organism – the notion of bureaucracies and organizations as living bodies. This idea goes back into antiquity, with conceptions of states and churches as bodies, and with the legal fiction of corporations as persons. This metaphor also has explanatory power, in that it fits with many observed characteristics of organizations – characteristics which do not have 'machine-like' qualities. If organizations are organisms, we can expect them to grow rapidly in their early years, reach a peak and then decline. We can discuss their demographics in terms of births, marriage/divorce, reproduction and deaths. If they are organisms, we can expect them to struggle for survival when they are attacked or threatened. We can expect them to compete in battles for the possession of territory, and to adapt to the environment. None of these are 'machine-like' properties, yet they may be seen as central to the understanding of organization and bureaucracy. Indeed, Morgan (1980, 615) claims that the development of the 'contingency theory' approach to organizational analysis in the 1960s and 1970s carried the organism metaphor to its logical conclusion, focusing on the internal arrangement of 'organs' within each entity in relation to the environmental conditions that those entities face.

Like the machine metaphor, the metaphor of organism has been a fertile source of explanation and interpretation. A case in point is the set of ideas associated with a life-cycle – notions of birth, death, climacterics, mating behaviour. A well-known example of the application of such ideas is Marver Bernstein's (1955) famous 'life-cycle' explanation of the way that US regulatory agencies behave over time. Bernstein argued that these organizations are begotten by strong political sentiments, and that the first stage of their life-cycle is marked with an abundance of youthful enthusiasm, energy and impetuosity. Later, as the organizations grow older, they start to show the experience and greater caution of maturity; the life-cycle concludes with the organization degenerating into the feebleness and inaction of old age (though not actual death). Anthony Downs (1967) also used a life-cycle metaphor to explain the behaviour of bureaucracies over time, and in particular the phenomenon of rapid growth and high 'infant mortality' in early years. This metaphor is deeply rooted in what Mary Douglas calls 'reason and nature'.

Another application of the living body metaphor for interpretation and explanation is the concept of 'diseases' and 'dysfunctions' of organizations and bureaucracies. From that it is a short step to the idea of cures and treatments for such diseases, and even to the idea of 'doctors' who can bring a healing touch to a sick organization. This is an old theme, which has recently been explicitly revived by Hogwood and Peters (1985). They classify and describe the numerous 'pathologies' of public policy, describing the various elements as if they were diseases of the body (terminal illness or chronic illness). The metaphor of sickness in turn leads to the notion of 'policy doctors'; and, just like any successful medical practitioner, the policy doctors are urged to pay close attention to their 'bedside manner' in their efforts to cure these ills.

Another contemporary application of the traditional organism metaphor is the notion of population–ecology systems. In this view, organizations are seen as competing for niches in an environment, with rival candidates being weeded out and changing by evolutionary selectors (Hannan and Freeman 1977). Another example is the application of evolutionary ideas to the development of policy, using the metaphor of 'trophic niches'. Such a framework has been used to explain why government law enforcement and tax collection mechanisms are more effective in some times and circumstances than others (see Hood 1985).

V   IMPLICATIONS FOR ADMINISTRATIVE ARGUMENT

Summary of the Argument

We began this chapter with an epigraph giving two rival views about metaphor and fiction. We have argued for a position somewhere between Aristotle's and Bentham's – and Bentham's approach to fictions was less antagonistic to Aristotle's than may appear at first sight, in that Bentham's ire was mainly directed against *tatemae* rather than against explanatory or philosophical fictions.

Our argument goes like this. First, we argued in section II of this chapter that fictions and figures of speech seem to be central to the achievement of persuasiveness in administrative argument. Analytic approaches which carry 'clout' and prestige into administrative argument - such as law, mathematics and economics – tend to be riddled with fiction and metaphor. CFR approaches seem to have less rhetorical power.

Of course, fiction and metaphor can be hard to recognize as such, and indeed their effectiveness for persuasive purposes may depend on this. A case in point is the use of statistical significance tests to lend to conclusions drawn from tabular data an air of technical authority which is not open to lay questioning (McCloskey 1985, 163–7). Perhaps this shows that the most effective rhetoricians are those who are innocent, on the Nietzschean principle that understanding inhibits effective action, or perhaps on the Hegelian principle that cunning precedes reason, as any parent can affirm.

Second, we argued in section III that there has been a strong bias in favour of CFR in mainstream Public Administration, a bias which could have been prompted by several factors. It could be argued that this characteristic is the main thing which has prevented mainstream Public Administration from being seen as a 'discipline' in the same sense as economics, and that this has stunted its persuasive force. Its intellectual weakness was encapsulated in Dwight Waldo's description of Public Administration as 'a subject-matter in search of a discipline' (in Charlesworth 1968, 2).

Third, we argued in section IV that metaphor and fiction are a – perhaps *the* – crucial device in both practical and intellectual development in administration. They appear to be an important ingredient of persuasiveness. And they are central to development, both in administrative practice and in explanation and interpretation.

The case should not be overstated. It is true that mainstream Public Administration could be counted as a 'discipline' in some weak senses of that term. For one thing, it is a relatively defined and well-established field of study. And it could be counted as a 'discipline' in the slightly stronger sense of being an organized and self-conscious academic community with a socially recognized institutional structure, marked by accreditation, specialized conferences and journals, formally organized groups of teachers and practitioners. Perhaps it was even a 'discipline' in the sense that it has contained a band of disciples sharing the same cognitive map, in that they agreed on the problems and variables which are taken to be important, and on the causal relationships between the variables (Axelrod 1976).

But this CFR mainstream is not a discipline in the stronger senses of the term, and this fact could account for its weak persuasiveness in administrative argument. Beginning students in the field were not made to undergo anything comparable to the 'discipline' of the formal dancer or the religious novice: the maintenance or development of standards through suffering or punishment, the striving towards some definition of analytic or performance perfection, through an arduous process of painful correction. There was never enough agreement on what analytic perfection would mean or even what would be progress towards it. Nor did the CFR mainstream of Public Administration count as a discipline in the sense of trained narrowness – the adoption of a consciously one-eyed mode of analysis. To the extent that the mainstream of Public Administration is programmed to reject fiction and metaphor as 'simplistic', we argue that this has weakened the subject's persuasive power and impoverished it intellectually.

From CFR to Persuasiveness?

The implication of this argument is that mainstream Public Administration can never match the persuasiveness of the 'econocracy' in administrative argument as long as it makes CFR its cardinal virtue. To produce winning arguments in administration, it would need plausible but stereotyped assumptions and lines of argument based on apparently arcane reasoning, particularly 'number magic'. To match the repute and position of the econocrats, it would need to achieve the trained narrowness that follows from the self-conscious adoption of false assumptions.

This means that mainstream Public Administration faces a choice. It can stay 'poor but honest' – and politically marginal. Or it can take over the intellectual devices which have led to the success of the econocrats and the consultocrats. To do that would require an alteration in its conventional attitude to the worth of fictions. It would need to be recognized that fictions are not necessarily to be equated with lies designed deliberately to deceive, nor with simple mistakes or errors.

This issue deserves some serious debate, but it has scarcely received it. There has been a degree of confused discussion as to whether doctrines like 'ministerial responsibility' or the 'policy-administration dichotomy' should be dismissed as poor descriptions of reality which serve some sinister obscurantist interest (the Benthamite argument), or whether they should be evaluated by the different test of whether, even as consciously false descriptions, they may nevertheless have utility. Certainly, the persistence and repeated re-invention of such ideas, against all the evidence of what administrative life is really like, suggests that they answer to some need.

The doctrine of scientific objectivity and the fact-value dichotomy which Simon and his fellow positivists took as their scientific credo, could itself be profitably discussed in these terms. Judged as a true-to-life description of how scientists actually behave or what research is really like, the doctrine is obviously implausible. There are simply too many well-documented counter-examples (Kuhn 1962; Medawar 1967; Watson 1968).

Considered as a fiction – a consciously false description of reality – the test must be utility or convenience. That is, even though it is consciously false, the doctrine might still be convenient, even useful, because if scholars did not do their best to behave *as if* facts could be distinguished from values or *as if* prescriptions could be distinguished from predictions, there are no secure grounds for maintaining intellectual honesty, in the sense of thorough investigation, careful justification of arguments, the attempt to demolish an opponent's position by the accumulation of rigorous evidence, even dialogue and debate in the face of public scrutiny (Reichenbach 1966, 231).

We draw two conclusions from our review of metaphor and fiction. First, metaphor and fiction are essential parts of how *persuasion* works in practice. If mainstream Public Administration adopts a CFR orientation, there will be a vacuum in persuasive doctrines about administration which will be filled by the metaphors of economics and management. The implication is that mainstream Public Administration may need to become less, not more, 'true to life'.

Second, fiction and metaphor are tools for *discovery*. They help to explain how the world works, in examples ranging from the double helix to the public service bargain. Only by these tools can we order and reinterpret the palpable confusion of 'reality'. And persuasion and discovery ultimately go together, because the first person who needs to be persuaded by an insight is its discoverer.

The lock of acceptance and the lock of discovery both seem to respond to metaphor and fiction. Accordingly, metaphor and fiction are essential to administrative argument, 'exactly as swindling is to trade' – but hardly in the sense that Bentham intended it.

PART IV
CONCLUSION

...we're on dangerous ground;
Who knows how the fashions may alter?
The doctrine, today, that is loyalty sound
Tomorrow may bring us a halter!
(Robert Burns, Address to Wm. Tytler, Esq., of Woodhouselee)

8 Two Administrative Philosophies: From the Leading Edge and the Lumber Room

The ever-arising prophets of the cult constantly seek to find new ways in order to succeed where the old leaders have failed...there is hardly a month that passes without...another prophet arising... to preach the cult of cargo. (Lawrence 1964, vi)

In this chapter, we move to the level of administrative *philosophies*, the peak of the isoceles triangle that we used to depict the world of administrative argument in Chapter 2. Having explored a set of doctrines and justifications in Part II and having pursued the 'acceptance factor' in Part III, we now look at administrative philosophies by comparing two key specimens in the sphere of public management, namely the 'new public management' (NPM) boom of the 1980s and the late cameralist movement of the eighteenth century.

I   NEW PUBLIC MANAGEMENT (NPM) AND LATE CAMERALISM

NPM is 'the doctrine, today, that is loyalty sound', and cameralism was in a real sense the first 'new public management' movement in modern Europe. Cameralism rested its ideas on claims to scientific authority, and it was every bit as influential in eighteenth-century Europe as NPM is today. So a comparison of NPM with cameralism has at least three things to teach us about administrative argument.

First, we can gauge the 'newness' of NPM by comparing its doctrines with the precepts of a far earlier philosophy of public management. Second, we can learn something about the 'acceptance factor', by exploring whether there were common factors which led to these two philosophies becoming received ideas. And the fate of cameralism (oblivion) reminds us that public management philosophies can go out of fashion as well as into it. Third, we can ascertain whether administrative argument has 'progressed' in the direction desired by Simon. In short, such a comparison can demonstrate important and relatively unchanging features of administrative argument.

New Public Management

NPM is a neologism - a convenient but imprecise shorthand term to denote a philosophy of administration which came to dominate the agenda of public administration in the 1980s in the UK, New Zealand and Australia. There are also Canadian and American variants which have some family resemblance.[1]

Like cameralism, the term NPM is necessarily a loose one. It can bear more than one interpretation – as a literally descriptive label, as a term deeply tinged with irony (like the Emperor's New Clothes, which to some observers it resembles), even as a *paranym* (in that sceptics claim that NPM's content is essentially hackneyed and recycled). Moreover, whether there is in fact a single 'new public management', or whether NPM is better seen as something like a 'flu virus, continuously mutating and having several different strains at once, is debatable. Here we shall tentatively assume that NPM in some sense can be regarded, like cameralism, as a generic movement, crossing different policy sectors as well as national boundaries.

Commentators such as Aucoin (1990) see NPM as broadly characterized by advocacy of:

- a shift from *policy* to *management* (in the sense of increasing the emphasis on cost-conscious direction of public service organization and away from policy development);
- a shift from *aggregation* to *disaggregation* in public service organization (from 'U-form' monopoly systems to disaggregated budgets, internal markets and rivalry);
- a shift from *planning* and *public service welfarism* to a stress on *cost-cutting* and *labour discipline*;[2]
- a shift from *process* to *output* in controls and accountability mechanisms (particularly through the development of quantitative methods of performance and efficiency measurement);
- a divorce of *provision* from *production* (or 'delivery') in public policy. This division is associated with a shift from permanent public bureau production to term contracts and private sector delivery (consultancy firms instead of in-house policy advice and management troubleshooting, contract or franchisee arrangements instead of 'monopoly bureaus').

Such doctrines were applied in a number of different contexts – notably general public service management, the management of school and tertiary education, and health care management.

Like cameralism, NPM was a school involving practitioners as much as theorists. Many of the innovations came from practice and from the private sector, not from the groves of academe. There is no single classic text which definitively sets out NPM ideas. Significantly, what is perhaps the landmark text comes from an official document – the New Zealand Treasury's treatise *Government Management* produced in 1987 (NZ Treasury 1987).

Like cameralism, NPM had both conservative and radical strains. The conservative strain lies in the fact that the movement was an explicit reaction against the more wide-ranging concern with 'policy studies' which overshadowed academic Public Administration in the 1970s, and indeed represented a return to the traditional (pre policy analysis) focus of Public Administration, back to its early roots in cameralism. NPM's radical strain comes in its challenge to the middle-class professions, which has some parallels with the challenge presented by late cameralism to the German 'home towns' and the guilds in the eighteenth century[3] once 'police science' had been developed as cameralism's central thrust.[4]

Like cameralism, NPM built on an eclectic intellectual base. To some extent it drew on the 'new' economic institutionalism which had burgeoned since the 1940s. How far such ideas had direct influence on the practice of government is debatable,[5] though they were certainly part of a broad climate of attitudes to the state and the public sector within which NPM developed. NPM drew some of its glamour from the fashionable 'corporate culture' doctrines of the 1980s (notably Peters and Waterman 1982; see Aucoin 1990, 118). But in many ways NPM can be seen as a development of the international scientific management movement, with its concern to eliminate waste and measure work outputs as a precondition for effective control. This is a preoccupation going back to Taylor's and even Bentham's ideas about public management (cf. Taylor 1916; Merkle 1980; Hume 1981).

Late Cameralism

Cameralism is a set of administrative doctrines of which few current students or even teachers of administration have even heard. It belongs in the 'lost causes' category of administrative thought, and its devotees today can be seen as the administrative-science equivalents of vintage car or steam train enthusiasts. However, for the exploration of the acceptance factor, its fate is instructive.

Cameralism is an administrative philosophy which reached its flower in the eighteenth century, though the plant began to grow fully two centuries before that (Parry 1963, 180; Raeff 1975, 1232; Maier 1986). The term 'cameralism' developed from the word for the treasure-chest or chamber in which taxes were collected, later denoting the science of effective fiscal management and, by a further extension, the administrative sciences more generally (Small 1909, 18). Highly influential in the Europe of its day, cameralism is little discussed now except as an appendage of the German version of mercantilism. It lingers only in the 'lumber room' of administrative thought (ibid., vii).

Like NPM, cameralism is an imprecise term. Many writers and administrators can loosely be described as cameralists. And, like NPM, late cameralism was both conservative and radical. It was conservative in that it took Christian absolutism as the natural order of society, that it assumed a static social structure with a fixed standard of living appropriate to each social class (ibid., 590) and that it drew on the knowledge of estate management that had underwritten the old regime. It was radical in that it purported to be a science of state-led economic development, designed to bring Germans into step with the modern world through industrialization.

Commentators such as Small (1909), Sommer (1930), Tauscher (1956a), Kasnacich-Schmid (1958), Parry (1963) and Walker (1971) see cameralism as broadly characterized by advocacy of:

- a shift from *noble birth* and political connections to *meritocracy* as the basis for recruiting public managers (Small 1909, 335 and 429), with meritocracy being reflected in entrance examinations from 1770;
- a shift from knowledge of feudal *law* (for adjudication of conflicting claims) to knowledge of *administrative science* (comprising the study of fiscal management, natural resource management and economic regulation) as the skill base of public managers (Parry 1963, 180);
- a shift from *local particularity* to *standardized principles* of economic management, applying throughout the territory, intended to sweep away the past and based on the tenets of 'police science for the common weal' (Walker 1971, 170–1);
- a shift from ad hoc *traditionalism* to a more *formalized* and *professionalized* system of administration, based on university training (Armstrong 1973, 163), explicit procedures for ensuring the proper discharge of duties by administrators, continuity in service on the basis of fixed salaries and a relative separation of the operational levels of the bureaucracy (organized in collegial form at decision-making levels) from the high policy level of government, represented by the monarch and the highest ministers of state.

This is a proto-bureaucratic philosophy of administration, anticipating the thrust of many later ideas about bureaucratic government, from Bentham to Weber. It rested on five key assumptions:

1   that the foundation of a strong state lay in its degree of economic development;
2   that economic development and social order was not spontaneous, but required the active management of government;
3   that to be equipped to promote development, government needed to be based on a professional public service which was loyal to the state rather than to any particular caste, class or guild and whose officials were thoroughly schooled in the sciences of administration and economic development;
4   that intermediary organizations in the state (guilds, local autonomous units) were generally harmful to economic development (Walker 1971, 167);
5   that economic development, social well-being and the interests of a strong, enlightened national leader will tend to be synonymous.

These assumptions in their most general form are far from dead today, in ideas such as realist international relations theory, in ideas about the 'new industrial state' as the key to economic progress, in ideas of intermediary organization as tending to lead to economic sclerosis and in faith in strong leadership. Indeed, they formed an orthodoxy of development nostrums for the third world from the 1960s to the 1980s. But their European origin is usually forgotten.

Like NPM, cameralism involved both practitioners and theorists (the 'cameralists of the books', who worked out the ideas for publication and training). Many cameralists had direct experience in government, giving them a 'practical agenda' (and also sometimes leading them to make powerful enemies, as with the case of von Justi himself, who ended his days in prison).[6] Like NPM, there is no single definitive text encompassing the ideas of the school, though many commentators (such as Small 1909) have taken Justi's work as the most systematic exposition of its ideas.[7]

II   NPM AND LATE CAMERALISM AS SETS OF DOCTRINES

There are seven interesting similarities between NPM and late cameralism as sets of administrative doctrines. The similarities illustrate the point made in Chapter 2 that different administrative philosophies may have doctrines in common, and show how recurrent are some of the basic doctrines of administration. These similarities are:

* the use of the *term* 'public management' (*Staatswirtschaft*, *Haushaltungskunst*);
* the stress on *administrative technology* as the key to effective state management;

- the view that *execution* can and should be separated from high *policy*;
- the view that *thrift* is the monarch of administrative virtues, and the central emphasis given to the financial system of the state;
- the preference for *avoiding direct state management of* complex transactions or processes;
- the essentially *top-down and centralist* nature of both schools in practice;
- the *lack of questioning* of the parameters of social and political order within which public management operates.

It is these seven shared features which could be used for an interpretation of NPM as a 'new cameralism'.

However, there are also important differences in the substantive doctrines advanced by each school. For example, NPM tended to stress the one-boss principle, while cameralism was associated with collegial decision-making in the upper reaches of the bureaucracy; NPM tended to favour 'empowerment of managers' to leave them 'free to manage', while cameralism favoured decision by rule and rote; NPM tended to favour limitation of tenure and the linking of reward to performance, while cameralism favoured tenure and fixed salaries.

The similarities and differences are easiest to summarize by representing both NPM and cameralism as subsets of the 99 commonest doctrines of administration which were discussed in Part II, and comparing the two philosophies in terms of their doctrinal composition. In these terms, NPM could be expressed as a bundle of doctrines as A3.1, A3.2, H2.1, H2.1B, J1.2, K2, L1, M2, N2, O1, P2.2B, R2.2B, R2.2C, T2.1, T2.2A, V2, X2.3, X3.1. Cameralism by contrast could be expressed as A1, A3.1, B1, C2, G7, H2.2A, J1.2, K1, N2, Q1, R2.1, T1, X2. These constituents are summarized in Table 4.1.

III   NPM AND LATE CAMERALISM AS STYLES OF ARGUMENT

It could be argued, however, that the real similarities between NPM and cameralism lie not so much in the content but in the *packaging* – that is, the way that the doctrines were justified rather than in the substance of the doctrines themselves. This links to our earlier discussion of the way in which administrative doctrines become persuasive.

Walker (1971, 145) has described cameralism as 'a baroque science'. It was 'baroque' in more than one sense. Cameralism constantly invoked 'science', but its style of argument consisted essentially of a long series of stories told in encyclopaedic detail and of philosophical presumptions about the underlying harmony of the universe which were related to Leibnitz's metaphysics (ibid., 146). Its 'science' was the declaration of rules of thumb.

Table 8.1   NPM and late cameralism: some contrasts

	NPM	CAMERALISM
Who-type Doctrines		
Selection	Q1 for managers? Q2 for others?	Q1
		G7 (select by objective test)
Promotion	P2.2B (subj merit)	
Reward	R2.2C (performance linked pay)	R2.1 (fixed pay)
Tenure	T2.2A (limited)	T1 (career tenure)
Skills	N2 (admin skills)	N2 (admin skills)
Experience		E2 (raw recruits)
Deployment		D1 (continuity)
What-type Doctrines		
Conditions	U2 (varying)	
Agency type		A1 (classic b'cracy)
	A2 (independent public agency)	
	A3 (subsidiarity)	A3 (subsidiarity)
Rivalry	O1.1 (competition for the field)	
	M2.1 (multi-source)	
	M2.2 (M-form rivalry)	
Size		B1 (large scale)
Configuration		C2.2 (like with like)
How-type Doctrines		
Authority	H2.1B (one boss, delegate power)	H2.2A (collegial direction)
Procedure	K2 (managerial discretion)	K1 (decide by rule & rote)
	X2.3 (control by business methods)	X2 (special safeguards
	X3.1 (result oriented)	
Make/buy	O1 (contract-oriented)	
Specialism	J1.2 (sep pol & execution)	J1.2 (sep pol & execution)

Its argument was conducted in a flowery style of rhetoric, replete with platitude and generalization.[8]

As a 'space-age' philosophy of administration, we might naively suppose that NPM's style of argument would be very different. We might expect the adoption of NPM doctrines to have followed a set of carefully controlled experiments comparing 'test' and 'control' groups and 'before' and 'after' periods, in order to demonstrate in proper Simonian fashion the benefits associated with administrative design on NPM principles.

In fact, there existed little such evidence. There were no such experiments. Pilot studies were rare and ambiguous. A strategy of piecemeal controlled experiment, and the time and money needed to evaluate it properly, was generally rejected by NPM reformers as a needless brake upon progress (or an unfair discrimination among consumers in different areas). NPM was no more grounded in systematic hard-data demonstration of the effects of alternative administrative design principles than was cameralism. Like most administrative reform proposals, NPM typically involved what Spann (1981) called 'following the swing' and 'administrative cloning' (i.e. if one organization has a feature that is thought to be successful or desirable, insist that *every* organization has one).

IV   'SIX KEYS TO PERSUASION': NPM AND LATE CAMERALISM COMPARED

To explain, therefore, why the NPM key 'fitted the lock' in the 1980s (as well as why cameralism fitted the lock in the eighteenth century, but lost its power in the nineteenth century), we need to turn back to the six items identified in Chapter 2 in relation to the 'acceptance factor'. These were, it will be recalled, 'symmetry', metaphorical force, ambiguity, private benefit successfully presented as public good, selective evidence rather than the production of irrefragable proofs from systematic analysis of hard data, and suspension of disbelief. Looking at NPM and late cameralism in the light of these elements can give us a pointer to the way that the 'acceptance factor' operated in these cases. A summary of the discussion is presented in Table 8.2 below.

1   Symmetry

As we saw in Part I, one of the traditional (if somewhat tautological) ways in which analysts explain the 'acceptance factor' is the idea of symmetry between the persuasive doctrines on offer and the problems experienced by the community to be persuaded.

Cameralism could be said to be 'symmetrical' with its eighteenth-century social context in several respects. One was its association with German state

Table 8.2   Six keys to persuasion: NPM and late cameralism

	NPM	Cameralism
1. Symmetry	Attack on career tenure linked with changes in campaign technology	Stress on economic development linked with attempt to build strong German state
	Stress on lean govt and contract provision linked with 'post-industrial' social trends	Emphasis on 'police science' and merit bureaucracy linked with the centralizing claims of the monarchy
2. Metaphor	State organization as private corporate management	State as large family estate Society as a factory
3. Ambiguity	Vague & multi-faceted catch-phrases	Assumption of harmony among elements of society
	Mix of radicalism and conservatism	Mix of radicalism and conservatism
4. Public Good & Private Interests	*Public*: better & cheaper public services. *Private*: cent. agencies, higher managers, management 'brokers'	*Public*: social harmony & progress. *Private*: monarchy, educated middle class, cameralist professors
5. Selectivity in Argument	Argument by example: waste & failure in old management system, successes in private sector	Detailed selective examples. Selective use of argument from Enlightenment authors Use of historically particular events as evidence of general truths
6. Suspension of Disbelief	*Ad hominem/ feminam* argument, evocation of crisis, cargo-cultism, amnesia/ 'Newism'	'Scientific' authority in a 'technical' subject 'Newism'

building, in the sense of the attempt to build a strong German state to match the capacity of the great powers of the day – France, Russia, Britain. Eighteenth-century Germany was politically divided among more than 300 self-governing units. Even the strongest states – Prussia and Austria – lacked the resource base of the surrounding great powers. Hence the appeal of ideas linking economic development with a strong state. For Frederick the Great and his officials, the key to improving the relative performance of their conscripts in battle with their French, British and Russian counterparts was the improvement of the peasants' diet (Johnson 1975). Hence the 'symmetry' of cameralism's doctrine that government should play the role of estate manager, which fitted with schemes such as the ill-fated attempt of successive Prussian governments to grow Irish potatoes in Pomerania. After witnessing the terror of the French Revolution and then being defeated by Napoleonic armies, many German leaders were sure that change was necessary for two reasons. One was that a revolution from above was needed to prevent a revolution from below. The other reason for change was the need to strengthen Germany against France and Prussia.

The other element of symmetry was the way that cameralism fitted with the attempt to develop monarchical power and weaken the power of rival forces in the state. Late cameralism's emphasis on 'police science' and the royal bureaucracy buttressed the centralizing claims of the monarchy against the dispersal of authority to the home towns. Cameralism also offered an administrative philosophy (related to the more general philosophy of thinkers such as Kant and Krause) which justified bypassing the traditional landed gentry to recruit the middle class for service in the state bureaucracy. The Prussian kings were not alone in finding their hands tied by the feudal nobility. More than one crowned head in the German states wanted to dispense with the traditional aristocracy's hold on government, judicial and military office by entitlement of birth. The cameralist doctrine of paper qualifications for bureaucratic office matched these ambitions. And cameralism developed ideas for royal control over the new bourgeois officials, by its doctrine of administrative performance by rule and rote (Dorn 1931; Johnson (1964) terms this the 'routine duty concept').

It is perhaps easier to discern the symmetry of an administrative philosophy with the benefit of two centuries of hindsight than it can be for a contemporary movement. The 'symmetry' of NPM can therefore only be tentatively identified, but there are at least three possible aspects of symmetry.

One, most simply, is that NPM fitted a desire for a change in the fashions, for the appearance of something new, with a different slant from the planning and social engineering ideas of the 1960s and 1970s. Perhaps the most dramatic example of NPM as 'new look' was its emergence in New Zealand with the foreign exchange crisis and change of government in 1984 (see Jesson 1989).

A second possible aspect of symmetry was the way in which NPM's emphasis on 'management' and abandonment of tenure fitted with trends in political campaign technology (Mills 1986; Hood 1990). This means the emerging system of policy-making by intensive opinion polling, with special pollsters and professional political strategists playing a larger part in policy making relative to the traditional players in the world of political advice. The aim of the new machine politics is to identify and target key swinging groups in the electorate, with the objective of tailoring public policy to those key groups. Some have argued that this new technology of policy-making has enabled some governments (such as the Hawke government in Australia and the Thatcher government in the UK) to stay in office longer than would otherwise have been possible.

Such a development would imply declining demand from elected politicians for policy advice from professional bureaucrats on the basis of long experience. The traditional 'mandarin' policy advisor, with the qualities of 'character' and 'independence' prized by the Northcote–Trevelyan Report (Nethercote 1989a) would be squeezed between the professional pollsters and party strategists on the one hand and the public service managers on the other.

Third, NPM could perhaps be interpreted as 'fitting' the broader socio-technical changes of the late twentieth century, which go variously under the title of post-industrialism, the fifth Kondratiev cycle and post-Fordism.[9] Such developments are nebulous, and we will not here go into the fine distinctions between the terms. All that we need to note for the purposes of this argument is that most expositions of these changes involve (a) a change in frontier technology, with microelectronics, materials and biotechnology displacing older frontier technologies (b) a change in economic structure away from standardized mass production towards services and flexibilization of production (c) a change in the composition of the labour force and electorate, with a decline in the proportion of semi-skilled blue-collar workers and an increase in the proportion of white-collar, college-educated workers.

Changes such as these could affect the context of public services in two ways. First, the shift towards a more polarized, less homogenous labour force may help to destroy the electoral viability of high and rising public spending as the basis of public policy. In conditions where there is a pyramidal income distribution structure and the median voter has less than the mean income, it is electorally viable to build a coalition for high public spending based on taxes on those with average or higher incomes.[10] But if polarization of the labour force and electorate results instead in a diamond-shaped income distribution pattern (particularly with the onset of two-career families), the median voter will not necessarily have less than the mean income, and hence the electoral power of resistance to extra taxation will grow, creating the conditions instead for a tax-sensitive majority coalition of voters, opposed by a tax-insensitive underclass which is not electorally viable. NPM's promise of cost-cutting, no-frills government could be seen as symmetrical with that changing trend.

Second, NPM, as a set of doctrines associated with advocacy of contracting out and 'slimming down' could be seen to fit with changes in the private business sector from traditional manufacturing and service activities to a system based on the frontier technologies of the fifth Kondratiev cycle, particularly microelectronics. Such a change creates the conditions for more contracting out of government activities than in the past, since it tends to destroy the traditional differences between what the mainstream private economy does and what government does. It also destroys the conditions traditionally associated with a 'productivity growth gap' between the public and private sector,[11] and hence may remove or reverse one of the factors which has been identified as leading to public bureaucracy growth in the past.

2   Metaphor

The idea of metaphor as a key to acceptance may also have some applicability to both NPM and cameralism. Cameralist ideas incorporated two powerful metaphors. The primary and older metaphor was the image of the state as a large family estate, and government as the estate manager. Like the manager of an aristocratic estate, its responsibility was to protect the resources for the owner (at first, clearly the king, later a more abstract idea after Frederick the Great declared himself to be the first servant of the Reich). It followed that a professional public bureaucracy was needed to echo on a bigger scale the division of labour on a large landed estate.

The secondary and later cameralist metaphor was a mechanical one. Society was portrayed as a factory in which everyone had a productive role to play. Government was conceived as the machinery of the factory. For example, von Justi made a detailed study of a needle factory, discussing the advantages of specialized labour[12] and repeatedly drew an analogy between government and machinery (see Small 1909, 462; Parry 1963, 182). Since German leaders at this time were trying to imitate the British factory system, this metaphor was likely to strike home. The factory image of society was one in which there was no clear place for the provincial landed gentry, but in which the monarch can be seen as '... the foreman, the mainspring, or the soul – if one may use the expression - that sets everything in motion' (Justi 1761, III, 86–7).

Though NPM may at first sight seem like 'soulless cost accounting', NPM involved some telling metaphors too. Examples include the equestrian image which is embedded in the word 'management' itself, with its overtones of skill, determination and mastery, and the equation of bureaucratic cost cutting with 'leanness and fitness' (Gray and Jenkins 1982, 47). The latter metaphor was perhaps particularly apt for the non-smoking health-faddist 1980s.

However, NPM's primary metaphor was that of the direction of state organization as private corporate management. Whether or not NPM radically changed the reality of work 'down the line' in government is debatable. But what it did do (and this is an index of its persuasive power) was to change the language in which senior officials talked in public, from 'public bureaucratese' to 'corporate managementspeak'. The new language fitted with ideas such as 'freedom to manage', 'managing for results' and the general 'aggrandizement of management' within the public sector (Martin 1983). It fitted with the pervasive importation of the language of private sector management into public bureaucracy, the idealization of the Japanese model (or rather of the popular myth of 'Japan Inc.'), and the avalanche of private sector management consultants into public sector work.

3 Ambiguity

If ambiguity is what it takes to achieve persuasiveness, both cameralism and NPM had some of the necessary ingredients.

Cameralism's chief ambiguity lay in its assumption that all the diverse parts of German society were or could be essentially harmonious. This enabled it to square the circle between the centralizing ambitions of the state governments and the local privileges of the 'home towns' – at least until the point when state administration became sufficiently strong for the conflict to become stark (Walker 1971). Part of the way in which opposite forces were reconciled was by the idea that bureaucracy offered a way to represent the nation in government, by an educated bourgeoisie who would transcend their class of origin, and (in some versions) by a degree of election to the bureaucracy (Mueller 1984, 131).

Both philosophies were ambiguous to the extent that combined radical and conservative elements, as has already been mentioned. Cameralism drew on Enlightenment ideas and thinkers (such as Montesquieu), but at the same time treated absolutism as the only conceivable form of government. It followed both the general happiness principle and the principle of monarchical government, without acknowledging the possible conflicts between the two.

Part of the appeal of NPM, too, could be explained by the capacity of its ideas to appeal to different groups at the same time. As Pollitt (1985, 12–13) points out, the rhetoric of 'performance', as a *leitmotif* of NPM, is a vague and multi-faceted concept which carries a wide array of potential meanings (effectiveness, economy, efficiency, quality, availability, consumer satisfaction). Hence 'improving performance' can be interpreted as a code-word for financial parsimony (improving *financial* performance) and as a code-word for service quality.

The same goes for 'accountability', another of NPM's catch-phrases; and even for the equally common idea of 'excellence', so much invoked in the aftermath of Peters' and Waterman's (1982) best-seller *In Search of Excellence*. NPM was ambiguous as to whether the goal was for excellence in the public service by hiring the best and brightest or whether, on the contrary, national economic 'excellence' required that the quality of the talent available to the public service be average or inferior, so that the best and brightest would instead be attracted to the private 'wealth-creating' sector. It is the sub-text, what is read into deeply ambiguous words like 'performance', 'accountability' and 'excellence', which counts.

4   Public Good and Private Interests

It is said to be a condition of effective persuasion that proposals must be presented in terms of public good, not of private benefit. Indeed, a cynical definition of effective rhetoric might be '... the art of converting self-interest into an issue of high principle' (Gittins 1988).

Cameralism presented its ideas as a recipe for social harmony and progress. Enlightened government would raise individual capacities as well as the collective wealth. The private interests to be served by the adoption of its doctrines were not stressed. Nevertheless, all members of society did not stand to gain equally from the adoption of cameralist doctrines: there were winners and losers. The prospective 'winners' included the monarchy, the educated middle class and the professors of cameralism themselves, since the effect of the doctrines was to close the public service to all but the 'credentialled'. Walker (1971, 170–1) describes Justi's notion of a police science for the common weal as 'a slogan that supported their ambitions and gave them dignity: a watchword, a calling.'

NPM was also presented as a formula for collective benefit. In this case, the collective benefit lay in the promise of better and cheaper public services to taxpayers and citizens at large. These benefits would be delivered as a result of professional management allied with other standard NPM doctrines, such as privatization, corporatization, performance measurement and merit pay.

On close examination, of course, this public good seems hard to demonstrate clearly. Many of the public benefits of NPM are imponderable and contested. It is much easier to demonstrate the private and quasi-private benefits of NPM which do not figure in the justificatory arguments.

A quasi-private (but not privately-appropriable) benefit from the adoption of NPM flows to central controlling agencies. Indeed, NPM is sometimes interpreted, by line bureaucrats as well as lobby groups, simply as neo-Treasury control, a set of doctrines which serve to reassert the power of central controlling departments and high bureaucrats against the 'spenders' and professionalized 'service deliverers' in the public service. The new corporate management/public choice language gives a new base for the activities of those departments in cutting back staff and spending, in reducing the power of public sector labour unions and of the service professions.

At the more 'private' level of benefit, NPM fits with Dunleavy's (1986) conditions for the success of a 'policy boom'. These conditions map roughly on to James Wilson's (1980) earlier concept of 'client politics' as a condition for public regulation in order to benefit private interests. In 'client politics', benefits arising from public regulatory power are concentrated on a small, easily-mobilized group, while the costs are paid by a group which is larger and more diffuse, and hence harder to mobilize.

Which groups could fit these conditions for NPM? Actual or potential private providers for public services could do so only if they were smaller in number and encountered fewer collective-action difficulties than the corresponding bureaus and public service labour unions. The same goes for the managerialism industry and upper-middle-level executives, since NPM represents an 'aggrandizement of management' (Martin 1983), and a route to greater rewards, attention, prestige, and personal power to managers through the doctrine of 'freedom to manage'.

The privatization and corporatization *brokers* (financial intermediaries, investment banks, insurance institutions, and the associated consultants) are perhaps more likely to fit those conditions. This group combines comparative advantage in collective action (through geographical and informational concentration) with material interest in the introduction of private ownership rights in public utilities – fee and commission income, the 'unbundling' and privatization of insurance liability (by abandonment of the tradition of government underwriting its own risks), even first-mover advantages, as in the case of those banks which handled the early Thatcher privatizations in the UK and which were later able to turn that experience to profit world-wide (Letwin 1988).

The same applies to the topmost public bureaucrats, according to Dunleavy (1985). On Wilson's assumptions this group is better placed for collective action than the more numerous executive group. And Dunleavy claims that, contrary to the normal stereotype of senior bureaucrats as culturally resistant to the 'philistine' doctrines of managerialism and to the normal economics-of bureaucracy stereotype of the staff-and-budget maximizing bureaucrat (Niskanen 1971), rational senior bureaucrats will aim to improve the quality of their own personal working environment (and, perhaps, their own subsequent employment opportunities) by hiving off or contracting out work from their bureaus as much as possible. This removes senior staff from potentially conflict-laden and stressful supervision of lower-level staff, involves them in more involvement with high level peers and high status people in politics, and gives them contacts with private industry which may enhance their own career options.

5   Selectivity in the Argument

A fifth element identified earlier as a link to acceptance is a carefully selective use of example and maxim rather than demonstration from hard-data analysis. Both cameralism and NPM built their arguments on such a basis. For instance, in its attempt to show how social harmony could be engineered by enlightened government, cameralism piled detail upon detail, in huge multi-volume treatises which substituted altitude for argument (at least in the sense that Toulmin (1958) defines 'argument'). Despite the constant harping on 'science' in cameralist texts, those texts did not offer arguments so much as tell stories, selected to make the point. Enlightenment authors such as Montesquieu were selectively quoted where they were convenient for the argument. For instance, Justi (1760, 482–97) used Montesquieu's argument that there could be no universal constitution, but not Montesquieu's argument for federalism. Historically particular events were used as 'evidence' of general 'truths' (Small 1909, 322).

Much the same applied to NPM. Like cameralism, the case for NPM typically rested on examples, authorities and maxims. Its advocacy was rich in anecdotes about extravagant failure or waste in the 'old' public management. NPM followed the same style as earlier advocates of bringing 'business efficiency' to public management, by picking stirring examples of success and failure and ignoring cases that did not fit the desired stereotypes. Rival doctrines which contradicted the ideas of NPM – for example, A1, M2.3, O2 – were not confronted and refuted, but ignored.

6   The Suspension of Disbelief

The sixth link to acceptance discussed earlier is the ability to suspend well-founded disbelief – in the same way as a successful theatrical performance needs to suspend disbelief (traditionally by means such as the use of scenery, costume, turning off house lights).

Both cameralism and NPM were potentially vulnerable to disbelief. Cameralism was vulnerable to disbelief on the grounds that it was bogus science (Small 1909, 470); that the vast tracts produced by the cameralist professors were no more than aggregations of random pieces of information (Walker 1971, 146); that skill in administration was not a technical subject which could be imparted in college classes to raw recruits; that entrusting government administration to the middle class rather than the aristocracy meant that the state was in the hands of those who had less to lose from revolution or military defeat; that the interests of a princely ruler were by no means the same as the interests of the people as a whole.

Equally, NPM was vulnerable to disbelief on the grounds that its case was not proven; that the shift to corporatization and privatization mainly benefited managers and politicians rather than public service consumers; that the decentralist biases of 'free to choose' were incompatible with the centralist biases of 'free to manage' (see Passmore 1989); that NPM advocates tended to inconsistently argue for private-sector comparisons for rewards of politicians and top managers while rejecting exactly the same argument for workers down the line in the public sector; that NPM's concept of 'accountability' was an impoverished and apolitical one (see Nethercote 1989b, 9); that NPM constituted a possible recipe for socially-created disasters through its advocacy of measures which encouraged information-distortion and public risk-taking (through devices such as measurable performance targets, financial pressure and deregulation) and muffled the voice of caution, experience and independence in the policy advice system. The idea of modelling public management on the recipe for 'excellence' found in Peters' and Waterman's *In Search of Excellence* (1982) was vulnerable to disbelief on the grounds that the cases were all American, such that any 'lessons' to be drawn from them might not translate to other contexts any better than Irish potatoes did to Pomerania; and that 'excellence' might be a transient phenomenon, to be followed by disaster (more than half of the companies identified as 'excellent' by Peters and Waterman had collapsed less than ten years after their book was published).

One of the features of cameralism's suspension of disbelief was the sheer bulk of its written product – which might serve (recalling Sterne) to silence, if not to convince – and by its claims that administration was a scientific or technical subject, associated with 'vitality', 'progress', 'energy' and the sweeping away of an outmoded past (Mueller 1984, 127). Even so, in the event, late cameralism was unable to sustain the suspension of disbelief. The defeat of Prussia by Napoleon weakened its credibility; the abandonment of mercantilist for liberal ideas seems to have done damage by association to the 'management' ideas of the cameralists; the assertion of home town claims by conservative critics of late cameralism such as Möser gained the political ascendancy over the centralizing ambitions of von Justi's 'police science' (Parry 1963, 188–91).

Whether NPM will be able to suspend disbelief in the long run more successfully than late cameralism did, remains to be seen. Unlike cameralism, NPM did not rely on bulk to suspend disbelief, though it did tend to claim that management was a technical and portable skill. In addition, NPM advocates used four main methods in their attempt to suspend disbelief.

1   *Ad hominem (or feminam)* arguments, dealing with sceptics through character assassination – attacking the doubters as *people* rather than dealing centrally with their arguments. Thus the doubters were portrayed as out of tune with the times/self-interested mouthpieces of vested interests/impractical dreamers or academic theorists, without 'hands on' experience of their subject. In discussing the use of these tactics by

NPM's advocates in Australia, Nethercote (1989c, 364) notes that an early criticism of Adam Smith's *Wealth of Nations* ran that Smith was no more qualified to write about his subject than a lawyer upon medicine, since he had never been 'in trade' himself.

2   The assertion of *time pressure*, building up a sense of crisis and urgency in order to quash 'try before you buy' objections calling for piecemeal experimentation or controlled experiment before wholesale adoption of NPM doctrines.

3   *Cargo-cultism*, as in the linking of national economic performance with the quality of public management. Cargo-cultism is used here to denote the recurring belief (and not only among the remote tribes of Melanesia) that material progress can be achieved by essentially ritual activity, as recalled in the epigraph to this chapter (cf. also Worsley 1968). For example, Michael Heseltine, one of the political leaders of NPM in the early Thatcher era in the UK, asserted in 1980:

> Efficient management is a key to the (national) revival...And the management ethos must run right through our national life – public and private companies, civil service, nationalized industries, local government, the National Health Service.... (Heseltine 1980, quoted by Pollitt 1985, 10)[13]

4   *Amnesia*: the presentation of NPM's doctrines as new, in order to avoid disbelief on the grounds that the same doctrines have been tried before, shown to be unsatisfactory in particular cases, and abandoned. In reality, of course, 'better public management', through the adoption of business-type methods, is a doctrine which has a long and chequered history.[14] And many of NPM's individual doctrines have a long history, as was indicated when we encountered them in our brief exploration of some of the commonest 'who', 'how' and 'what' doctrines of administration in Part Two (particularly J1.2, N2, U2). For example, schoolteachers in the UK were paid on performance up to 1902, with pay being linked to tests of the ability of their pupils in the 'three Rs'. University teachers were rewarded from fees paid by those attending their classes, and merit pay in education is also a doctrine with a past in the USA (cf. Majone 1989, 176). Tax-collectors were traditionally paid on poundage; much of law enforcement was effectively privatized in eighteenth-century Britain and in the Western part of the USA in the nineteenth century. If we look closely at historical experience of this kind, we learn something about the limitations of that kind of system (for instance, the problem with the old UK payment-on-performance scheme for schoolteachers was that it set up pressures to narrow the curriculum and encouraged teachers to concentrate their energies on pushing the brightest pupils while ignoring the slower learners).

The advantage of contrived institutional forgetting (Douglas 1987) as an antidote to disbelief is that it gives the ruling doctrines an air of freshness, as new ideas and a new approach for new times; and repels the kinds of doubts that can creep in if historical experience is carefully examined.

V ASSESSING THE ACCEPTANCE FACTOR

The discussion above shows that there is a good case for suggesting that NPM and cameralism both built their appeal on comparable bases for winning administrative arguments. Each of the six elements examined above seems to give us some explanatory 'purchase' on the rise of cameralism and NPM. We could perhaps think of them as *complementary*, like the tumblers of a lock, all of which must be turned in order for a doctrinal key to open the door of acceptance. Alternatively, we could think of them as *substitutable*, with not all needing to be activated for the achievement of persuasion. Or we could think of them as an *hierarchy*, with some elements carrying far more weight than others.

We would need many more cases before that question could be answered with any confidence. In these cases, there is an attractiveness at first sight in explaining their success parsimoniously, simply by reference to the combination of private interest with claims of public good. It is a normal expectation of the rhetorical approach to administrative argument that people will tend to pick the doctrine that happens to serve their own interests. Certainly, sheeting NPM and cameralism home to private benefit gives us an apparently powerful explanation for their rise to greatness. For instance, the rise of NPM seems to fit with a firmer grip on the public sector by central finance ministries than at any time in the post-World War II period. And for both philosophies we can identify a broader group of interests combining strong private stakes in the doctrines with relatively low collective action costs.

However, putting all our explanatory eggs in that basket leaves some important questions unexplained. For instance, it does not really help us understand why NPM 'boomed' in the 1980s rather than in the 1880s, when the same potential private benefits could presumably have been obtained from it. It is open to the same objections which lie against explaining the rise of large corporations in the twentieth century by businessmen's desire for monopoly.[15] 'Symmetry', in the sense of fitting a larger historical lock, seems important in explaining what a narrower interest-based approach cannot do, namely why the rise of NPM ideas came in the 1980s rather than at an(y) earlier time.

Many commentators, too, stress presentational factors such as metaphorical skill and calculated ambiguity in determining the success or failure of doctrines like cameralism and NPM. For instance, Kenneth Minogue (1986) sees such factors as important in understanding the rise or fall of political doctrines in what he calls 'loquocentric society' – that is, a society in which ideas and doctrines can boom on the basis of their persuasive power, without having a close relation to material interests. Minogue argues (ibid., 342) that in the modern world the link between interests and public action has been broken: 'Politics swings freely subject only to the ebb and flow of persuasion.' Presentation rather than interest might not be sufficient, on Minogue's argument to explain the rise of cameralism; but it would perhaps be sufficient to explain the NPM boom. Peter Aucoin (1990, 118) seems to be following this line of thought when he attributes a large part of the success of NPM doctrines in the 1980s to the detailed way in which those ideas were *packaged* by their advocates – for example, in the way that the ideas were presented from the perspective of managers rather than of administrative scientists and in the way that they were disseminated through popular media and professional seminars rather than through academic channels.

For these two cases, it is not difficult to identify aspects of all of the six 'acceptance factor' elements, and so we cannot dismiss the possibility that they operate in conjunction, like the tumblers of a lock. Looking at administrative argument through such a framework may not help us narrowly to predict doctrinal success in any hard-science sense, but it helps us to build up the profile of a 'winner' and to 'retrodict' more successfully, at least in explaining the rise and fall of administrative philosophies like cameralism and NPM.

NOTES

1   See Overman 1984.
2   See Nethercote 1989, 14; Aucoin 1990, 115.
3   See Walker 1971; Justi 1760, I, 439–40 and 444–6 and also III, 406–9.
4   See Justi 1782.
5   For a sceptical view, see Bobrow and Dryzek 1987, 58.
6   See Walker 1981, 205.
7   On Justi, see Tauscher 1956b and Klein 1961.
8   See Small 1909, 298ff; Raeff 1975.
9   Cf. Aglietta 1976; Piore and Sabel 1984; Jessop 1988a, 4–5 and Jessop 1988b, 4.
10   Tocqueville 1946, 149–56; see also Peacock 1979.
11   Cf. Baumol 1967.
12   It has been suggested that it may be this study which prompted Adam Smith to use needle production in his famous example of economies of scale; see Walker 1971, 167.
13   The linkage can conveniently be presented as self-evident, and few have questioned it, even though there is no evidence for such a link; and indeed, if high productivity, dynamism and high ethical standards in public management were really prerequisites for economic performance, Japan, the USA and the Federal Republic of Germany would hardly have become economic superpowers.
14   It stretches back via the US city-manager movement of the 1890s, and the ideas of writers such as Chester Barnard and Mary Parker Follett in the 1920s and 1930s (Aucoin 1990) to even earlier roots in nineteenth-century utilitarianism and even to cameralism itself. What is 'new' about NPM is the packaging, not the content.

15   That is, business people have *always* desired monopoly: why should that desire have been met in the twentieth century rather than at other times? (cf. Hannah 1976, 6.)

9 Review and Conclusion

There ought to be a law in Vanity Fair ordering the destruction of every written document (except receipted tradesmen's bills) after a certain brief and proper interval.... (Thackeray 1848, 244-5)

I REVIEW

Our argument in Part I of this book can be summarized in the following seven claims:

1 Many ideas about administration are better described as *doctrines* than as *theories*.
2 Doctrines are what-to-do ideas which come somewhere between 'policy' and 'theory'.
3 Though doctrines are multiple and contradictory, they are not infinite in number. The commonest of them recur with striking regularity in spite of changes in terminology, and they can be collected and catalogued.
4 Doctrines usually rise and fall in social favour through some process other than conclusive 'hard data' demonstration.
5 Herbert Simon recognized the 'doctrinal' character of administrative argument and claimed that the proper way for administrative science to progress was by hard-data experimentation designed to produce robust and grounded generalizations about administration.

6   This agenda has had only limited success in over 40 years, at least in that it appears to have had little effect on the way that administrative argument is conducted in practice.
7   It is therefore worth trying out additional lines of analysis.

Building on these claims, we set out a two-point 'manifesto'.

a)   Instead of neglecting administrative doctrines as part of a disreputable past, we should take them seriously. We should catalogue and map them systematically as basic units of analysis for administrative science. The same approach needs to be applied to justifications and philosophies as the other basic elements of administrative argument. Such a programme is not inconsistent with Simon's approach, but it adds an extra dimension to it.

b)   Instead of concentrating exclusively on the link between administrative *design* and administrative *performance*, administrative analysis should also pay attention to the link between *argument* and *acceptance*, as a relationship analogous to that of key and lock. Though conventionally viewed as a 'black art', like reading palms or holding a *séance*, this process is not, we argue, beyond the reach of analysis.

II   CONCLUSION: UNDERSTANDING ADMINISTRATIVE ARGUMENT

At the outset of this book, we happened upon three lay philosophers who were passing by in the street and asked them for their views on the best way to get organized. One of them advanced a stereotype of military doctrine, another a stereotype of business doctrine, a third a stereotype of religious or collegial doctrine.

In the interest of evaluation we called back each of the philosophers and asked them to go carefully through the analysis laid out in the intervening pages. What have they learned?

Our military-minded consultant philosopher gave us a terse debriefing. When reviewing the set of doctrines and their justifications discussed in Part II, this philosopher was most at home with justifications based on the maintenance of robustness or reliability even in unexpectedly adverse worst-case conditions. Earlier, we termed such precepts as lambda-type justifications, and they chime with military preoccupations with ensuring resilience when the going gets tough.

The administrative philosophy that struck our military consultant as most closely built on this type of justification was cameralism, as discussed in the last chapter. Born of the desire of the German states to make themselves proof against French power on one side and Russian expansion on the other, cameralism is an administrative philosophy built on valuing the avoidance of catastrophe above all else.

Overall, the military philosopher noted three points. First, administrative argument – philosophy, doctrine, justification – is like weaponry. Second, this consultant noticed that the approach to understanding administrative argument which is used here is remarkably like the way that soldiers are trained to understand weapons. Taking administrative arguments apart and naming their constituent elements is rather like disassembling a weapon. Third, awareness of the range and pedigree of administrative doctrines and justifications is itself a weapon. Such knowledge is useful for refutation, deconstruction and the generation of alternative strategies on the administrative battlefield. It is not just of antiquarian interest.

Our business-minded philosopher, after some haggling over the consultancy fee, also offered us several conclusions from this analysis. When reviewing the doctrines discussed in Part II, this consultant was most at home with justifications based on the matching of resources to task, and on the competent or efficient use of resources in the pursuit of defined aims. Earlier, we named these sigma-type justifications, and they fit with business preoccupations with cost, resources, 'delivering the goods'.

The administrative philosophy that struck our business-minded consultant as built most clearly on this type of justification is New Public Management, as discussed in the last chapter. NPM's preoccupations with cutting costs, delivering defined services effectively, valuing output over process, are essentially sigma-type precepts.

The business-minded philosopher offered three general conclusions. First, it seemed to this consultant that administrative ideas are like products in a market. Second, this consultant reminded us, market share and popularity usually depend on more than the intrinsic merits of a product. So any administrative science which purports to understand the market in administrative ideas needs to pay close attention to the role of packaging and presentation in determining winners and losers. Third, this philosopher concluded that, just as in business, most administrative argument relates to action which needs to be taken in circumstances where time-horizons are too short and resources too tight for the production of incontrovertible evidence from hard data. So we need an approach to administrative science that helps us to understand how that process of persuasion works and to judge its efficacy, and not to reject it in favour of a hard-science approach that is often inapplicable (cf. Lindblom and Cohen 1979; Majone 1989).

Our advocate of religious-style organization spent some time in contemplation before coming to any conclusion. In reviewing the range of doctrines described in Part II, this philosopher was most at home with justifications based on the avoidance of error, the prevention of oppression or unfairness or abuse of office. Earlier, we termed such precepts as theta-type justifications, and they fit with religious preoccupations with checking human propensities to fallibility and corruption.

Neither of the two administrative philosophies discussed in the last chapter seemed to fit closely with theta-type justifications to the religious-minded philosopher. But this philosopher was drawn to some of the tenets of utilitarian administrative philosophies which appeared in the discussion of doctrines in Part II, and if space had permitted an exposition of these philosophies as well as cameralism and NPM, the third philosopher might have identified them as built most nearly on theta-type justifications.

Overall, our religious-minded philosopher concluded that, just as in the spiritual life, there are very few ideas in administration which are genuinely novel. Most supposedly new doctrines are reinventions of ideas which have a past – and often an heretical past, at that. This consultant has concluded that in administration, just as in religion, anyone trying to take a long view needs to be healthily sceptical of claims to novelty. A close awareness of the finite range of doctrines available is the only basis for making sense of the ceaseless change of fashion in administrative nostrums. It is the first stage of literacy in administrative argument.

All three of our consultant philosophers have seen what they want to see, as we all do sometimes. We summarize their conclusions in Table 9.1 below. But, though their conclusions differ in point of emphasis, they are not necessarily incompatible. We think that all of their conclusions are valid.

In addition, it turned out that there were three points on which all of the philosophers were agreed. First, they have all learned from Part II that there are a lot more ways to get organized than they had originally supposed when advising us in the first chapter, before our platoon of researchers got to work.

Second, they have learned that the justifications with which they are most at home are not the sole basis for administrative argument. To take on the other philosophers on their own ground, each philosopher must grapple with different justifications.

Third, though they recognize that this book is an exploratory exercise, not the last word on administrative argument, all three philosophers conclude that a better understanding of doctrine, justification and philosophy is important for administrative science.

> Whatever the nature of the assertion may be...in each case we can challenge the assertion, and demand to have our attention drawn to the grounds (backing, data, facts, evidence, considerations, features) on which the merits of the assertion are to depend. We can, that is, demand an argument; and a claim need be conceded only if the argument which can be produced in its support proves to be up to standard. (Toulmin 1958, 11–12)

In matters of administration, we still do not demand an argument often enough. If the how-to-get-organized question of administration can never be

Table 9.1   Three perspectives on administrative argument

	'Military' Philosopher	'Business' Philosopher	'Religious' Philosopher
Image of Administrative Argument	Battlefield	Market	Clash of faiths
Most Familiar Type of Justification	Lambda-type (precepts based on resilience and reliability)	Sigma-type (precepts based on matching of resources to task)	Theta-type (precepts based on fairness, mutuality, accountability)
Most Closely Related Philosophy	Cameralism	New Public Management	Possibly some aspects of utilitarian or socialist admin. philosophies (not fully discussed in this book)
Conclusions For Admin. Science	See admin. ideas as weapons Learn to name their parts and identify their contraries	See admin. ideas as products Learn to understand packaging as well as content	See admin. ideas as faiths Learn to see through claims to novelty

answered once and for all, it is all the more important that we systematically analyze the range of available doctrines, justifications and philosophies, to chart their dialectic and understand what makes them rise and fall.

References

Aglietta, M. (1976) *A Theory of Capitalist Regulation*, New Left Books, London.

Allott, A. (1980) *The Limits of Law*, Butterworths, London.

Appleby, P. H. (1949) *Policy and Administration*, Alabama UP, Alabama.

Arendt, H. (1964) *Eichmann in Jerusalem*, rev edn, Viking, New York.

Aristotle (1984) *The Complete Works of Aristotle*, ed. J.Barnes, Vol. 2, Princeton UP, Princeton NJ.

Aristotle (1932) *Rhetoric* (tr. and ed. L. Cooper), Appleton-Century, New York.

Armstrong, J. A. (1973) *The European Administrative Elite*, Princeton UP, Princeton.

Atkin, R. H. (1977) *Combinatorial Connectivities in Social Systems*, Birkhaeuser, Basel.

Aucoin, P. (1990) 'Administrative Reform in Public Management: Paradigms, Principles, Paradoxes and Pendulums' *Governance* **3**, 115–37.

Austin, J. L. (1962) *Sense and Sensibilia*, Oxford UP, Oxford.

Avineri, S. (1972) *Hegel's Theory of the Modern State*, Cambridge UP, Cambridge.

Axelrod, R. (1976) *Structure of Decisions*, Princeton UP, Princeton.

Bagehot, W. (1963) *The English Constitution*, Collins, London.

Bahmueller, C. F. (1981) *The National Charity Company*, California UP, Berkeley.

Bardach, E. and Kagan, R. A. (1982) *Going by the Book*, Temple UP, Philadelphia.

Baumol, W. J. (1967) 'Macro-Economics of Unbalanced Growth' *American Economic Review* **57**, 415–26.
Beer, S. (1972) *Brain of the Firm*, Allen Lane, London.
Bendix, R. (1966) *Max Weber*, Methuen, London.
Bennett, J. M. (1983) 'Large Computer Project Problems and their Causes' *Australian Computer Bulletin* **7(3)**, 18–27.
Bentham, J. (1931) *The Theory of Legislation*, ed. G. K. Ogden, tr. R. Hildreth from the French of E. Dumont, Routledge, London.
Bentham, J. (1962) *The Works of Jeremy Bentham* (Bowring edn), Book II, Russell and Russell, Inc., New York.
Bernstein, M. (1955) *Regulating Business by Independent Commission*, Princeton UP, Princeton, NJ.
Black, D. (1958) *The Theory of Committees and Elections*, Cambridge UP, Cambridge.
Bobrow, D. B. and Dryzek, J. S. (1986) *Policy Analysis by Design*, Pittsburgh UP, Pittsburgh, PA.
Borges, J. L. (1974) 'The Library of Babel' in J. L. Borges *Fictions* (ed. A. Kerrigan), Calder and Boyars, London, 72–80.
Brams, S. J. (1975) *Game Theory and Politics*, Free Press, New York.
Braybrooke, D. (1974) *Traffic Congestion Goes Through the Issue Machine*, Routledge, London.
Breyer, S. (1982) *Regulation and Its Reform*, Yale UP, New Haven.
Broom, L. and Cushing, R. (1977) 'A Modest Test of an Immodest Theory' *American Sociological Review* **42**, 157–69.
Brown, R. H. (1978) 'Bureaucracy as Praxis', *Administrative Science Quarterly*, **23**, 365–82.
Brown, R. H. (1983) 'Theories of Rhetoric and the Rhetorics of Theory', *Social Research* **50(1)**, 126–57.
Burke, K. (1950) *A Rhetoric of Motives*, Prentice-Hall, New York.
Burnheim, J. (1985) *Is Democracy Possible?*, Polity, Cambridge.
Carnap, R. (1966) *The Philosophical Foundations of Physics*, Basic Books, New York.
Cassese, S. (1988) 'PGOs in Italy' in Hood and Schuppert 1988, 108–19.
Cd. 9230 (1918) *Report of the Machinery of Government Committee*, London, HMSO
Chadwick, E. (1854) Memorandum in *Papers Relating to the Re-Organisation of the Civil Service*, HMSO, London.
Chandler, A. D. (1962) *Strategy and Structure*, MIT Press, Cambridge, Mass.
Chaples, E., Nelson, H. and Turner, K. (eds) (1985) *The Wran Model*, Oxford UP, Melbourne.
Chapman, R. and Greenaway, J. R. (1980) *The Dynamics of Administrative Reform*, Croom Helm, London.
Charlesworth, J. C. (ed.) (1968) *Theory and Practice of Public Administration*, American Academy of Political and Social Science/American Society

for Public Administration, Philadelphia.

Clark, L. D. (1975) *The Grand Jury*, Quadrangle/The New York Times Book Co., New York.

Clausewitz, C. von (1968) *On War* (ed. A. Rapoport), Penguin, Harmondsworth.

Cmd. 9613 (1955) Royal Commission on the Civil Service 1953–5. *Report*, HMSO, London

Cmnd. 3638 (1968) *The Civil Service Vol 1 Report of the Committee*, HMSO, London.

Corbett, D. (1965) *Politics and the Airlines*, Allen and Unwin, London.

Cornford, F. M. (1908) *Microcosmographia Academica*, Bowes and Bowes, London.

Cornwell, J. (1989) *A Thief in the Night*, Viking, New York.

Craig, G. A. (1955) *The Politics of the Prussian Army*, Oxford UP, London.

Crain, W. M. and Ekelund, R. B. (1976) 'Chadwick and Demsetz on Competition and Regulation' *Journal of Law and Economics*, **19**, 149–62.

Dahl, R. A. (1984) *A Preface to Economic Democracy*, Yale UP, New Haven.

Dahl, R. A. (1985) *Controlling Nuclear Weapons*, Syracuse UP, Syracuse, NY.

Dale, P. N. (1986) *The Myth of Japanese Uniqueness*, Croom Helm, London.

Demsetz, H. (1968) 'Why Regulate Utilities?', *Journal of Law and Economics*, **11**, 55–65.

Deutsch, K. W. (1963) *The Nerves of Government*, Free Press, New York.

Dickens, C. (1910) *Little Dorrit*, The Educational Book Co., London.

Dixon, N. (1976) *On The Psychology of Military Incompetence*, Jonathan Cape, London.

Dore, R. (1973) *British Factory–Japanese Factory*, Allen and Unwin, London.

Dorn, W. (1931) 'The Prussian Bureaucracy in the Eighteenth Century, I, II and III', *Political Science Quarterly*, **46**, 402–23 and **47**, 75–94 and 259–73.

Douglas, M. (1987) *How Institutions Think*, Routledge, London.

Douglas, M. and Wildavsky, A. (1982) *Risk and Culture*, California UP, Berkeley.

Downs, A. (1967) *The Economics of Bureaucracy*, Little, Brown, Boston.

Downs, G. W. and Larkey, P. D. (1986) *The Search for Government Efficiency*, Temple UP, Philadelphia.

Dunlay, T. (1982) *Wolves for the Blue Soldiers*, Nebraska UP, Lincoln.

Dunleavy, P. (1985) 'Budgets, Bureaus and the Growth of the State', *British Journal of Political Science*, **15**, 299–328.

Dunleavy, P (1986) 'Explaining the Privatisation Boom', *Public Administration*, **64**, 13–34.

Dunn, W. N. (1981) *Public Policy Analysis*, Prentice Hall, Englewood-Cliffs.

Dunsire, A. (1973a) *Administration*, Robertson, London.

Dunsire, A. (1973b) 'Administrative Doctrine and Administrative Change', *Public Administration Bulletin*, **15**, December, 39–56.

Dunsire, A. (1978) *The Execution Process Vol 2 Control in a Bureaucracy*, Robertson, Oxford.

Dunsire, A. (1989) 'Holistic Governance', Frank Stacey Memorial Lecture, PAC Conference, University of York, September 1989.

Earl, P. E. (1984) *The Corporate Imagination*, Wheatsheaf, Brighton.

Eaton, J. (1986) *Card-Carrying Americans*, Rowman and Littlefield, Totowa, NJ.

Edelman, M. (1964) *The Symbolic Uses of Politics*, Illinois UP, Urbana.

Edmondson, R. (1984) *Rhetoric in Sociology*, Macmillan, London.

Edwards, S. (ed.) (1973) *The Communards of Paris 1871*, Thames and Hudson, London.

Efficiency Unit [UK] (1988) *Improving Management in Government: the Next Steps*, HMSO, London.

Eichhorn, P. with Boehret, C. (1985) *Verwaltungslexicon*, Nomos, Baden-Baden.

Esser, J. (1969) *Wert und Bedeuting des Rechtsfiktionen*, 2nd edn, Klostermann, Frankfurt am Main.

Farrell, J. G. (1985) *The Siege of Krishnapur*, Fontana, Glasgow.

Ferguson, K. E. (1984) *The Feminist Case Against Bureaucracy*, Temple UP, Philadelphia.

Feyerabend, P. K. (1978) *Against Method*, Verso, London.

Finer, S. E. (1952a) 'Patronage and the Public Service', *Public Administration*, **30**, 329–60.

Finer, S. E. (1952b) *The Life and Times of Sir Edwin Chadwick*, Methuen, London.

Fortescue, S. (1988) 'Building Consensus in the Japanese and Soviet Bureaucracies', University of New South Wales, mimeo.

Fromkin, D. and Chace, J. (1985) 'What *are* the lessons of Vietnam?', *Foreign Affairs*, **63**, 722–46.

Fuller, L. (1967) *Legal Fictions*, Stanford UP, Stanford.

Galbraith, J. K. (1967) *The New Industrial State*, Hamish Hamilton, London.

George, A. L. (1972) 'The Case for Multiple Advocacy in Making Foreign Policy', *American Political Science Review*, **66**, 751–85.

Gerth, H. H. and Mills, C. W (1948) *From Max Weber*, Routledge, London.

Gittins, R. (1988) 'The Madness of Strike-it-Lucky Housing Welfare', *Sydney Morning Herald*, 2.11.88, 21.

Gottlieb, G. (1968) *The Logic of Choice*, Allen and Unwin, London.

Gray, A. and Jenkins, W. I. (1982) 'Efficiency and the Self-Evaluating Organization – the Central Government Experience', *Local Government Studies*, **8**, 41–53.

Gray, G. (1984) 'The Termination of Medibank', *Politics* (Journal of the Australasian Political Studies Association) 19, 1–17.

Gray, J. C. (1921) *Nature and Sources of the Law*, Columbia UP, New York.

Greenaway, J. R. (1984) 'British Administrative Reform in Historical Perspective' paper to PAC Conference, University of York, September 1984.

Griffith, J. A. G. (1985) *The Politics of the Judiciary*, 3rd edn, Fontana, Glasgow.

Gulick, L. (1937) 'Notes on the Theory of Organization' in Gulick and Urwick 1937, 3–45.

Gulick, L. and Urwick, L. (1937) *Papers on the Science of Administration*, Institute of Public Administration, New York.

Gustafsson, B. ed. (1979) *Post-Industrial Society*, Croom Helm, London.

Hage, J. (1974) *Communication and Organizational Control*, Wiley, New York.

Hague, D. C., MacKenzie, W. J. M. and Barker, A. (1975) *Public Policy and Private Interests*, Macmillan, London.

Halberstrom, D. (1972) *The Best and the Brightest*, Fawcett Crest, New York.

Halbrook, S. P. (1984) *That Every Man Be Armed*, New Mexico UP, Albuquerque.

Hannah, L. (1976) *The Rise of the Corporate Economy*, Methuen, London.

Hannan, M. T. and Freeman, J. H. (1977) 'The Population Ecology of Organizations', *American Journal of Sociology*, **82**, 929–64.

Hanusch, H. (ed.) (1983) *Anatomy of Government Deficiencies*, Springer Verlag, Berlin.

Hart, H. L. A. (1961) *The Concept of Law*, Clarendon, Oxford.

Hatch, S. and Mocroft, I. (1979) 'The Relative Costs of Services Provided by Voluntary and Statutory Organizations', *Public Administration*, **57**, 397–405

Heirs, B. and Pehrson, G. (1982) *The Mind of the Organization*, rev edn, Harper and Row, New York.

Heller, J. (1964) *Catch-22*, Corgi, London.

Henderson, D. (1986) *Innocence and Design*, Blackwell, Oxford.

Heseltine, M. (1980) 'Ministers and Management in Whitehall', *Management Services in Government*, **35**.

Hill, D. M. (1974) *Democratic Theory and Local Government*, Allen and Unwin, London.

Hirschman, A. O. (1970) *Exit Voice and Loyality*, Harvard UP, Cambridge, Mass.

Hogwood, B. W. and Peters, B. G. (1985) *The Pathology of Public Policy*, Clarendon, Oxford.

Holdich, R. (1989) *Fair Enough*, AGPS, Canberra.

Homer (1950) *The Iliad* (tr. E. V. Rieu), Penguin, Harmondsworth.

Hood, C. (1978) 'Keeping the Centre Small', *Political Studies*, **XXVI(i)**, 30–46.

Hood, C. (1985) 'British Tax Structure Development as Administration Adaption', *Policy Sciences*, **18**, 3–31.

210   *Administrative Argument*

Hood, C. C. (1986) *Administrative Analysis*, Wheatsheaf, Brighton.
Hood, C. (1990) 'De-Sir-Humphrey-fying the Westminster Model of Bureaucracy', *Governance*, 3, 205–14.
Hood, C. C. and Schuppert, G-F. (1988) *Delivering Public Services*, Sage, London.
Howard, A. (1978) *Welfare Rights*, Bedford Square Books, London.
Hume, L. J. (1981) *Bentham and Bureaucracy*, Cambridge UP, Cambridge.
Isensee, J. (1968) *Subsidiaritätsprinzip und Verfassungsrecht*, Duncker and Humblot, Berlin.
Jackson, M. W. (1972) 'The Application of Method in the Construction of Political Science Theory', *Canadian Journal of Political Science*, 5, 402–17.
Jackson, M. W. (1984) 'Eichmann, Bureaucracy and Ethics', *Australian Journal of Public Administration*, 43, 301–6.
Jackson, M. W. (1989) 'Rules versus Responsibility in Morality', *Public Affairs Quarterly*, 3, 27–40.
Jackson, P. M. (1983) *The Political Economy of Bureaucracy*, Philip Allan, London.
Janis, I. I. (1972) *Victims of Groupthink*, Houghton Mifflin, Boston.
Jesson, B. (1989) *Fragments of Labour*, Penguin, Auckland.
Jessop, B. (1988a) 'Conservative Regimes and the Transition to Post-Fordism', *Essex Papers in Politics and Government*, 47, Department of Government, University of Essex.
Jessop, B. (1988b) 'Regulation Theories in Retrospect and Prospect' Zentrum für interdisziplinäre Forschung, Research Group 'Staatsaufgaben', Preprint Series No. 1, University of Bielefeld, December 1988.
Johnson, H. C. (1964) 'The Concept of Bureaucracy in Cameralism', *Political Science Quarterly*, 79, 378–402.
Johnson, H. C. (1975) *Frederick the Great and his Officials*, Yale UP, New Haven.
Justi, J. H. G. (1760) *Die Grundfeste der Macht und Glückseligkeit der Staaten*, J. H. Hartungs, Königsberg.
Justi, J. H. G. (1761) *Gesammelte Politische und Finanzschriften*, Rothenschen, Kopenhagen.
Justi, J. H. G. (1782) *Grundsätz der Polizeywissenschaft*, Wittwe Vandenhoek, Göttingen.
Jones, J. M. (1980) *Organisational Aspects of Police Behaviour*, Gower, Farnborough.
Kanter, R. M. (1989) *When Giants Learn to Dance*, Simon and Schuster, London.
Karl, B. D. (1963) *Executive Reorganization and Reform in the New Deal*, Harvard UP, Cambridge, Mass.
Kasnacich-Schmid, J. (1958) 'Grundsätz Kameralistischer Geldpolitik', *Weltwirtschaftliches Archiv*, 80, 90–130.

Kassem, M. S. and Hofstede, G. (eds) (1976) *European Contributions to Organization Theory*, Van Gorcum, Assen.

Kaufmann, F-X., Majone, G. and Ostrom, V. eds. (1986) *Guidance, Control and Evaluation in the Public Sector*, De Gruyter, Berlin.

Keating, M. (1989) 'Quo Vadis' based on an address by Michael Keating [Secretary, Department of Finance, Australian Commonwealth Government] to the Royal Australian Institute of Public Administration, Perth, 12 April 1989.

Keynes, J. M. (1936) *The General Theory of Interest, Employment and Money*, Macmillan, London.

Keynes, J. M. (1952) *Essays in Persuasion*, Macmillan, London.

Kingsley, J. D. (1944) *Representative Bureaucracy*, Antioch, Yellow Springs, Ohio.

Klein, E. (1961) 'Johann Heinrich Gottlob Justi und die Preussische Staatswirtschaft' *Vierteljahrshrift für Sozial und Wirtschaftgeschichte*, 48, 145–202.

Kochen, M. and Deutsch, K. W. (1980) *Decentralization*, Oelgeschlager, Gunn and Hain, Cambridge, Mass.

Kuhn, T. S. (1962) *The Structure of Scientific Revolutions*, Chicago UP, Chicago.

Kunst, H. (ed.) (1975) *Evangelisches Staatslexicon*, 2nd edn, Kreuz, Stuttgart.

Lacey, R. (1986) *Ford*, Heinemann, London.

Landau, M. (1969) 'Redundancy, Rationality and the Problem of Duplication and Overlap', *Public Administration Review*, 29(4), 346–58.

Lane, F. C. (1966) *Venice and History* (ed. by a committee of colleagues and former students), Johns Hopkins UP, Baltimore.

Larsen, E. (1980) *Wit as a Weapon*, Frederick Muller, London.

Lawrence, P. (1964) *Road Belong Cargo*, Manchester UP, Manchester.

Lebra, T. S. and Lebra, W. P. (1986) *Japanese Culture and Behavior*, 2nd edn, Hawaii UP, Honolulu.

Legendre, P. (1968) *Histoire de l'Administration de 1750 à Nos Jours*, Presses Universitaires de France, Vendôme.

Leggett, G. (1985) *The Cheka*, Clarendon, Oxford.

LeGuin, U. (1974) *The Dispossessed*, Gollancz, London.

Lenin, V. I. (1933) *State and Revolution*, Martin Lawrence, London.

Letwin, O. (1988) *Privatising the World*, Cassell, London.

Levine, C. H. (1988) 'Human Resource Erosion and the Uncertain Future of the US Civil Service', *Governance*, 1(2), 115–43.

Levitt, B. and March, J. G. (1988) 'Organizational Learning', *Annual Review of Sociology*, 14, 319–40.

Lindblom, C. E. (1965) *The Intelligence of Democracy*, Free P, New York.

Lindblom, C. E. and Cohen, D. K. (1979) *Usable Knowledge*, Yale UP, New Haven.

Machiavelli, N. (1961) *The Prince* (tr. G Bull), Penguin, Harmondsworth.
Mackenzie, W. J. M. and Grove, J. M. (1957) *Central Administration in Britain*, Longmans, London.
MacLean, F. (1978) *Holy Russia*, Weidenfeld and Nicholson, London.
Maier, H. (1986) *Die Ältere Staats- und Verwaltungslehre*, 2nd edn, Deutscher Taschenbuch, München.
Majone, G. (1986) 'Mutual Adjustment by Debate and Persuasion', Ch 21 in Kaufmann, Majone and Ostrom 1986, 445–58.
Majone, G. (1989) *Evidence, Argument and Persuasion in the Policy Process*, Yale UP, New Haven.
Marini, F. (1971) *Toward a New Public Administration*, Chandler, Scranton, Penn.
Marshall, G. (1984) *Constitutional Conventions*, Clarendon, Oxford.
Martin, S. (1983) *Managing without Managers*, Sage Beverly Hills.
Mashaw, J. (1983) *Bureaucratic Justice*, Yale UP, New Haven.
McCloskey, D. N. (1985) *The Rhetoric of Economics*, Wisconsin UP, Madison, Wisconsin.
McCurdy, H. E. and Cleary, R. E. (1984) 'Why can't we resolve the Research Issue in Public Administration?', *Public Administration Review*, **44**, 49–55.
McNeill, W. H. (1974) *Venice*, Chicago UP, Chicago.
Medawar, P. B. (1967) *The Art of the Soluble*, Methuen, London.
Merkle, J. (1980) *Management and Ideology*, California UP, Berkeley.
Metcalfe, L. and Richards, S. (1983) 'The Impact of the Efficiency Strategy: Political Clout or Cultural Change?' *Public Administration*, **62**, 439–54.
Michels, R. (1949) *Political Parties*, Free Press, Glencoe, Ill.
Mill, J. S. (1854) Memorandum in *Papers Relating to the Reorganisation of the Civil Service*, HMSO, London.
Mill, J. S. (1910) *Representative Government*, J. M. Dent, London.
Mills, S. (1986) *The New Machine Men*, Penguin, Ringwood.
Minogue, K. (1986) 'Loquocentric Society and its Critics', *Government and Opposition*, **21(3)**, 338-61.
Mintzberg, H. (1979) *The Structuring of Organizations*, Prentice-Hall, Englewood Cliffs, NJ.
Mintzberg, H. (1990) *Mintzberg on Management*, Free Press, New York.
Montesquieu, Baron C de S (1977) *The Spirit of Laws*, ed D. W. Carrithers, California UP, Berkeley.
More, Sir T. (1965) *Utopia*, Penguin, Harmondsworth.
Morgan, G. (1980) 'Paradigms, Metaphors and Puzzle Solving in Organization Theory' *Administrative Science Quarterly*, **25**, 605–22.
Morrison, H. (1933) *Socialisation and Transport*, Constable, London.
Mueller, H. E. (1984) *Education and Monopoly*, California UP, Berkeley.
Mulgen, G. (1988) 'New Times', *Marxism Today*, December 1988, 24–31.

Nader, R., Petkas, P. and Blackwell, K. (1972) *Whistle Blowing*, Grossman, New York.

Nethercote, J. (1989a) 'Public Service Reform' paper presented to conference of Academy of Social Sciences of Australia on the Public Service, University House, Australian National University, 25 February 1989.

Nethercote, J. (1989b) four articles in *The Canberra Times*, June 1989.

Nethercote, J. (1989c) 'The Rhetorical Tactics of Managerialism', *Australian Journal of Public Administration*, **48**, 363–7.

Niskanen, W. A. (1971) *Bureaucracy and Representative Government*, Aldine Atherton, Chicago.

Niskanen, W. A. (1980) 'Competition among Government Bureaus' in Weiss and Barton 1980, 167–74.

Niskanen, W. A. (1983) 'Bureaucrats between Self-Interest and Public Interest', Ch 7 in Hanusch (1983), 111–16.

Nitti, F. S. (1974) *Discorsi Parlamentari di Francesco S Nitti*, pubblicati per deliberazione della Camera dei deputati, Vol. 2, Grafica editrice romana, Rome.

Norris, C. (1985) *Contest of Faculties*, Methuen, London.

NZ Treasury (1987) *Government Management*, 2 Vols., NZ Treasury, Wellington.

Oakeshott, M. (1964) 'Political Laws and Captive Audiences' in Urban 1964.

Ogden, C. K. (1932) *Bentham's Theory of Fictions*, Routledge, London.

O'Leary, B. (1989) 'The Limits to Coercive Consociationalism in Northern Ireland', *Political Studies*, **37**, 562–88.

Olson, M. (1982) *The Rise and Fall of Nations*, Yale UP, New Haven.

Ostrom, V. (1974) *The Intellectual Crisis in American Public Administration*, 2nd edn, Alabama UP, Alabama.

Ostrom, V. (1987) *The Political Theory of a Compound Republic*, 2nd edn, Nebraska UP, Lincoln.

Overman, E. S. (1984) 'Public Management', *Public Administration Review*, **44**, 275–9.

Oyen, E. (1982) 'The Social Functions of Confidentiality', *Current Sociology*, **30**, 1–37.

Painter, M. (1987) *Steering the Modern State*, Sydney UP, Sydney.

Parris, H. (1969) *Constitutional Bureaucracy*, Allen and Unwin, London.

Parry, G. (1963) 'Enlightened Government and Its Critics in Eighteenth-Century Germany', *The Historical Journal*, **V1(2)**, 178–92.

Passmore, J. (1989) 'Hearing Voices' (review of M. Oakeshott, *The Voice of Liberal Learning*, Yale UP, New Haven 1989), *Times Literary Supplement* May 26–June 1 1989, 567–8.

Peacock, A. (1979) 'Public Expenditure Growth in Post Industrial Society' in Gustafsson 1979, 80–95.

Perrow, C. (1984) *Normal Accident*, Basic Books, New York.

Perry, J. and Kraemer, K. (1983) *Public Management*, Mayfield, Palo Alto, Calif.

Peters, B. G. (1988) *Comparing Public Bureaucracies*, Alabama UP, Tuscaloosa.

Peters, T. and Waterman, R. (1982) *In Search of Excellence*, Harper and Row, New York.

Piore, M. J. and Sabel, C. F. (1984) *The Second Industrial Divide*, Basic Books, New York.

Pocock, J. G. A. (1971) *Politics, Language and Time*, Methuen, London.

Pollitt, C. (1984) *Manipulating The Machine*, Allen and Unwin, London.

Pollitt, C. (1985) '"Performance" in Government and the Public Services', paper presented to the JUC Public Administration Committee Conference, University of York, UK, September 1985.

Posner, R. A. (1977) *Economic Analysis of Law*, 2nd edn, Little, Brown, Boston.

President's Committee on Administrative Management (1937) *Report of the Committee with Studies of Administrative Management in the Federal Government*, US Government Printing Office, Washington, DC.

Price, J. L. (1968) *Organizational Effectiveness*, J..L. Irwin, Homewood, Ill.

Raeff, M. (1975) 'The Well-Ordered Police State and the Development of Modernity in Seventeenth and Eighteenth Century Europe', *American Historical Review*, **80**, 1221–43.

Rapoport, A. (1968) 'Introduction' in Clausewitz 1968, 11–80.

Rapoport, A. and Chammah, A. M. (1965) *Prisoner's Dilemma*, Michigan UP, Ann Arbor, Mich.

Rawls, J. (1971) *A Theory of Justice*, Belknap, Cambridge, Mass.

Reichenbach, H. (1966) *The Rise of Scientific Philosophy*, California UP, Berkeley.

Reid, M. (1988) *All-Change in the City*, Macmillan, London.

Reischauer, E. (1977) *The Japanese*, Belknap Press, Cambridge, Mass.

Report on the Organization of the Permanent Civil Service, together with a Letter from the Rev B. Jowett (1854) HMSO, London.

Review of NSW Government Administration (1982) *Unfinished Agenda*, Further Report, Government Printer, Sydney.

Rihs, C. (1973) *La Commune de Paris 1871*, Seuil, Paris.

Rodger, S. (1986) *Pay Fixing in the State Sector*, Ministry of State Services, Wellington.

Rorty, R. (1979) *Philosophy and the Mirror of Nature*, Princeton UP, Princeton.

Rosenberg, N. (1960) 'Some Institutional Aspects of the Wealth of Nations', *Journal of Political Economy*, **68**, 557–70.

Rourke, F. E. (1980) 'Bureaucratic Autonomy and the Public Interest' in Weiss and Barton 1980, 103–12.

Royal Commission on Australian Government Administration (1976) *Report*, AGPS, Canberra.

Sarah, E., Scott, M. and Spender, D. (1989) 'The Education of Feminists: The Case for Single-Sex Schools' in Spender and Sarah 1989, 55–66.

Savigny, F. C. von (1967) *Vom Beruf Unserer Zeit für Gesetzgebung und Rechtswissenschaft*, 2nd edn, Georg Olms, Hildesheim.

Schaffer, B. (1973) *The Administrative Factor*, Frank Cass, London.

Schumacher, E. F. (1973) *Small is Beautiful*, Blond and Briggs, London.

Schumpeter, J. (1952) *Capitalism, Socialism and Democracy*, 5th edn, Allen and Unwin, London.

Scott, G. and Gorringe, P. (1988) 'Reform of the Core Public Sector' paper presented to the national conference of the Royal Australian Institute of Public Administration, November 1988.

Self, P. (1975) *Econocrats and the Policy Process*, Macmillan, London.

Selznick, P. (1949) *TVA and the Grass Roots*, California UP, Berkeley.

Sennett, R. (1977) *The Fall of Public Man*, Cambridge UP, Cambridge.

Shapiro, D. (1978) 'The Policy Implications of Treasury Organization' paper presented to the PAC conference, University of York, September 1978.

Sharkansky, I. (1979) *Wither the State?* Chatham House Publishers, Chatham, N.J.

Shubik, M. (1986) 'Appendix 1: A Note on Biology, Time and the Golden Rule' in Kaufman, Majone and Ostrom 1986, 245–8.

Simon, H. A. (1946) 'The Proverbs of Administration' *Public Administration Review*, **6**, 53–67.

Simon, H. A. (1957) *Administrative Behavior*, 2nd edn, Free Press, New York.

Simon, H. A., Smithburg, D. W., and Thompson, V. A. (1950) *Public Administration*, A. A. Knopf, New York.

Small, A. W. (1909) *The Cameralists*, Chicago UP, Chicago.

Smith, A. (1937) *The Wealth of Nations*, Modern Library Edition, Random House, New York.

Smith, A. (1978) *Lectures in Jurisprudence*, ed. R. L. Meek, D. D. Raphael, P. G. Stein, Clarendon, Oxford.

Smith, N. L. (ed.) (1981) *Metaphors for Evaluation*, Sage, Beverly Hills.

Snellen, I. T. M. and van de Donk, W. B. H. J. (1989) *Expert Systems in Public Administration*, Elsevier, Amsterdam.

Sommer, L. (1930) 'Cameralism', *Encyclopaedia of the Social Sciences*, Macmillan, New York, Vol III, 158–61.

Spann, R. N. (1966) 'Clichés in Political Science', *Politics* (the journal of the Australasian Political Studies Association), **1**, 3–16.

Spann, R. N. (1981) 'Fashions and Fantasies in Public Administration', *Australian Journal of Public Administration*, **XL**, 12–25.

Spender, D. and Sarah, E. (1989) *Learning to Lose*, 2nd edn, Women's Press, London.

Spinoza, B. de (1951) *A Theologico-Political Treatise and a Political Treatise* (tr. R.H.M. Elwes), Dover, New York.

Spinoza, B. de (1958) *The Political Works* (ed. and tr. A.G. Wernham), Clarendon, Oxford.

Sterne, L. (1983, ed. I. C. Ross) *The Life and Opinions of Tristram Shandy, Gentleman*, Oxford UP, Oxford.

Stigler, G. J. (1958) 'The Economies of Scale', *Journal of Law and Economics*, **1**, 54–71.

Subrananiam, V. (1967) 'Representative Bureaucracy', *American Political Science Review*, **61**, 1910–19.

Sykes, T. (1988) *Two Centuries of Panic*, Allen and Unwin, Sydney.

Tauscher, A. (1956a) 'Kameralismus', *Handwörterbuch der Sozialwissenschaften*, Fischer, Stuttgart, Vol V, 463–7.

Tauscher, A. (1956b) 'Justi, Johann Heinrich Gottlob', *Handwörterbuch der Sozialwissenschaften*, Fischer, Stuttgart, Vol V, 452–4.

Taylor, F. W. (1911) *The Principles of Scientific Management*, Harper, New York.

Taylor, F. W. (1916) 'Government Efficiency', *Bulletin of the Taylor Society*, December 1916, 7–13.

Thackeray, W. M. (1848) *Vanity Fair*, Nelson, London.

Thomas, R. (1978) *The British Philosophy of Administration*, Longman, London.

Thompson, V. A. (1975) *Without Sympathy or Enthusiasm*, Alabama UP, Alabama.

Thompson, V. A. (1976) *Bureaucracy and the Modern World*, General Learning Press, Morristown NJ.

Titmuss, R. M. (1971) 'Welfare Rights, Law and Discretion' *Political Quarterly*, **42**, 113–42.

Tivey, L. (1978) *The Politics of the Firm*, Robertson, Oxford.

Tocqueville, A. de (1946) *Democracy in America*, Oxford UP, London.

Tocqueville, A. de (1949) *L'Ancien Régime*, Clarendon P., Oxford.

Tocqueville, A. de (1954) *Democracy in America* (ed. H. Reeve), Vintage, New York.

Toulmin, S. (1958) *The Uses of Argument*, Cambridge UP, Cambridge.

Townsend, R. (1970) *Up the Organization*, Knopf, New York.

Tullock, G. (1965) *The Politics of Bureaucracy*, Public Affairs Press, Washington.

Turkle, S. (1984) *The Second Self*, Granada, London.

Turner, B. A. (1976) 'How to Organize Disaster', *Management Today*, March 1976, 56–7 and 105.

Turner, B. A. (1978) *Man-Made Disasters*, Wykeham, London.

Twining, W. and Miers, D. (1976) *How to Do Things with Rules*, Weidenfeld and Nicholson, London.

Urban, G. R. (1964) *Talking to Eastern Europe*, Eyre and Spottiswoode, London.

Vincent, K. S. (1984) *Pierre-Joseph Proudhon and the Rise of French Republican Socialism*, Oxford UP, New York.

Voslensky, M. (1984) *Nomenklatura*, Bodley Head, London.

Wagner, R. E. (1973) *The Public Economy*, Markham, Chicago.

Walker, G. de Q. (1986) *Initiative and Referendum*, Centre for Independent Studies, Sydney.

Walker, M. (1971) *German Home Towns*, Cornell UP, Ithaca.

Walker, M. (1981) *John Jakob Möser and the Holy Roman Empire of the German Nation*, North Carolina UP, Chapel Hill.

Watson, J. (1968) *The Double Helix*, Signet, New York.

Wegener, R. (1978) *Staat und Verbände im sachbereich Wohlfahrtspflege*, Duncker and Humblot, Berlin.

Weiss, C. and Barton, A. H. (1980) *Making Bureaucracies Work*, Sage, Beverly Hills.

Weller, P. and Fraser, S. (1987) 'The Younging of Australian Politics or Politics as First Career', *Politics* (Journal of the Australasian Political Studies Association), 22, 76–83.

Wettenhall, R. L. (1968) 'Government Department or Statutory Authority?', *Public Administration* (Sydney), 17, 350–9.

Wildavsky, A. (1985) 'Trial without Error', *CIS Occasional Papers*, 13, Centre for Independent Studies, Sydney.

Wilenski, P. (1977) Review of NSW Government Administration, *Directions for Change*, Interim Report, Government Printer, Sydney.

Wilenski, P. (1986) *Public Power and Public Administration*, RAIPA/Hale and Iremonger, Sydney.

Williamson, O. E. (1975) *Markets and Hierarchies*, Collier Macmillan, London.

Wilson, J. Q. (ed) (1980) *The Politics of Regulation*, Basic Books, New York.

Wilson, W. (1887) 'The Study of Administration', *Political Science Quarterly*, 2, 197–222.

Worsley, P. (1968) *The Trumpet Shall Sound*, 2nd edn, MacGibbon and Kee, London.

Wright, M. (1969) *Treasury Control of the Civil Service 1854–1874*, Clarendon P., Oxford.

Index